Karen Brown's
California
Charming Inns & Itineraries

Written by

CLARE BROWN, JUNE BROWN, and KAREN BROWN

Illustrations by Barbara Tapp
Cover Painting by Jann Pollard

Karen Brown's Guides, San Mateo, California

Karen Brown Titles

Austria: Charming Inns & Itineraries

California: Charming Inns & Itineraries

England: Charming Bed & Breakfasts

England, Wales & Scotland: Charming Hotels & Itineraries

France: Charming Bed & Breakfasts

France: Charming Inns & Itineraries

Germany: Charming Inns & Itineraries

Ireland: Charming Inns & Itineraries

Italy: Charming Bed & Breakfasts

Italy: Charming Inns & Itineraries

Mexico: Charming Inns & Itineraries

Mid-Atlantic: Charming Inns & Itineraries

New England: Charming Inns & Itineraries

Pacific Northwest: Charming Inns & Itineraries

Portugal: Charming Inns & Itineraries

Spain: Charming Inns & Itineraries

Switzerland: Charming Inns & Itineraries

For Pam & Ann

Editors: Anthony Brown, Karen Brown, JuneEveleigh Brown, Clare Brown, Iris Sandilands, Lorena Aburto Ramirez, Debbie Tokumoto, Courtney Gaviorno.

Technical support: Michael Fiegel, Gary Meisner.

Illustrations: Barbara Tapp.

Maps: Michael Fiegel.

Distributed by Fodor's Travel Publications, Inc., 1745 Broadway, New York, NY 10019, USA.

Distributed in Canada by Random House Canada, 2775 Matheson Boulevard. East, Mississanga, Ontario L4W 4P7, Canada, phone: (905) 624 0672, fax: (905) 624 6217.

Distributed in the United Kingdom, Ireland, and Europe by Random House UK, 20 Vauxhall Bridge Road, London, SW1V 2SA, England, phone: 44 20 7840 4000, fax: 44 20 7840 8406.

Distributed in Australia by Random House Australia, 20 Alfred Street, Milsons Point, Sydney NSW 2061, Australia, phone: 61 2 9954 9966, fax: 61 2 9954 4562.

Distributed in New Zealand by Random House New Zealand, 18 Poland Road, Glenfield, Auckland, New Zealand, phone: 64 9 444 7197, fax: 64 9 444 7524.

Distributed in South Africa by Random House South Africa, Endulani, East Wing, 5A Jubilee Road, Parktown 2193, South Africa, phone: 27 11 484 3538, fax: 27 11 484 6180.

A catalog record for this book is available from the British Library.

ISSN 1535-4032

Contents

INTRODUCTION   1–10
    Introduction   1
    About Itineraries   2–3
    About Inn Travel   4–10

ITINERARIES   11–96
    Leisurely Loop of Southern California   11–26
    San Francisco to Los Angeles via the Coast   27–48
    North from San Francisco, almost to the Oregon Border   49–60
    Wandering through the Wine Country   61–80
    Yosemite, the Gold Country & Lake Tahoe   81–96

PLACES TO STAY
    Inns Listed Alphabetically by Town   97–260

INDEX   261–272

MAPS
    Places to Stay & Itineraries   Color Section at Back of Book

Introduction

San Francisco Cable Car

California, the Golden State, is fascinating with its diverse regions, dramatic scenery, exciting places to visit, and appealing places to stay. There is almost too much—it can be confusing to decide the most important sights to see and the most special inns to choose. This book is written to help you through the maze: we have done your homework for you. The first section of the book presents five detailed driving itineraries that spider-web across the state. The second section features our personal recommendations of places to stay, written with the sincere belief that where you lay your head each night makes the difference between a good and a great vacation.

About Itineraries

Five driving itineraries map and describe a route through the various regions of California so that you can choose one that includes the area you have your heart set on visiting. These itineraries are outlined on the maps at the back of the book. Each routing can easily be tailored to meet your own specific needs by leaving out some sightseeing, or linking several itineraries together if you wish to enjoy a longer vacation.

CAR RENTAL

The itineraries are designed for travel by car. If you are staying in San Francisco at the beginning of your trip, it is not necessary to pick up a rental car until you leave the city since the public transportation system is so convenient and this is a wonderful town for walking. However, if your vacation begins in Los Angeles, you will need a car within the city to get from place to place and should pick it up on arrival at the airport.

DRIVING TIMES

California is a large state, approximately 1,000 miles from tip to toe. If you stay on the freeways, you can quickly cover large areas of territory, but if you choose to savor the beauty of the coast along California's sensational Hwy 1 or dip into the countryside along scenic back roads, plan on traveling about 30 miles in an hour and remember to allow extra time for stopping to enjoy countryside vistas.

MAPS

The colored map section at the back of the book shows all the towns in which we have a recommended place to stay and the driving itineraries' routings: Map 1 *Leisurely Loop of Southern California*, Map 2 *San Francisco to Los Angeles via the Coast*, Map 3 *North from San Francisco almost to the Oregon border*, Map 4 *Wandering Through the Wine Country*, and Map 5 *Yosemite, The Gold Country and Lake Tahoe*. For detailed trip planning it is essential to supplement our maps with comprehensive maps. Rand McNally maps are available on our website, *www.karenbrown.com*.

PACING

At the beginning of each itinerary we suggest our recommended pacing to help you decide the amount of time to allocate to each one. The suggested time frame reflects how much there is to see and do. Use our recommendation as a guideline only, and choreograph your own itinerary based on how much leisure time you have and whether your preference is to move on to a new destination each day or settle in and use a particular inn as base.

WEATHER

At the beginning of each itinerary a brief note is given on what you can expect to encounter weather-wise in the various regions. In California a whole new climate emerges in just a short distance. The idea that the entire state is sunny and warm year-round can all too quickly be dispelled when the summer fog rolls into San Francisco or 3 feet of winter snow falls in the High Sierras.

Introduction—About Itineraries

3

About Inn Travel

We use the term "inn" to cover everything from a simple bed and breakfast to a sophisticated resort. A wide range of inns is included in this guide: some are great bargains, others very costly; some are in cities or well-trafficked areas, others in remote locations; some are quite sophisticated, others extremely simple. The common denominator is that each place has some special quality that makes it appealing. Our descriptions are intended to give you an honest appraisal of each property so that you can select an accommodation based on your personal preferences. The following pointers will help you appreciate and understand what to expect when traveling the "inn way."

AFFILIATIONS:

If a property is a member of either Select Registry or Relais & Châteaux we reference this on the hotel description page.

BATHROOMS

We do not specify whether the bath is equipped with stall-shower, tub-shower, tub only, or Jacuzzi, so you'll need to ask when you make your reservation. Some inns offer guestrooms that share a bath with other rooms, or rooms that have a private bath but locate it down the hall so you'll need to ask about that, too.

BREAKFAST

Breakfast is usually included in the room rate, and we make note if it is not. Although innkeepers take great pride in their morning offerings, know that breakfast can range from a gourmet "waddle-away" feast (as proudly described by one innkeeper-chef) to muffins and coffee. Sometimes breakfast is limited to a Continental in your room or a hot breakfast with others in the dining room, and sometimes both. Breakfast times vary as well—some innkeepers serve a hot breakfast at a specified time, while others replenish a buffet on a more leisurely schedule. Breakfasts are as unique as the inns themselves.

CANCELLATION POLICIES

Although policies vary, inns are usually more rigorous than large chain hotels about their cancellation policies. Understand their terms when securing a reservation.

CHARM

It is very important to us that an inn has charm. Ideally, an inn should be appealing in several ways: perhaps in an historic building, tastefully decorated, lovingly managed, and in a wonderful location. Few inns meet every criterion, but all our selections have something that makes them special and are situated in memorable surroundings. (We have had to reject several lovely inns because of a poor location.) Small inns are usually our favorites, but size alone did not dictate whether or not a hostelry was chosen.

CHECK-IN

Inns are usually very specific about check-in time—generally between 3 and 6 pm. Let your innkeeper know if you are going to arrive late so that (s)he can make special arrangements, such as leaving a door key and a note with directions to your room under a potted plant. Also, for those who might wish to arrive early, note that some inns close their doors between check-out and check-in times. Inns are frequently staffed only by the owners themselves and that window of time between check-out and check-in is often the one opportunity to shop for those wonderful breakfasts they prepare in addition to running their own personal errands.

CHILDREN

Many places in this guide do not welcome children. Inns cannot legally refuse accommodation to children but, as parents, we really want to stay where our children are genuinely welcome, so ask when making reservations. In the inn descriptions on our website (*www.karenbrown.com*) we have an icon that indicates at what age children are welcome.

COMFORT

As influential as charm, comfort plays a deciding role in the selection of inns recommended. Firm mattresses, a quiet setting, good lighting, fresh towels, scrubbed bathrooms—we do our best to remember the basics when considering inns. The charming decor and innkeeper will soon be forgotten if you do not enjoy a good night's sleep and comfortable stay.

CREDIT CARDS

Whether or not an establishment accepts credit cards is indicated in the list of icons at the bottom of each description by the symbol CREDIT. We have also specified in the accommodation description which cards are accepted as follows: AX–American Express, MC–MasterCard, VS–Visa, or simply, all major.

FOOD

The majority of places featured in this guide do not have restaurants, but innkeepers are always very knowledgeable about and happy to recommend local favorites. Most inns do serve breakfast, however: quite often a sumptuous one. Frequently, in addition to breakfast, tea or wine and hors d'oeuvres are served in the afternoon or evening either at a specific time or on a self-serve basis at your leisure. Sometimes, if you request it in advance, a picnic lunch can also be prepared.

If you have any special dietary requirements, most innkeepers will gladly try to accommodate you. Not having the resources a restaurant would have, they usually plan a breakfast menu that features one entrée, making sure to have the necessary ingredients on hand. It is best to mention any special requests at the time you make your reservation, both as a courtesy and from a practical point of view. The innkeeper will want the chance to stock items such as low-fat dairy products, egg substitutes, and sugar-free syrups.

ICONS

We use these icons in the guidebooks and more on our website, *www.karenbrown.com.*
❄ Air conditioning in rooms, ☕ Breakfast included in room rate, ♨ Cooking classes
offered, CREDIT Credit cards accepted, ☎ Direct-dial telephone in room, 🐾 Dogs by special
request, 🛗 Elevator, 🏋 Exercise room, 🔥 Fireplaces in some bedrooms, @ Internet
access, ⅄ Mini-refrigerator in room, 🚭 Non-smoking rooms, P Parking available, 🍴
Restaurant, ❀ Spa, 🏊 Swimming pool, 🎾 Tennis, 📺 TV—cable or satellite, 💒
Wedding facilities, ♿ Wheelchair accessible, ⚓ Beach nearby, 🏛 Archaeological site
nearby, 🏌 Golf course nearby, 🥾 Hiking trails nearby, 🏇 Horseback riding nearby, 🎿
Skiing nearby, 🏄 Water sports nearby, 🍷 Wineries nearby.
Icons allow us to provide additional information about our recommended properties.
When using our website to supplement the guides, positioning the cursor over an icon
will in many cases give you further details. For easy reference an icon key can be found
at the back of the book.

PROFESSIONALISM

The inns we have selected are run by professional innkeepers. We recommend only inns that offer privacy for their guests, not places where you'd have to climb over family clutter to reach the bathroom.

RESERVATIONS

The two best ways to make a reservation are to telephone or, if an inn participates in our website, to connect to them on line. Another convenient and efficient way to request a reservation is by fax. When planning your trip, be aware that many inns require a two-night stay on weekends and over holidays. Conversely, discounted midweek and off-season rates are often available, so do ask about them.

RESPONSIBILITY

All of the inns featured have been visited and selected solely on their own merits. Our judgments are made based on the charm of the inn, its setting, cleanliness, and, above all, the warmth of welcome. Each property has its own appeal, and we try to present you with a very honest appraisal. However, no matter how careful we are, sometimes we misjudge an inn's merits, or the ownership changes, or—unfortunately—inns just do not maintain their standards. If you find that an inn does not meet the standards we promise, please let us know, and accept our sincere apologies.

ROOM RATES

Rates can vary often, between high-season, low-season, midweek, weekend, and holiday pricing. We have quoted only high-season rates for 2004, generally a range from the lowest-priced bedroom for two people (singles usually receive a very small discount) to the most expensive suite, including breakfast. The rates given are those quoted to us by the inn. Please use these figures as a guideline and be certain to ask at the time of booking what the rates are and what they include.

We have not given prices for "special" rooms such as those that can accommodate three people traveling together. Discuss options with the innkeeper. We make a note of all exceptions, e.g., when an inn does not include breakfast with the price of your room. The rates we quote do not include tax.

SMOKING

Most inns have an extremely strict non-smoking policy. A few inns permit smoking in restricted public areas or outside, but in general it is best to assume that smoking is not appropriate. If you need a place where smoking is allowed, be sure to ask the hotel about the specifics of their policy.

SOCIALIZING

Inns usually offer a conviviality rarely found in a "standard" hotel. The gamut runs from intimate gatherings around the kitchen table to sharing a sophisticated, elegant cocktail hour in the parlor. Breakfast may be a formal meal served at a set hour when the guests gather around the dining-room table, or it may be served buffet-style over several hours where guests have the option to sit down and eat alone or join other guests at a larger table. Some inns will bring a breakfast tray to your room.

After check-in, many inns offer afternoon refreshment, such as tea and cakes or wine and hors d'oeuvres, which may be seen as another social opportunity. Some inns set out the refreshments buffet-style where guests are invited to meander in and out mixing or not mixing with other guests as they choose, while others orchestrate a more structured gathering, often a social hour, with the innkeeper presiding. Choose the inn that seems to offer the degree of intimacy or privacy that you desire. It's entirely possible to find inns that downplay the social aspect of your visit, if privacy is what you're after.

WEBSITE

Please supplement this book by looking at the information provided on our Karen Brown website (*www.karenbrown.com*), which serves as an added dimension to our guides. Most of our favorite inns are featured on the site (web participation is an inn's choice) and on their web page you can usually link to their email so that making a reservation is a breeze. Also featured on our site are comments, feedback, and discoveries from you, our readers; information on our latest finds; post-press updates; contest drawings for free books; special offers; unique features such as recipes and favorite destinations; and special savings offered by certain inns.

WHEELCHAIR ACCESSIBILITY

If an inn has *at least* one guestroom that is accessible by wheelchair, it is noted with the symbol ♿. This is not the same as saying it meets full ADA standards.

Leisurely Loop of Southern California

Disneyland

Los Angeles and San Diego are popular destinations, attracting travelers from around the world to a wealth of sightseeing treats. But in addition to visiting these justifiably famous cities, we hope to entice you to venture out into the countryside to explore lesser-known sightseeing gems: quaint Balboa Island with its handsome yachts, charming La Jolla with its idyllic beaches, picturesque Julian exuding its Gold Rush heritage, secluded Idyllwild nestled in the mountains, glamorous Palm Springs where movie stars still steal away, beautiful Arrowhead with its crystal-clear lake. Perhaps nowhere else can you discover within only a few short miles such a rich tapestry of places to visit—all so different, all so appealing. White-sand beaches, forests with towering pines, deserts rimmed with snow-peaked mountains, bountiful orchards, historical mining towns, and shimmering blue lakes all await your discovery.

Recommended Pacing: Greater Los Angeles is an enormous metropolis of cities and suburbs connected by an overwhelming maze of very busy freeways—during the commuter rush hours it can take hours to get from one side of the city to the other. Choose a hotel or motel close to the principal attraction you are visiting in Los Angeles and use it as a base for your other sightseeing. If you are just visiting Disneyland, stay in the area for two nights—the more attractions you want to include, the longer the recommended stay: if you include San Diego or La Jolla, add two nights; if you visit Palm Springs, add another and possibly include one additional night for Lake Arrowhead. **The itinerary route is outlined on Map 1 at the back of the book.**

Weather Wise: The weather along the coast is warm year-round and there is very little winter rain. Julian has a more temperate climate—though sometimes in the summer it has the odd very hot day and in the winter the occasional snowfall. Palm Springs can be boiling hot, but with a dry heat, during the summer, and is ideal in the winter, with warm days and cool mountain-desert nights. Lake Arrowhead is a mountain resort with warm summer weather and snow in winter.

If you are going to be staying for an extended period of time in **Los Angeles**, supplement this guide with a book totally dedicated to what to see and do. There is also a wealth of free information available from the Los Angeles Visitors Bureau—213-624-9746, *www.lacvb.com*—they will send you a very useful packet of information. We are not going to attempt to detail all of Los Angeles's sightseeing possibilities, but just briefly mention a few highlights.

Disneyland: The wonderland created by Walt Disney needs no introduction. What child from two to ninety-two has not heard of this Magic Kingdom, home to such lovable characters as Mickey Mouse, Donald Duck, Pluto, and Snow White? The park is a fantasyland of fun, divided into various theme areas. You enter into Main Street, USA and from there it is on to Tomorrowland, Fantasyland, Frontierland, and Adventureland, each with its own rides, entertainment, and restaurants. California Adventure, Disney's newest theme park, is located right next door to the main park. Disneyland is open every day of the year and is located at 1313 Harbor Boulevard in Anaheim. (714-781-4565, *www.disney.go.com*)

The J. Paul Getty Museum: Climbing aboard the electric tram that takes you up to the Getty's mountaintop location, you soon realize that this is not your usual museum visit. Arriving at the central plaza of gleaming white travertine rock and walking up the broad staircase, you soon discover there is so much more than museum exhibits. There is the architecture to admire, exquisite gardens to stroll in, inviting tree-lined pathways to follow, places to dine, quiet corners for contemplation, reflecting pools to gaze in, and spectacular views across the city to the ocean. The exhibition galleries house collections of European paintings (Van Gogh's *Irises*, Monet's *Wheatstacks,* and David Hockney's *Pearblossom Hwy No 2* being amongst the more well known), drawings (Michelangelo's *The Holy Family with Infant St. John the Baptist*), sculpture (lots of Greek and Roman antiquities), illuminated manuscripts, decorative arts (there's a wonderful collection of Louis XIV furniture), photographs, and changing exhibits. Admission is free. You do not need a reservation for the museum BUT you do need a parking reservation ($5 fee for parking). Often parking reservations have to be made several weeks in advance. There is no convenient street parking. Buses—MTA Metro bus #561 (213-626-4455, *www.mta.net*) and Santa Monica Big Blue Bus #14 (310-451-5444, *www.bigbluebus.com*)—stop at the Getty Center. Closed Mondays and holidays, the museum is open weekends 10 am to 9 pm and weekdays 10 am to 6 pm or 9 pm. (310-440-7300, *www.getty.edu*)

Huntington Library, Art Gallery, and Botanical Gardens: The home and 207-acre estate of the late Henry Huntington are open to the public and should not be missed by any visitor to the Los Angeles area. Huntington's enormous home is now a museum featuring the work of French and English 18th-century artists. What makes the museum especially attractive is that the paintings are displayed in a homelike setting surrounded by appropriately dramatic furnishings. Nearby, in another beautiful building, is the

Huntington Library—a real gem containing, among other rare books, a 15th-century copy of the Gutenberg bible, Benjamin Franklin's handwritten autobiography, and marvelous Audubon bird prints. The gardens of the estate merit a tour in themselves and include various sections such as a rose garden, a Japanese garden, a camellia garden, a cactus garden, an English garden, and a bonsai garden. Located at 1151 Oxford Road in San Marino, the estate is open Tuesday through Friday noon to 4:30 pm, and Saturday and Sunday 10:30 am to 4:30 pm. For information on special events and shows call 626-405-2100, *www.huntington.org.*

NBC Television Studios: Los Angeles is the television capital of the world. To get an idea of what goes on behind the screen, visit the NBC Television Studios and take their one-hour tour that gives you a look at where the stars rehearse, how costumes are designed, how stage props are made, and what goes into the special effects. The tour also visits some of the show sets. The studios are located at 3000 West Alameda Avenue in Burbank. (818-840-3537)

The Norton Simon Museum of Art: The Norton Simon Museum of Art is without doubt one of the finest private art museums in the world, set in a beautiful Moorish-style building accented by a reflecting pool and manicured gardens. Norton Simon and his actress wife, Jennifer Jones, share their incredible collection of art including paintings by such masters as Rubens, Rembrandt, Raphael, Picasso, and Matisse. The museum, open Thursday through Sunday noon to 6 pm, is located at 411 West Colorado Boulevard in Pasadena. (626-449-6840, *www.nortonsimon.org*)

El Pueblo de Los Angeles: With all the tinsel of modern-day Los Angeles, it is easy to forget that this city was originally a *pueblo* founded in 1781 to grow food for the Spanish soldiers guarding this distant territory for their king. You catch a glimpse of the town's history in El Pueblo de Los Angeles, a little bit of Mexico where Hispanic people sell colorful Mexican souvenirs and operate attractive restaurants. The 42-acre complex of old buildings (some dating back to the 1780s) has been restored and is now a state park.

El Pueblo is located at 125 Paseo de la Plaza, Los Angeles. (213-628-1274, *www.cityofla.org/elp*)

The *Queen Mary*: If you take Hwy 710 west to Long Beach, the freeway ends at the waterfront with the *Queen Mary* docked alongside: you can go aboard and wander through the biggest ocean liner ever built. A portion of the ship is a hotel, the rest a museum, re-creating the days of splendor when the *Queen Mary* was queen of the seas.

Universal Studios: Visiting Universal Studios, the biggest, busiest movie studio in the world, is like going to a vast amusement park and there is so much to see and do that you must spend a whole day here. Included in the admission price is a two-hour tram journey that takes you around the 420-acre lot, out of the real world and into make-believe: along the way you venture inside the Curse of the Mummy's Tomb, encounter the howling fury of King Kong, and tremble in a terrifying 8.3 earthquake. Water World, a live sea war spectacular, Back to the Future, a time-travel ride from the age of the dinosaurs to 2015, and Backdraft's raging firestorm thrill you with their excitement, while the Animal Planet Live show and the re-creation of the zany Lucille Ball sitcoms give you the chance to laugh away all that adrenaline in your blood. New in 2002 is the Spider Man Rocks rock 'n' roll stunt show. The studios are just off the Hollywood Freeway at the Universal Center Drive exit. (818-508-9600, *www.universalstudios.com*)

It takes only a couple of hours to whip down the freeway between Los Angeles and San Diego but, instead, follow our sightseeing suggestions and dawdle along the way to enjoy some of southern California's coastal attractions en route.

Drive south from Los Angeles on Hwy 405, the San Diego Freeway, until you come to Hwy 73, the Corona del Mar Freeway, which branches to the south toward the coast. Take this, then in just minutes you come to Hwy 55, Newport Boulevard. Exit here and stay on the same road all the way to **Newport Beach**. Soon after crossing the bridge watch for the sign to your right for Newport Pier. (In case you get off track, the pier is at the foot of 20th Street.) Try to arrive mid-morning so that you can capture a glimpse of yesteryear when the **Dory Fleet** comes in to beach, just to the right of the pier. The dory fleet, made up of colorfully painted, open wooden fishing boats, has been putting out to sea for almost a hundred years. It is never certain exactly what time the fleet will come in (it depends upon the fishing conditions), but if you arrive mid-morning, the chances are you will see the fishermen preparing and selling their catch-of-the-day from the back of their small boats. If seeing all the fresh fish puts you in the mood for lunch, walk across the street to the **Oyster Bar & Grill**—the food is excellent and the clam chowder truly outstanding.

From Newport Beach, continue south along the long, thin peninsula: the next community you come to is **Balboa**. In the center of town there is a clearly signposted public parking area next to Balboa Pier: leave your car here and explore the area. The beach is beautiful, stretching the entire length of the peninsula, all the way from the southern tip to beyond Newport Pier. Stroll along the beach and then walk across the peninsula (about a two-block span) to the Balboa Pavilion, a colorful Victorian gingerbread creation smack in the center of the wharf. Next to the pavilion are several booths where tickets are sold for cruises into the harbor. One of the best of these excursions is on the *Pavilion Queen*, which makes a 45-minute loop of the bay. Buy your ticket and, if you have time to spare until the boat leaves, wander around the nostalgic, honky-tonk boardwalk with its cotton candy, Ferris wheel, saltwater taffy shops, and penny arcade. But be back in time to board your boat because the Balboa harbor cruise should not be missed. The trip is a boat fancier's dream: over 9,000 yachts are moored in the harbor. Also of interest are the opulent homes whose lawns stretch out to the docks where their million-dollar cruisers are moored.

A block from the Balboa Pavilion is the ferry landing—you cannot miss it. After your cruise, retrieve your car and follow signs to the Balboa Ferry. You might have to wait in line a bit because the little old-fashioned ferry takes only three cars at a time. When your turn comes, it is just minutes over to **Balboa Island**, a delightful, very wealthy community. Park your car on the main street and poke about in the pretty shops, then walk a few blocks in each direction. The homes look quaint and many seem quite small and simple, but looks are deceiving—the price tags are very high.

From Balboa Island there is a bridge across the harbor to the mainland. Almost as soon as you cross the bridge, turn right, heading south on Hwy 1 through the ritzy community of **Corona del Mar**. Although there is still a quaintness to the area, exclusive boutiques, expensive art galleries, palatial homes, and trendy shops hint at the fact that this is not the sleepy little town it might appear to be.

From Corona del Mar, Hwy 1 parallels the sea, which washes up against a long stretch of beach bound by high bluffs. The area seems relatively undeveloped except for its beach parks. About 11 miles south of Corona del Mar the road passes through **Laguna Beach**, famous for its many art galleries, pretty boutiques, and miles of lovely sand. In summer, from mid-July through August, Laguna Beach is usually packed with tourists coming to see the Pageant of the Masters, a tableau in which town residents dress up and re-create paintings. Two dozen living paintings are staged each evening and viewed by spectators in an outdoor amphitheater.

Continue south along the Coastal Hwy. Soon after passing Dana Point, take the turnoff to the east on Hwy 5 to **San Juan Capistrano**. Watch for signs directing you off the freeway two blocks to **Mission San Juan Capistrano**. This mission, founded by Father Junipero Serra in 1776, has been carefully restored to give you a glimpse of what life was like in the early days of California. Although located in the center of town, the mission creates its own environment since it is insulated by lovely gardens and a complex of Spanish adobe buildings. Another point of special interest at San Juan Capistrano is that the swallows have chosen it as "home," arriving every March 19th (Saint Joseph's Day) and leaving October 23rd. Visit the mission and then retrace your route to Hwy 5 and continue south about an hour to **San Diego**.

The San Diego Visitors Bureau—619-232-3101—will send you a packet of valuable information for touring its many attractions. The San Diego Trolley makes it easy and fun to get around San Diego and its environs—you can actually ride from Old Town to the Mexican border. San Diego offers a wealth of attractions and amusements—on the following pages we feature some of our favorites. (Find out more at *www.sandiego.org*.)

Balboa Park: Balboa Park is without a doubt one of the highlights of San Diego. One of the most famous attractions within the park is the **San Diego Zoo**, one of the finest in the world (619-234-3153, *www.sandiegozoo.org*). For a good orientation of the zoo take either the 40-minute bus tour or the aerial tramway. Most of the more than 3,000 animals live within natural-style enclosures with very few cages. The Children's Zoo is especially fun, with a nursery for newborn animals and a petting zoo. But Balboa Park offers much more than its splendid zoo. There are fascinating museums and exhibits within the 1,400-acre park: the Museum of Man, the Aerospace Museum, the San Diego Museum of Art, the Timken Art Gallery, the Natural History Museum, the Reuben H. Fleet Space Theater and Science Center, the Hall of Champions, the Museum of Photographic Arts, the Lily Pond, and the Botanical Building. Most of the museums are housed in picturesque Spanish-style buildings. (619-239-0512, *www.balboapark.org*)

Coronado: While in San Diego take the bridge or the ferry over to Coronado, an island-like bulb of land tipping a thin isthmus that stretches south almost to the Mexican border. Here you find not only a long stretch of beautiful beach, but also the Del Coronado Hotel, a Victorian fantasy of gingerbread turrets and gables. The Del Coronado, locally referred to as "The Del," is a sightseeing attraction in its own right and makes an excellent choice for a luncheon stop or place to settle in at the beach.

The Embarcadero: The Embarcadero is the downtown port area located along Harbor Drive. From here you can take a harbor cruise or visit one of the floating museums tied up to the quay, part of the San Diego Maritime Museum, such as the *Star of India*, built in 1863, a dramatic tall-masted ship that carried passengers and cargo around the world and the *Medea*, a luxury steam yacht built in 1904 which has had a very colorful history. (619-234-9153, *www.sdmaritime.com*)

Heritage Park: Just adjacent to Old Town is Heritage Park, where some of San Diego's Victorian heritage is preserved. Next to the spacious village green, a street lined with fabulous Victorian houses slopes gently uphill. The buildings were moved here from other areas of San Diego to save them from the bulldozers and now these intricate creations house small shops and offices (do not miss the doll shop with a wonderful collection of doll houses and antique toys).

La Jolla: Be sure to visit La Jolla, "The Jewel," a sophisticated town just north of San Diego. Classy shops and restaurants line the streets and on a warm sunny day there is nowhere more perfect for an informal lunch and water views than George's Ocean Terrace (858-454-4244). La Jolla is home to a branch of the University of California and within its Scripps Institution of Oceanography are an excellent aquarium and museum featuring marine life from California and Mexico. Another very interesting museum is the Museum of Contemporary Art San Diego with its spectacular ocean views, interesting exhibits, and delightful café (858-454 3541, *www.mcasandiego.org*). However, what really makes La Jolla so special is her setting—beautiful white-sand beaches sheltered in intimate little coves. You may prefer to stay here rather than in San Diego.

Legoland: A Mecca for children between the ages of two and eight, this is the first Legoland in the United States and is modeled on the famous one in Denmark. All the attractions are built of or themed on the colorful Lego bricks. From fun rides to opportunities to see the production of the famous bricks and the chance to buy every available Lego product, this is a theme park that Lego enthusiasts will not want to miss. (760-918-5346, *www.legoland.com*)

Mexico: Mexico lies just south of San Diego. Do not judge Mexico by its border town of Tijuana, but if you would like to have a *taste* of Mexico, take one of the "shopping and sightseeing" tours that leave from downtown for the short drive to the border. You can drive across the border, but the bus tour removes the hassle from the trip.

Old Town: Old Town is where San Diego originated. Just southeast of the intersection of Hwys 5 and 8 you see signposts for the oldest sections of San Diego. The area has been designated as a city park and several square blocks are accessible to pedestrians only. Make the Historical Museum your first stop and orient yourself by viewing a scale model of San Diego in its early days. Although small in area, Old Town is most interesting to visit as many of the buildings are open as small museums, such as the

Mission San Diego de Alcala

Machado-Stewart Adobe, the Old School House, and the Seeley Stables (an 1860s stage depot with a good display of horse-drawn carriages). If you are in Old Town at mealtime, you can choose from many attractive restaurants. (619-291-4903)

Mission San Diego de Alcala: The oldest of the chain of missions that stretches up the coast is Mission San Diego de Alcala. The mission was originally closer to San Diego but was moved to its present site (10818 San Diego Mission Road) in 1774. To reach the mission, head east on Hwy 8—it is signposted to the north of the highway beyond the intersection of Hwy 15. (619-283-7319, *www.missionsandiego.com*)

Seaport Village: Just a little way south of the Embarcadero is Seaport Village, a very popular tourist attraction and fun for adults and children alike. Situated right on the waterfront, it has little paths that meander through 23 acres of a village of shops and restaurants built in a colorful variety of styles from Early Spanish to Victorian. Street artists display their talents to laughing audiences. An old-time merry-go-round (an import from Coney Island) jingles its gay melody, irresistibly beckoning the child in all of us to climb aboard.

Sea World: San Diego's marine display is in Mission Bay Park. Set in a 150-acre park which includes a 1-acre children's playland, Sea World features one of California's famous personalities, Shamu, the performing killer whale who delights everyone with her wit and aquatic abilities. Penguin Encounter is a particularly fun exhibit where you watch comical penguins waddling about in their polar environment, while Shark Encounter presents one of the largest displays of sharks in the world and provides the terrifying thrill of being surrounded by these efficient killing machines as you walk through an acrylic tube. (619-226-3901, *www.seaworld.com*)

Wild Animal Park: This is a branch of the San Diego Zoo 30 miles north of the city near Escondido—truly a zoo on a grand scale. The animals roam freely in terrain designed to match their natural habitat. You feel as if you are on a safari in Africa as you watch for lions and other animals while you tour the park on the Wgasa Bushline Monorail tour. There are also several open theaters where animal shows are presented. (619-234-6541)

Leaving San Diego, Hwy 8 takes you east and winds through shrub-filled canyons dotted with ever-expanding housing suburbs. About 30 minutes after you leave the city, watch for the sign for Hwy 79 where you turn north toward Julian. The road weaves through an Indian reservation and the scenery becomes prettier by the minute as you climb into the mountains and enter the **Cuyamaca Rancho State Park**. There are not many opportunities to sightsee en route, but if you want to break your journey, you can pause at the park headquarters and visit the Indian museum or the museum at the **Old Stonewall Mine**. Leaving the park, the road winds down into Julian.

Julian is a small town that can easily be explored in just a short time. What is especially nice is that, although it is a tourist attraction, the town is not "tacky touristy." Rather, you get the feeling you are in the last century as you wander through the streets and stop to browse at some of the antique shops, visit the small historical museum in the old brewery, and enjoy refreshment at the soda fountain in the 1880s drug store. If you want to delve deeper into mining, just a short drive (or long walk) away on the outskirts of town is the **Eagle Mine**, founded by pioneers from Georgia, many of them soldiers who came here after the Civil War. Tours are taken deep into the mine and a narration gives not only the history of the mine, but the history of Julian.

If you are in Julian in the fall, you can enjoy another of Julian's offerings—apples. Although you can sample Julian's wonderful apples throughout the year (every restaurant has its own special apple pie on the menu), the apple becomes king during the fall harvest. Beginning in October and continuing on into November, special crafts shows and events are held in the Julian Town Hall, and, of course, apples are featured at every restaurant. If you visit one of the packing plants on the edge of town you can buy not only apples, but every conceivable item that has apples as a theme.

It is only a short drive north from Julian on Hwy 79 to **Santa Ysabel** where you turn right at the main intersection. At this junction you see **Dudley's Bakery**, a rather nondescript-looking building that houses a great bakery: loyal customers drive all the way from San Diego just to buy one of their 21 varieties of tasty bread. As you leave Santa Ysabel you come to **Mission Santa Ysabel**, a reconstructed mission that still serves the Indians. This is one of the less interesting missions, but you may want to see the murals painted by the local Indians.

About 7 miles after leaving the mission, Hwy 79 breaks off to the east and you continue north on Hwy 76. In five minutes you come to Lake Henshaw. Just beyond the lake turn northeast (right) on East Grade Road, which winds its way up the mountain to the **Palomar Observatory**. Just near the parking area is a museum where you learn about the observatory through photos and short films. It is a pleasant stroll up to the impressive white-domed observatory, which houses the Hale telescope—the largest in the United States. A flight of steps takes you to a glass-walled area where you see the giant telescope whose lens is 200 inches in diameter, 2 feet thick, and took 11 years to polish. You cannot see the telescope in operation because it is used only at night, but it is fun to imagine scientists scanning the heavens.

After viewing the observatory, loop back down the twisting road to the main highway and when it intersects with Hwy 76 turn northwest (right), driving through hills covered with groves of avocado and orange trees. In about 12 miles you come to **Pala** and the **Mission San Antonio de Pala**. Established in 1810, it is one of the few remaining active *asistencias* (missions built in outlying areas to serve the Indians). The mission is small, but the chapel is very beautiful in its rugged simplicity enhanced by thick adobe walls, rustic beamed ceiling, and Indian paintings. A bell tower stands alone to the right of the chapel, a picturesque sight. To the left are a simple museum and a souvenir shop.

From Pala it is about a ten-minute drive north on S16 to Temecula. Just before you enter town the road intersects with Hwy 79 and you head east for 18 miles to Aguanga where Hwy 371 takes you northeast for 21 miles to Hwy 74. As you head north on 74 the mountain air becomes sweeter and the scenery increasingly prettier as you enter the forest. In about 12 miles you see signs for **Idyllwild** to the northeast. Turn here on Hwy 243 and very soon you come to the small resort tucked into the mountains high above Palm Springs. Homely little restaurants, antique stores, and fascinating gift shops make up the town.

Leaving Idyllwild, continue north on Hwy 342 to Banning where you turn east (right) on Hwy 10. In about 12 miles you come to Hwy 111 where you turn right and follow signs to Palm Springs (about a ten-minute drive). **Palm Springs** was first discovered by the Indians who came to this oasis to bathe in the hot springs, which they considered to have healing qualities. The same tribe still owns much of Palm Springs and rents their valuable real estate to homeowners and commercial enterprises. The hot springs are still in use today.

During the winter season the town is congested with traffic and the sidewalks are crammed with an assortment of people of every age, size, and shape dressed in colorful, sporty clothes. Palm Springs used to be deserted in summer when the days are very hot. However, more and more tourists are coming in June, July, and August, attracted by the lower hotel rates. Although the temperature in the summer months is frequently well above 110 degrees, it is a dry heat and not unbearable in the mornings and balmy evenings. In fact, due to the altitude, evenings often require a sweater. So if your visit is in summer, plan your sightseeing for early and late in the day and spend midday in the comfort of your air-conditioned inn.

In addition to the pleasures of basking in the sun or playing on one of the many golf courses in the area, Palm Springs offers a variety of sightseeing. The most impressive excursion is to take the **Aerial Tramway** (located just north of town off Hwy 111) from the desert floor up 2½ miles into the San Jacinto Mountains. In summer you go from sizzling heat to cool mountain forests, while in winter you go from desert to snow. The weather atop the mountain is often more than 40 degrees cooler than in Palm Springs, so remember to take the appropriate clothing. At the top are observation decks with telescopes, a restaurant, and miles of hiking trails. (760-325-1391 or 888-515-TRAM, *www.pstramway.com*)

If you enjoy deserts, be sure not to miss the **Living Desert Wildlife and Botanical Park** (open only in the mornings in summer) where 6 miles of trails wind through different types of desert that are found in the United States. Tour booklets are available at the entrance to assist you along the trails (760-346-5694). If you are interested in the rich and famous, join a bus tour that drives by the outside of their magnificent homes. Many movie stars have second homes in Palm Springs.

Palm Springs is a convenient place to end this itinerary because it is a quick, easy drive on the freeway back to Los Angeles. But, if time permits, squeeze in one more contrasting destination, the exclusive Alpine resort of Lake Arrowhead.

Aerial Tramway, Palm Springs

Leave Palm Springs and head north on Hwy 111 for about 10 miles to Hwy 10 and turn west for Banning. Approximately 20 miles past Banning at Redlands, exit from the freeway on Hwy 30 and drive north for a few minutes until Hwy 38 travels into the hills. As the road begins to climb up from the valley the scenery becomes prettier with every curve—the dry desert brush is gradually left behind, replaced by evergreen trees. At the town of Running Springs turn west on Hwy 18. This is called the "**Rim of the World Highway**," a road where sweeping vistas of the valley floor can be glimpsed through the clouds. Be aware that fog often hovers around this drive and then, instead of admiring beautiful views, you creep along in thick, gray mist.

Lake Arrowhead village is a newly built cluster of restaurants and shops along the lakefront. The lake is bordered by magnificent estates of the wealthy from southern California. The magnet of Lake Arrowhead is not any specific sightseeing, but rather the outdoors experience: although lakefront and beach access is restricted and private, you can take leisurely walks through the forest, picnic in secluded parks, explore the lake by paddle boats, or rent bicycles for a bit of fresh-air adventure. You must also take the hour-long ride on the nostalgic steamer that circles the lake.

When it is time to complete your itinerary, retrace your path back to the valley and follow Hwy 10 back into Los Angeles. Unless you encounter unexpected traffic, the trip should take about two hours.

San Francisco to Los Angeles via the Coast

Golden Gate Bridge

You can drive between San Francisco and Los Angeles in a day or fly in an hour. But rather than rushing down the freeway or hopping aboard an airplane, drive leisurely along the coast between these two metropolises and enjoy the quaintness of Carmel, the charm of Santa Barbara, the splendor of the Big Sur coastline, the opulence of William Randolph Hearst's hilltop castle, and the fun of experiencing a bit of Denmark in Solvang. Also intertwined in this itinerary are stops to appreciate a piece of California's colorful heritage—her Spanish missions. This routing roughly follows the footsteps of the Spanish padres who, in the 1700s, built a string of missions (about a day's journey on horseback apart) along the coast of California from the Mexican border to just north of San Francisco. Today many of these beautiful adobe churches and their surrounding settlements have been reconstructed and are open as museums, capturing a glimpse of life as it was lived by the Spaniards and the Indians in the early days of colonization.

Recommended Pacing: We recommend a minimum stay of two or three nights in San Francisco, affording two full days for a quick introduction to the city, and definitely more time if your schedule allows. San Francisco is a beautiful city and there is much to explore and enjoy. From San Francisco, if you take the direct route, you can easily drive to Carmel in about three hours. However, located just south of San Francisco is the Año Nuevo Reserve, where you can observe the enormous elephant seals in their natural habitat. It takes several hours to walk around the secluded beaches where the seals congregate, so if you want to visit the reserve en route to Carmel, we recommend an early start from the city. Plan on at least two to three nights (or again, if possible, more) in the Carmel, Pacific Grove, or Monterey area. One day can easily be devoured exploring the Monterey Bay Aquarium, Cannery Row, and the wharf. Another full day is needed to drive the gorgeous Seventeen-Mile Drive, walk the spectacular Point Lobos State Park, visit the beautiful Carmel Mission—and we have yet to even discuss shopping in downtown Carmel! From Carmel, you can drive the dramatic coastline of Big Sur and on to Santa Barbara in four to five hours, but plan to overnight in Cambria if you want to include even just one of the tours of Hearst Castle and visit the cute artists' town of Cambria—it's too much to do in one day. From Cambria you can go directly to Santa Barbara or tarry for a couple of days and explore the the wine region around Paso Robles. Santa Barbara is a beautiful, charming city with an expanse of lovely beach. You'd be disappointed if you didn't plan at least two nights in the area before continuing on to Los Angeles. **The itinerary route is outlined on Map 2 at the back of the book.**

Weather Wise: San Francisco and the coast are often foggy during June, July, and August. The farther south you go, the earlier in the day the fog burns off. The northern California coast is cool and rainy during the winter. In southern California the weather is warmer year-round and traditionally less rain falls during the winter.

When you ask travelers around the world, "What is your favorite city?" many times the answer is "San Francisco." And it is no wonder: **San Francisco** really is special, a magical town of unsurpassed beauty—spectacular when glistening in the sunlight, equally enchanting when wrapped in fog. But the beauty is more than skin deep: San

Francisco offers a wealth of sightseeing, fabulous restaurants, splendid shopping, and a refreshing climate.

There are many large, super-deluxe hotels in San Francisco and we recommend a marvelous selection of small, intimate inns. Study our various recommendations to see what most fits your personality and pocketbook. Be advised that hotel space is frequently tight, so make reservations as far in advance as possible.

A good way to orient yourself in San Francisco is to take a half-day city sightseeing tour (brochures on these tours should be available at your hotel) and then return to the destinations that most catch your fancy. If you like to study before you arrive, there are entire guidebooks devoted to San Francisco and the Visitors Bureau will send you an information packet on what to see and do (San Francisco Convention and Visitors Bureau, 900 Market Street , San Francisco, CA 94101, *www.sfvisitor.org,* 415-391-2000). To keep you on the right track, the following is an alphabetical listing of some of our favorite sights.

Alcatraz: Wreathed in mystery, the often fog-shrouded island of Alcatraz lies in the heart of San Francisco Bay, a scant mile and a quarter from the sights and sounds of downtown. The site of the first lighthouse on the west coast, in operation since 1854, "The Rock" has since been used as an army fortress and a jail. The latter, supposedly escape-proofed by the icy-cold waters and dangerous currents of the Bay, was home to criminals deemed "incorrigible" by the Federal penal system. Numbered among its inmates were Al Capone and Robert Stroud, the infamous "Birdman of Alcatraz." Access is by ferry from the San Francisco waterfront. Trips run daily but are extremely popular and should be booked well in advance contact TeleSails, 415-705-5555, *www.telesails.com*). The island is now under the control of the National Park Service and ranger-guided and audio-assisted tours provide a fascinating insight into the island's history, as well as affording spectacular views of San Francisco and its bridges. Be sure to wear sturdy, comfortable shoes and warm clothing.

Cable Cars: You cannot leave San Francisco without riding one of the colorful little trolleys that make their way up and down the breathtakingly steep city hills. Rather than touring by cab or bus, plan your sightseeing around hopping on and off cable cars. You can travel easily from the shopping district of Union Square past Chinatown and the "crookedest street in the world"—Lombard, and on to the Ghiradelli Square-Fisherman's Wharf area. For a behind-the-scenes look at this charmingly antiquated transit system, visit the Cable Car Museum at the corner of Washington and Mason Streets. Here you can view the huge cables that pull the cars from below the streets and a historical display that includes the very first cable car.

California Palace of the Legion of Honor: has a spectacular setting on a bluff in Lincoln Park overlooking the ocean. The original of Rodin's famous *Thinker* welcomes you to the San Francisco replica of the Palais de la Légion d'Honneur in Paris where Napoleon first established his new government. A self-guided audio tour is available to steer you through the galleries, which include one devoted to medieval art (there's a ceiling from a 15th-century Spanish palace), a British gallery with paintings by Gainsborough and Constable, and 19th- and 20th-century galleries with their popular works by Monet, Renoir, and Picasso. Located at 34th Avenue and Clement Street. (415-750-3600, *www.thinker.org*)

Chinatown: Just a few short blocks from Union Square you enter beneath the dragon arch (at the corner of Bush Street and Grant Avenue) into another world with street signs in Chinese characters, tiny grocery stores displaying Chinese vegetables and delicacies, apothecary shops selling unusual remedies, spicy aromas drifting from colorful restaurants, older women bustling about in traditional dress, and the surrounding hum of unfamiliar phrases. Of course, the streets are jammed with tourists and locals and there is a plethora of rather tacky, but fun-to-explore souvenir shops. Don't limit your exploration of Chinatown to the main thoroughfare of Grant Avenue: poke down the intriguing little alleys and side streets. Plan a visit to 56 Ross Alley, the Golden Gate Fortune Cookie Factory. Down another alley, at 17 Adler Place, is the Chinese Historical Society of America—a small museum portraying the story of the Chinese immigration.

The Chinese Cultural Center (415-986-1822, *www.c-c-c.org*), housed in the Holiday Inn at Kearny and Washington streets, offers fascinating docent-led heritage and culinary walks affording a glimpse of the "real Chinatown." It also has a wonderful small museum offering an ever-changing schedule of exhibits.

Coit Tower: Coit Tower, located at the top of Telegraph Hill, is a relic of old San Francisco and fun to visit—not only because of the great view, but because its story is so very "San Francisco." The money to construct the watch tower, which resembles the nozzle of a fire hose, was willed to the city by the wealthy Lillie Hitchcock Coit, a volunteer fireman (or should we say firewoman) who dearly loved to rush to every blaze wearing her diamond-encrusted fire badge. A mural on the ground floor provides a vivid depiction of early California life.

Fisherman's Wharf to Ghiradelli Square: This portion of the waterfront is very popular with tourists. **Pier 39** is lined with New England-style shops; nothing authentic, but a popular shopping and restaurant arcade complete with street performers and a beautiful two-tier carousel. Pier 39 is also home to a new aquarium and some very boisterous and amusing sea lions (415-981-7437, *www.pier39.com*). Pier 41 is where you purchase tickets for the popular excursion to Alcatraz (see listing). **Fisherman's Wharf**, where fishermen haul in their daily catch, has long been a favorite with tourists. It is difficult to find even the heart of Fisherman's Wharf behind all the trinket-filled souvenir shops and tourist arcades, but look carefully and sure enough, you will see the colorful fishing boats bobbing about in the water at the waterfront between Jones and Taylor Streets. Nearby, Fish Alley, a small pier extending out into the harbor, affords a good view of the fishing fleet and the aroma of fresh fish mingling with the salty air. At the corner of Leavenworth and Jefferson **The Cannery**, formerly a fruit cannery, is today an attractive shopping complex. At the foot of Hyde Street **Hyde Street Pier** is home to the Maritime Museum's fleet of historic ships, several of which can be boarded and explored. Our favorite is the *Balclutha* (1886), a three-masted merchant ship typical of the hundreds that came round the Horn to San Francisco. Inspect the comfortable captain's quarters and cramped crew's quarters and exhibits of nautical gear. Just beyond the **Hyde Street cable car turnaround** lies **Ghiradelli Square**, a lovely brick building that used to house the Ghiradelli chocolate factory, now a complex of attractive stores and restaurants. The ship-shaped building in Aquatic Park (in front of Ghiradelli Square) is the land base of the **Maritime Museum**, full of displays on the history of water transportation from the 1800s to the present, including marvelous photos of old San Francisco. (415-561-7100, *www.nps.gov/safr*)

Golden Gate Bridge and **Fort Point:** San Francisco's symbol is the Golden Gate Bridge with its graceful orange arches. The visitors' viewing area on the San Francisco side offers stunning views (if the fog is not in) and access to the pedestrian walkway across the bridge (2½ miles round trip, wear warm clothing). At the base of the Golden Gate Bridge's south pier, Fort Point, built in 1861 as one of the west coast's principal points of defense, provides a fascinating insight into military life during that period. (415-556-1693, *www.nps.gov/fopo*)

Golden Gate Park: You will need to take a bus or taxi to Golden Gate Park, but don't miss it. The park encompasses over 1,000 acres, so large you really cannot hope to see it all, but many attractions are located near one another. Wander through the traditional **Japanese Tea Garden** and enjoy tea and cookies Japanese-style at the tea house (415-752-1171). The **California Academy of Sciences** (415-750-7145, *www.calacademy.org*) houses the Museum of Natural History, the Steinhart Aquarium, and the Morrison Planetarium. The **Museum of Natural History** offers dioramas of wildlife from African to Californian (along with an impressive collection of gems and minerals), while the neighboring **Steinhart Aquarium** has all things fishy, from a tropical swamp with alligators and turtles to a fish roundabout—an enormous donut-shaped fish tank. The **Morrison Planetarium** offers visitors daily multimedia presentations about astronomy, such as a realistic simulation of the night sky as observed from any place on Earth. If you are hungry, you might want to consider the **Beach Chalet**, a restaurant on the ocean side of the park near the Dutch Windmill. The menu offers good, simple fare matched with their list of brewery selections. The building once served as the changing rooms for Ocean Beach. On the first floor are beautifully restored murals of San Francisco in its early days and guests enjoy unobstructed views of the surf from tables by the second-floor expanse of window. (415-386-8439)

Lombard Street: Lombard is an ordinary city street—except for one lone, brick-paved block between Hyde and Leavenworth where the street goes crazy and makes a series of hairpin turns as it twists down the hill. Pretty houses border each side of the street, and banks of hydrangeas add color. Start at the top and go down what must be the crookedest street in the world: it is lots of fun. The Hyde Street cable car makes a stop at the top of the hill and from here you can easily walk down to Fisherman's Wharf.

Mission San Francisco de Assisi: This mission at Dolores and 16th Streets is frequently referred to as the Mission Dolores. If you are interested in Californian missions, you will find a visit here worthwhile. It was on this spot that San Francisco was born when Father Francisco Palou founded his mission here in 1776. At one time this was a large complex of warehouses, workshops, granaries, a tannery, soap shop, corrals, Indian dwellings, and even an aqueduct. Today, all that is left is the chapel and next to it the garden where gravestones attest to the fragility of life. Although small, the chapel is beautiful in its simplicity with 4-foot-thick adobe walls and massive redwood timbers. (415-621-8203)

Museum of Modern Art (MOMA): A cylindrical, striped turret rising from blocks of red bricks gives a hint of what lies within this futuristic building at 151 Third Street. To help you appreciate the exhibits, an audio-cassette can be rented in the lobby to guide you through the museum's permanent collection of abstract expressionistic paintings and avant-garde photography. Even if you are not a fan of modern art, you will be awed by the building's interior: the space soars upwards from the lobby for seven stories to a broad catwalk that runs below the cylindrical glass skylight (415-357-4000, *www.sfmoma.org*). Just across the street from the MOMA lie the **Yerba Buena Gardens and Galleries**. The gardens are an oasis of tranquillity where a broad expanse of grass leads to a cascading sheet of water—a perfect place to relax and people watch. The galleries offer changing exhibits that showcase the San Francisco Bay Area's cultural diversity. On the top floor, encircled by windows and a spectacular view of the city skyline, is an ice-skating rink. (Open daily 1 pm to 5 pm and evenings with some limitations. 750 Folsom Street between 3rd and 4th, 415-777-3727, *www.skatebowl.com*.) Just round the corner (678 Mission Street) a turn-of-the-century hardware store houses the **California Historical Society** with its bookstore and changing exhibits of photographs, paintings, and objects documenting California's growth and change. (415-357-1848, *www.calhist.org*)

Sausalito and **Tiburon:** An enjoyable excursion is to take the ferry from Pier 43½ in San Francisco to Sausalito or Tiburon, small towns just across the bay full of intriguing shops, art galleries, and wonderful restaurants. As a bonus, en route you enjoy gorgeous vistas of San Francisco and the Golden Gate Bridge. For information call the Red and White Fleet at 415-447-2900, or visit their website at *www.redandwhite.com*.

Theater: For theater buffs, San Francisco offers an excellent variety of entertainment. Most theaters are located in the heart of the city within walking distance of Union Square. In addition, San Francisco has fine opera and ballet. The San Francisco Visitors Bureau (415-391-2000, *www.sfvisitor.org*) can send you a packet with information on what is going on. You can also call the "hot line" at 415-391-2001 for a recording of all current events.

Union Square: In the center of the city sits Union Square, hallmarked by a small park around which tower deluxe hotels and fancy department stores. Do not tarry too long at the "biggies" because just beyond the square lies every specialty shop imaginable from department stores to any number of designer boutiques. San Francisco's own exclusive and elegant Gumps at 135 Post Street certainly merits a visit. The Crocker Galleria at 50 Post houses collections from top names in international design and many fine specialty stores and restaurants.

Union Street: Union Street (between Laguna and Steiner), lined with lovely restored Victorian houses, offers a wonderful variety of quaint gift shops, elegant boutiques, beautiful antique stores, small art galleries, excellent restaurants, and a multitude of intriguing little shops hidden down tiny brick-paved lanes.

It's a three-hour drive south from San Francisco to Carmel taking the scenic Hwy 280 to San Jose and Hwys 17 and 1 on to Carmel. But rather than head directly to Carmel, we suggest you meander down the coast, following the contours of the spectacular coastline, enjoying a number of sights en route—a journey that will deserve a couple of days.

Leave San Francisco to the south on 19th Avenue to Hwy 280 and take Hwy 1 through Pacifica where the freeway ends and the road narrows to meander around the precipitous rocky promontory known as Devil's Slide to Moss Beach. Just to the south of Moss Beach, **Princeton Harbor**, with its mass of fishing vessels and sailboats, is one of California's last true commercial fishing harbors. Sport-fishing and whale-watching boats leave early in the morning from Princeton—bookings can be made through **Huck Finn Sport Fishing** (650-726-7133).

Detour off the Coastal Hwy to the east at Hwy 92 and take it for one block, making a right on **Half Moon Bay's** Main Street. Park just across the bridge and visit **Half Moon Bay Feed and Fuel**, an authentic country store selling saddles, rabbits, chickens, animal feed, and farm implements. Poke your head in the variety of shops, restaurants, and art galleries that line the street. Leaving Half Moon Bay, continue down Main Street to rejoin Hwy 1 to the south of town.

Thirty miles south of Half Moon Bay is the **Año Nuevo State Reserve**, home to elephant seals whose huge males with their trunk-like snouts reach a whopping 6,000 pounds. From mid-December to the end of March park docents conduct a 3-mile round-trip hike to the breeding grounds of these car-size mammals. Reservation lines open in October for the following season (800-444-7275). If you are not able to book several months in advance, call the park directly at 650-879-2025 and they may be able to advise you if last-minute tickets are available. We have, in the past, secured tickets by arriving at 8:30 am and queuing at the entrance booth for tickets for tours that day. Outside of the breeding season obtaining permits to view the seals (there are often also a great many sea lions in residence) is not a problem: tickets are issued on arrival and you follow the well-marked path to the distant beach where the seals are found. Outside of the breeding season, the best time to visit is during July and August when the juvenile males return to molt.

Ten miles south of Año Nuevo you come to the cluster of houses that makes up the town of **Davenport**. Fronting Hwy 1 is the **New Davenport Cash Store**, which sells everything from handmade jewelry to local pottery and whose restaurant offers a varied and healthful menu with excellent soups and tasty vegetarian dishes. (831-426-4122)

Downtown **Santa Cruz**, 11 miles south of Davenport, was badly damaged in the 1989 earthquake, but a newly revived Pacific Avenue demonstrates all the laid-back charm the town is noted for, with outdoor cafés, a variety of shops and galleries, and numerous street performers. Years ago this busy seaside town, with its bustling **boardwalk** and amusement park bordering a broad stretch of white-sand beach, was a popular day trip for workers in San Francisco. The rides include a heart-stopping wooden roller coaster and a wonderful old-fashioned carousel.

If you enjoy riding trains, you can take the old-fashioned diesel that departs from the boardwalk twice a day during the summer months for the 60-minute ride to Felton. Here you board an old steam train of the **Roaring Camp Railroad**, a train that winds up into a redwood forest. The train leaves several times a day from its main station in **Felton** (except on Christmas) along narrow-gauge tracks built to carry lumber out of the forest.

The conductor tells stories of the old days as the train circles up through the trees, making a brief stop at the "cathedral," a beautiful ring of redwoods that form a natural outdoor church, before heading back to the depot. It is possible to take a picnic with you, alight at the top, and take the next train back. Call for schedules and directions: 831-335-4400.

Leave Santa Cruz heading south on Hwy 1 and travel for about 20 miles to Hwy 129 where you head east. Continue on the 129 for approximately 16 miles through small farms and rolling hills to **San Juan Bautista** and its most attractive **mission**. There is far more to see here than just an old church, for an area of the town has been restored to the way it was 150 years ago with the mission as its focus. Facing the square is the restored Plaza Hotel, now a museum where tickets are sold for admission to the attractions in the park. The focal point of the sightseeing is, of course, the mission, but do not end your touring there. Directly across from the mission is a most interesting house, nicely restored, and furnished as it must have looked many years ago. Adjacent to this is a blacksmith's shop and stables where there is a colorful display of old coaches. Next door to the Plaza Hotel is another home now open as a museum with period furnishings.

Follow Hwy 156 west for a couple of miles until it merges with Hwy 101 going south to the Monterey Peninsula. As you pass through Prunedale, begin to watch for signs indicating a sharp right-hand turn on Hwy 156 west to the Monterey Peninsula. Along the way, fields of artichokes dominate the landscape as you near Castroville, the artichoke capital of the world. When you begin to smell the sea air, stay in the left lane following signs for Hwy 1 south to the Monterey Peninsula. As you approach Monterey, dunes lining the sweep of the bay come into view.

The main sightseeing attractions in **Monterey** are in two areas: the old town and the marina, and the Monterey Bay Aquarium and Cannery Row. A bayside walking and biking path runs from the Marina beside Cannery Row to the Aquarium and beyond to the adjoining town of Pacific Grove. A fun way to explore Monterey is to rent a side-by-side tricycle near the aquarium and pedal to the Marina.

Kayaking lets you enjoy another perspective of Monterey—looking back at the town and gorgeous beaches from the bay. Open-deck kayaks make the sport easy even for the inexperienced and paddling out amongst the seals and otters is quite memorable. We rented from **A B Seas Kayak** and found owner Geoff Hand and his team to be very helpful and accommodating. All equipment, loose-fitting rain gear (although plan on getting wet), life jackets, and instruction are included in the rental price. Geoff has generously offered any of our readers a 20% discount on the $30 per person, three-hour package if our guide is presented. A B Seas Kayak is conveniently located at 32 Cannery Row, on the coastguard pier. (831-647-0147)

In **Old Town** a 3-mile walking tour links the restored buildings of early Monterey. The old adobe structures are interesting and a sharp contrast to the bustle of nearby **Fisherman's Wharf**, a quaint wooden fishing pier lined with shops and restaurants. At the end of the pier huge sea lions vie for the fish cast off the fishing boats.

Cannery Row, once the center of this area's thriving sardine industry (the fish are long gone), and brought vividly to life by John Steinbeck in his novels featuring Doc and the boys, is now filled with small stores and tucked into an old warehouse are some outlet stores. The premier attraction in Monterey is the adjacent **Monterey Bay Aquarium**. The centerpieces of the Aquarium are the huge glass tanks that showcase the underwater world of the local offshore marine habitat from the diverse tidepools to the multitude of life in the Monterey Bay: one tank is populated by huge sharks and colorful schools of fish while another contains a mature kelp forest teeming with fish. The Outer Bay exhibit, a vast tank of water representative of the outer ocean, brings a new dimension to the Aquarium and leaves the visitor with a memorable impression of just how little is known about that massive body of water. (*www.montereybayaquarium.org, 831-648-4888*)

Monterey is all hustle and bustle (especially in summer) and it is nice to continue on to the neighboring, much quieter town of **Pacific Grove**. To reach Pacific Grove, follow the road in front of the Aquarium up the hill and make a right turn onto Ocean View

Boulevard, a lovely drive lined on one side with gracious Victorian homes and splendid views of the sea on the other. Besides being an affluent residential community, Pacific Grove is famous for the Monarch butterflies that return faithfully each October and cluster in the grove of trees next to Butterfly Grove Inn on Lighthouse Avenue.

Carmel lies just a few miles beyond Pacific Grove and there is no more perfect way to arrive than along the famous Seventeen-Mile Drive, which meanders around the Monterey Peninsula coastline between the two towns. The route is easy to find as the road that leads to the "drive" intersects Lighthouse Avenue and is appropriately called The Seventeen-Mile Drive.

The Seventeen-Mile Drive loops through an exclusive residential area of multi-million-dollar estates and gorgeous golf courses. Because the land is private a toll per car is levied at the entrance gate, where you'll receive a map indicating points of interest along the way. The scenic drive traces the low-lying shore, passes rocky coves where kelp beds are home to sea lions, sea otters, cormorants, and gulls (remember to bring your binoculars), and meanders through woodlands where Monterey pines gnarled by the wind stand sentinel on lonely headlands. Along the drive is the famous **Pebble Beach Golf Course**, site of the National Pro-Am Golf Championship each January.

Carmel—filled with Hansel-and-Gretel-style cottages nestled under pines and surrounded by flower-filled gardens—is one of California's most appealing towns. Tourists throng the streets lined with appetizing candy shops, beckoning bakeries, a wonderful selection of restaurants, enticing boutiques, pretty gift stores, and attractive art galleries. The picturesque combination of fairy-tale cottages and a sparkling blue bay makes Carmel so very special. Its main street slopes gently down the hill to a glorious white-sand beach crested by windswept dunes. Just south of town is the **Carmel Mission**, established in 1770 by Father Junipero Serra. Beautifully restored and fronted by a pretty garden, the mission was Father Serra's headquarters. It is from here that the stalwart little priest set out to expand the chain of missions. A small museum shows the simple cell in which Father Serra slept on a hard wooden bed. The church itself, with its

Moorish tower, star-shaped window, and profusion of surrounding flowers, has a most romantic appearance.

Located just south of Carmel on Hwy 1, **Point Lobos State Reserve** is, in our estimation, the premier place to enjoy the California coast. A small admission fee entitles you to day use of the park. Walk along the coastal trails and venture down wooden steps to secluded sandy beaches. Rocky coves are home to sea lions, harbor seals, and sea otters. Between December and May migrating gray whales surface and dive offshore. Bring your binoculars and head for Sea Lion Point and the headland on Cypress Grove Trail, the best places to see the whales. Walking trails and picnic areas are well marked and the times of guided nature walks are posted at the entrance gate. (831-624-4909, *www.ptlobos.org*)

Believe everything you ever read about the beauties of the **Big Sur Coastline**: it is truly sensational. However, hope for clear weather, because on foggy or rainy days an endless picture of stunning seascapes becomes a tortuous drive around precipitous cliff roads. (In poor weather, you may wish to take the inland route to Cambria by following the picturesque Carmel Valley road east to Hwy 101 where you then head south. When you come to Hwy 46, turn west. The road intersects with coastal Hwy 1 just south of Cambria.) As you drive south on Hwy 1, you have an indication that you are approaching Big Sur when you see the road sign "Hill Curves—63 miles," which is exactly what the road does as it clings precipitously to the edge of the cliff. While the road is quite narrow, there are plenty of turnouts and opportunities for taking photos.

If you have plenty of time, you might want to consider a very scenic 10-mile detour east off Hwy 1 following the **Old Coast Road** through beautiful redwood groves and country ranchland. To access the Old Coast Road, turn left just before crossing the dramatic span of Bixby Creek Bridge. You'll be on your own for most of the journey and the road will deposit you back on Hwy 1, across from the entrance to the wonderful **Andrew Molera State Park**. Allow approximately one hour for the adventure, and be aware that the road is not passable after heavy rains.

If you opt to remain on scenic Hwy 1, you will find its passage dramatic over the much-photographed, long concrete span of **Bixby Creek Bridge**. A few miles later, the rocky volcanic outcrop topped by the Point Sur lighthouse appears. About 40 miles south of Carmel is the **Pfeiffer Big Sur State Park** with its camping facilities and many miles of hiking trails among coastal redwood groves. (831-667-2315)

If you choose only one place to stop along the Big Sur drive, make it **Nepenthe**, about 3 miles south of the entrance to Pfeiffer Big Sur State Park. Nepenthe is a casual restaurant, with a '60s-style decor, perched on a cliff high above the ocean offering unsurpassed views (on a clear day) of the coast to the south (831-667-2345). Below Nepenthe, **The Phoenix Shop** has a wonderful selection of clothes, artwork, books, and gifts (831-667-2347). Interestingly, at the heart of the complex is a cottage that Orson Welles bought for his then wife, Rita Hayworth.

Another stop along the way where you can gain a closer view of this magnificent coastline is at the **Julia Pfeiffer Burns State Park**. The parking area is to the left of the road. Leave your car and take the short walk leading under the highway and round the face of the cliff, which overlooks a superb small cove with emerald-green water and a white-sand beach. From the rocky bluff a waterfall drops directly into the ocean and the restless sea beats against a craggy point. After the Ragged Point Inn, the bends become less frequent, and as the cliffs give way to the coastal plain, the driving becomes less arduous.

After the road begins to flatten out, watch for **Hearst Castle** impressively crowning the coastal hills. In 1919, William Randolph Hearst commissioned California's famous architect Julia Morgan to design a simple vacation home atop a hill on his estate overlooking the California coastline. Twenty-eight years and $10,000,000 later, he moved to Los Angeles and left his 100-room retreat, La Cuesta Encantada (the enchanted hill), which has never been completed. Hearst Castle continues to delight its millions of visitors: next to Disneyland, Hearst Castle is the most popular visitor attraction in California.

Hearst Castle

The number of visitors allowed on the hill during any one day is limited, so it is essential that you make reservations in advance. Hearst Castle is open every day except Thanksgiving, Christmas, and New Year's Day. Several different one-hour and forty-five-minute tours are available. Also from September through December, Hearst Castle offers at weekends a magical evening tour and program with a holiday theme. The castle is decorated for Christmas and the staff, dressed in appropriate and wonderful costumes, play the roles of William Hearst and his entourage of friends as they bring history alive. The evening tours are tremendously popular and must be booked well in advance. If traveling with children, inquire also about the special summer children's programs. Tickets for all tours are available for purchase up to eight weeks in advance. (800-444-4445, *www.hearstcastle.org*)

Plan on arriving at the visitors center at the foot of the hill at least half an hour before your scheduled departure, as the tours leave with clockwork-like precision and do not wait for stragglers. If you arrive early, you can browse through the small museum located next to the departure depot where groups assemble by number for their turn to be taken up the hill by bus. Here you also find an Imax Theater which shows a special documentary of Hearst Castle.

Of the daily tour programs, Tour 1, the overview of the castle, is the one recommended for first-time visitors. You walk through the gardens to the main house, La Casa Grande, to tour the rooms on the lower level. The sheer size and elaborate decor of the assembly room where Hearst gathered with his guests before dinner sets the opulent mood of this elegant establishment. In the adjoining refectory Hearst and his guests dined in a re-created medieval banquet hall—the bottles of Hearst's favorite ketchup on the table seem rather out of place. In the theater a short home movie of Hearst and some of his celebrity friends gives you an idea of life at the castle during the 1930s. A feeling for the opulence of the guest accommodation is given as you tour the guesthouse, Casa del Sol.

Tour 2 views suites of bedrooms, the kitchen, and the swimming pools. The indoor Roman pool has over half a million Italian mosaic tiles, vast amounts of gold leaf, and took over five years to complete. Tour 3 visits the guest wing of the castle, a guesthouse, and the pools. Tour 4, offered only in summer, does not go into the main house, but focuses on the estate's gardens.

From the Hearst-San Simeon State Historical Monument it is just an 8-mile drive south to Cambria. **Cambria** was once a whaling station and a dairy town that shipped butter and cheese to San Francisco. Now the main town lies away from the coast and encompasses two streets of art galleries, gift shops, antique stores, and restaurants.

Leave Cambria and the coast traveling east on 46 through the Santa Lucia coastal mountain range. We have always considered that Hwy 46 affords one of California's most beautiful drives through gorgeous stretches of farmland and lush, gently rolling, golden hills covered with oak trees and vineyards, and it is now the best route to explore the burgeoning **Paso Robles Wine Region**. Once known for cattle ranches and grain fields and historically as a mineral springs resort area, the Paso Robles region will captivate you. The Paso Robles area has a rich history of winemaking and grape growing—the first grapes were introduced to the region by Spanish conquistadors and the Franciscan missionaries and wine was produced in 1797 at the historic Mission San Miguel Arcángel. Approximately 13 miles inland from Cambria you begin to see farmland give way to row upon row and acre after acre of vineyards.

(Note: If you have the luxury of time, detour off Hwy 46 west on two separate roads to discover some of California's most beautiful scenery. Santa Rosa Creek Road offers a lovely ramble through pristine countryside to the back side of Cambria (approximately a 35-minute drive) and Old Creek Road is another charming drive (about a 20-minute trip), taking you by Whale Rock Reservoir to the beach city of Cayucos.)

Spend a few days here and you will enjoy not only drives along scenic, rural, uncrowded roads—most of the wineries are open for tasting (most are free) and a few offer self-guided tours. Clustered just off the 46, still on the outskirts of Paso Robles, are several wineries: **Summerwood** is beautiful and **Castoro** is a must for tasting. Castoro Winery also hosts concerts throughout the year. Other wineries not to miss are **Dover Canyon**, **Grey Wolf**, **Midnight Cellars**, **Dark Star**, and **Fratelli Perata**. **Sycamore Farms** is also a delightful stop to pick up herbs and gifts for house and garden.

To combine wine tasting with a drive through stunningly scenic countryside, take Vineyard Drive from the 46, traveling to the north, winding through the hills that were once home to Mennonite dairy farms, grain and nut farms, and cattle ranches. Venture on to two of the most picturesque wineries, Justin and Carmody McKnight. Stroll through Justin's lovely gardens and sample their award-winning wines. From **Justin Winery** head over to **Carmody McKnight**, an 1800s farmhouse with a pond in front, and enjoy your wine tasting while overlooking their gardens. A number of signs will tempt you off the main road down local roads to many family-run wineries. Follow Chimney Rock Road back to the heart of downtown Paso Robles.

Before continuing over to the east side of town to visit a number of the region's larger wineries, take some time to explore historic **Paso Robles**. Begin by taking a historical walk through downtown—a guide is available at the Chamber of Commerce office on Park Street (805-238-0506). The **Carnegie Library** in the center of the town park is home to a wonderful collection of local history and a Western Art Gallery. Not far away is the **Pioneer Museum** and there is also the **Estrella Warbird Museum**, which houses a collection of WWI and WWII military fighter planes. You will be thrilled to discover the many antique shops. History is being embraced with the opening of mineral spas. **Paso Robles Hot Springs** (located 3 miles east of town off Hwy 46 east) offers massage, facials, and therapeutic mineral baths in a serene lakeside setting.

To continue wine tasting, head out from Paso Robles on Hwy 46 east to many of the area's larger wineries. **Martin-Weyrich** has a feel of Tuscany and a wonderful gift shop and tasting room. **Eberle Winery** offers picnic baskets made to order with advance notice. Enjoy your picnic on their deck, sample award-winning wines, and take time to tour the Eberle caves. **Meridian Vineyards** has lovely gardens, a great tasting room, and a gift shop. Don't leave out **Tobin James,** with its real western-flavor tasting room, great hospitality, and award-winning wines. Follow your wine map, but don't miss **Wild Horse Vineyards** in Templeton and be sure to explore country roads like Neal Springs in this "El Pomar" area. The Paso Robles Vintners have a brochure, tel: 805-239-8463, fax: 805-237-6439, or visit their website at *www.pasowine.com.*

From Paso Robles travel south on Hwy 101 the short distance on to **San Luis Obispo.** If you want to visit every mission en route, when you reach San Luis Obispo take the Broad Street exit and follow signs to the **mission**, which lies at the heart of this bustling, charming college town.

About 10 miles south of San Luis Obispo, Hwy 101 returns to the coast where you take the exit for Hwy 1 and **Pismo Beach**, a 12-mile arc of white-sand beach backed in part by dunes. This is the home of the famous Pismo clam, which has unfortunately in recent years become rather scarce. As you travel south on Hwy 1, views of the beach are blocked by apartments and motels, but do not despair: 2 miles south of town, leave the freeway by turning right into **Pismo Beach State Park**. After paying the entrance fee, pass quickly over the soft sand. Once your tires hit the well-packed, damp sand, your way feels more secure as you drive along the beach, paralleling the crashing waves. From this vantage point you can really appreciate the beautiful sweep of this white-sand bay. While it is possible to drive about 5 miles south on the beach, the auto exit ramp lies 1 mile to the south.

Leaving Pismo Beach, follow Hwy 1 south passing flat, wide fields of vegetables and eucalyptus groves through Guadalupe, a rather poor agricultural town. The road becomes a divided two-lane road as Hwys 135 and 1 merge. After passing the gates of Vandenburg Air Force Base (on the approach to Lompoc), take a left turn onto Mission Purisma Road, which leads to **Mission La Purisma Concepcion**, founded in 1787 and now carefully restored and maintained by the state park system. A self-guided tour offers you the opportunity to see how the Indians practiced mission crafts such as leather working, candle making, and building. The simply decorated church with its sparse furnishings, rough floors, and stenciled walls is typical of Spanish and Mexican churches of the period. One of the nicest aspects of La Purisma Concepcion Mission is its lovely setting—deep in the countryside amidst rolling hills and flower-filled meadows.

Leaving the mission, follow signs for **Buelleton**, which has the redoubtable fame of being the home of split-pea soup—you come to **Andersen's Pea Soup Restaurant** just before Hwy 246 crosses Hwy 101. The menu has more to offer than soup, but it is still possible to sample a bowl of the food that put this little community on the map.

From Buelleton it is just a short drive into **Solvang,** a town settled originally by Danish immigrants, which has now become a rather Disneyfied version of how the perfect Danish village should look—a profusion of thatch-like roofs, painted towers, gaily colored windmills, and cobblestoned courtyards. The shops house a plethora of calorific bakeries and fudge and candy stores interspersed with lots of nifty-gifty Scandinavian-theme craft shops. Interestingly, a large portion of the town's residents truly are of Danish descent. Even if you are not a shopper, Solvang warrants a bakery stop.

Solvang

Leave Solvang and rejoin Hwy 246, following signs for Santa Barbara. This is another gorgeous region of horse ranches and neighboring vineyards. The towns are small, charming and country-western: **Santa Inez**, **Los Olivos**, **Ballard**—all with a main street, a few charming shops and restaurants, and the ever-present horse and feed store.

Just outside Santa Inez, Hwy 246 merges with Hwy 154, which takes you through the heart of this beautiful landscape and the lush green valley gives way to hills as the road climbs through the mountains up the San Marcos Pass. Rounding the crest of the pass, you see **Santa Barbara** stretched out below, hemmed between the mountains and the sea. The red-tile roofs and abundance of palm trees add an affluent look to this prosperous town. Santa Barbara is one of California's loveliest cities. The homes and public buildings show a decidedly Spanish influence and make such a pretty picture—

splashes of whitewashed walls, red-tiled roofs, and palm trees snuggled against the Santa Ynez Mountains to the east and stretching to blue waters of the Pacific to the west.

A pleasant introduction to Santa Barbara is to follow the driving tour published by the Chamber of Commerce. You can probably pick up a brochure at your hotel or by calling the Chamber of Commerce at 805-965-3023. You can also obtain information on the Internet at *www.sbchamber.org*. The route is well marked and gives you an overall glimpse of the city as you drive by beaches, the wharf, the old downtown area, and affluent suburbs. The brochure also outlines what is called the "Red-Tile Walking Tour," which guides you through the town's beautiful streets. It takes discipline to stay on the path as you pass the multitude of shops filled with so many tempting things to buy. The highlight of the tour is the **Santa Barbara County Courthouse**, a magnificent adobe structure with a Moorish accent. You definitely must not leave town without visiting the splendid **Mission Santa Barbara**, which is located at the rise of the hill on the northern edge of town. This beautiful church with two bell towers faces a large park laced with rose gardens. As in many of the other missions, although the church's main purpose is for religious services, a museum is incorporated into the complex with examples of how life was lived when the Spaniards first settled in California.

When your allotted stay in Santa Barbara draws to a close, it is a little less than a 100-mile drive to the Greater Los Angeles area. The vast **Los Angeles** basin is crisscrossed by a network of freeways, which confuses all but the resident Southern Californian. Frustrating traffic jams during the morning and afternoon rush hours are a way of life. Therefore, plot the quickest freeway route to your destination and try to travel during the middle of the day in order to avoid traffic. Los Angeles does not offer a wide selection of inns, but there are many attractive, modern hotels where you can stay. The Greater Los Angeles area has an incredible wealth of places to visit and things to do. Sightseeing suggestions are described in the *Leisurely Loop of Southern California* itinerary.

North from San Francisco, almost to the Oregon Border

Mendocino

If your heart leaps with joy at the sight of long stretches of deserted beaches, rugged cliffs embraced by wind-bent trees, sheep quietly grazing near crashing surf, and groves of redwoods towering above carpets of dainty ferns, then this itinerary will suit you to perfection. Nowhere else in California can you travel surrounded by so much natural splendor. Less than an hour after crossing the Golden Gate Bridge, civilization is left far behind you and your adventure into some of California's most beautiful scenery begins. The first part of this route includes many well-loved attractions: Muir Woods, the Russian River, Sonoma County wineries, the Mendocino Coast, and the Avenue of the

Giants. Then the route becomes less "touristy" as it reaches the Victorian jewel of Ferndale and the bustling town of Eureka, and concludes in the coastal hamlet of Trinidad.

Recommended Pacing: You can cover the distance between San Francisco and Mendocino in a day. It is approximately a four-hour drive if you are traveling inland on Hwy 101 and then cutting west over at Cloverdale on Hwy 128 back to the coast and Hwy 1 just south of Mendocino. It is approximately a six-hour journey if you follow Hwy 1 as it hugs the coast all the way north. However, if time allows, follow our routing and spend a night just north of San Francisco near Point Reyes National Seashore (more if you want to take advantage of the hiking and biking trails), and a night or two in the Healdsburg/Russian River area before arriving in Mendocino. Allow two nights for the Mendocino area and two nights for the Eureka area. **The itinerary route is outlined on Map 3 at the back of the book.**

Weather Wise: The weather along California's northern coast is unpredictable: beautiful warm summer days suddenly become overcast when the fog rolls in (July and August). The prettiest months are usually June, September, and October. Rain falls during the winter and spring, while fall enjoys beautiful crisp, clear days.

San Francisco, a city of unsurpassed beauty, is a favorite destination of tourists and it is no wonder: the city is dazzling in the sunlight, yet equally enchanting when wrapped in fog. The setting is spectacular: a cluster of hills on the tip of a peninsula. San Francisco is very walkable and if you tire, a cable car, bus, or taxi is always close at hand. In the *San Francisco to Los Angeles via the Coast* itinerary we give you enough sightseeing suggestions to occupy you for a week.

Avoiding commuter hours and congestion, leave San Francisco on the **Golden Gate Bridge** following Hwy 101 north. After you cross this famous bridge, pull into the vista point for a panoramic view of this most lovely city. For another spectacular detour, take the very first exit after the viewing area, Alexander Avenue, turn left back under the freeway, and continue as if you are heading back onto the Golden Gate Bridge but, instead, take a quick right to the **Marin Headlands**. Some of the city's most spectacular skylines are photographed from the vantage point of these windswept and rugged headlands looking back at the city through the span of the Golden Gate. The road continues through the park and eventually winds back to Hwy 101. Information and maps are available at the visitors center located in the old Fort Barry Chapel. Signs in the park direct you to the center, which is open daily, 9:30 am to 4:30 pm (415-331-1540). Not to be missed is the **Marine Mammal Center**, where injured seals and other marine animals are nursed back to health by a multitude of volunteers. (415-289-7325, *www.tmmc.org*)

After returning to Hwy 101, continue on to the Mill Valley exit. Circle under the freeway and follow signs for Hwy 1 north. As the two-lane road leaves the town behind and winds up through the trees, watch closely for a sharp right turn to **Muir Woods**. The road takes you high above open fields and down a steep ravine to the Muir Woods entrance and car park where a park volunteer gives out a map and information. Near the park entrance a cross section of a trunk of one of the stately giant coastal redwoods gives you an appreciation of the age of these great trees. Notations relate the tree's growth rings to significant historical occurrences during the tree's lifetime: 1066—the Battle of Hastings, 1215—the Magna Carta, 1492—the discovery of America, 1776—the Declaration of Independence. But this tree is only a baby—some date back over 2,000 years. Your brochure guides you on the walk beneath the redwoods or you can take a guided tour with one of the rangers. Allow about an hour for the park, longer if you take a long walk or just sit on one of the benches to soak in the beauty.

Leaving the park, continue west to the coastal road, Hwy 1. Turn left and then, almost immediately, right. There is a small sign marked **Muir Beach**, but it is easy to miss. Just before you come to the beach you arrive at the **Pelican Inn**, a charming re-creation of an English pub that fortunately also offers lodging (415-383-6000). The adjacent Muir Beach is a small half-moon beach bound at each end by large rock formations.

Return to Hwy 1 and head north along a challenging, winding section of this beautiful coastal road. The road descends to the small town of **Stinson Beach** where by entering the state park you can gain access to a fabulous stretch of wide white sand, bordered on one side by the sea and on the other by grassy dunes. This is a perfect spot to stretch and enjoy a walk along the beach.

Leaving Stinson Beach, the road curves inland bordering **Bolinas Lagoon**, a paradise for birds, and then leaves the water and continues north for about 10 miles to the town of Olema. At Olema you leave Hwy 1 and take the road marked to Inverness, just a short drive away.

If the weather is fine, allow time to explore **Point Reyes National Seashore**, a spectacular wilderness area stretching along the sea (*www.nps.gov/pore*). If you happen to be in the area on a weekend, in addition to taking advantage of the free ranger programs, call ahead on 415-663-1200 to inquire about special field trips (such as tidepool studies, bird watching, and sights and sounds of nature) that are offered for a fee. The ranger station, located in a handsome redwood building at the entrance to the

park, has maps, leaflets, books, a museum, and a movie theater where a presentation gives interesting information on the park. Be sure to stop here before your explorations to obtain a map and study what you want to see and do. A short stroll away from the ranger station is the "earthquake trail" where markers indicate changes brought about by the 1906 earthquake. Also within walking distance is the **Morgan Ranch** where Morgan horses are raised and trained for the park system. If the weather is clear, a drive out to **Point Reyes Lighthouse**

Point Reyes Lighthouse

is a highlight that should not be missed. As you drive for 45 minutes across windswept fields and through dairy farms to the lighthouse you realize how large the park really is. When you arrive, it is a ten-minute walk from the parking area to the viewing area. From there, steps lead down to the lighthouse. Be prepared: it is like walking down a 30-story building and once down, you have to come back up! In late fall and spring it is a perfect place from which to watch for migrating gray whales.

After a visit to the lighthouse, look on your map for **Drakes Bay**, one of the many beaches along this rugged strip of coast, and named for the explorer seeking lands for Queen Elizabeth I of England. He is purported to have sailed into the bay on the *Golden Hinde* and christened it Nova Albion, meaning New England. If you are hungry, there is a café at Drakes Bay where you can have a bite to eat. Another interesting stop is at the **Johnson Oyster Company** on Sir Francis Drake Boulevard—a sign directs you to it on the left on the drive toward Point Reyes Lighthouse. Stop to see the demonstration of how oysters are cultivated in the bay for 18 months before being harvested.

If you choose to continue on to the northernmost point of the peninsula, travel Pierce Point Road, which ends at the Tule Elk Range. Before 1860 thousands of tule elk roamed here but were hunted to extinction, then in 1978 two bulls and eight cows were successfully reintroduced and now the herd numbers over 300. Trails lead through this wilderness and research area to the Tomales Point Bluff or a shorter distance down to McClures Beach and Elephant Rock.

Retrace your route through the park to **Point Reyes Station** where the **Station House Café**, a delightful restaurant with delicious, imaginative food, beckons you into its dining room or tranquil, brick-paved, cottage-garden patio. Continue north on Hwy 1 as the road winds through fields of pastureland and dairies and then loops back and follows for a while the northern rim of **Tomales Bay**, providing lovely vistas across the water to the wooded hills and the town of Inverness. About a 20-minute drive brings you to the village of Marshall and soon after, the road heads inland through rolling ranch land bound by picket fences, passing the towns of **Tomales** (the **Tomales Bakery**, located in the old barbershop and open Thursday to Sunday, is worth visiting—rivaling anything you would sample in France) and Valley Ford before turning west to Bodega Bay and the small town of Jenner. From here it is about a 15-minute drive to **Fort Ross**. "Ross" means "Russian" and this is the site where the Russians, in the early part of the 19th century, built a fort to protect their fishing and fur interests in California. After browsing through the museum, follow the footpath through the woods and enter the courtyard bounded by the weathered wooden buildings where the settlers lived and worked. Be sure not to miss the pretty Russian Orthodox chapel in the southeast corner of the compound. When you have finished roaming through the encampment, take the dramatic walk along the bluffs above the ocean. (707-847-3286, *www.parks.sonoma.net/fortross.html*)

Leaving the fort, retrace your path to Jenner and follow Hwy 116 inland along the banks of the **Russian River**. This is a tranquil stretch of road, passing through dense forests that open up conveniently to offer views of the very green water of the Russian River. (In winter after heavy rains the river can become a rushing torrent—no longer green and tranquil.) On weekends this road is very congested, but midweek and off-season this is a very pretty drive. The largest resort along the river is **Guerneville** and just a few miles beyond the town you come to the **Korbel Winery** (13250 River Road, Guerneville), a picturesque, large building banked with flowers. Three Korbel brothers came to this area from Bohemia to harvest the redwoods and ended up harvesting grapes. Korbel is famous for sparkling wines and the tour and video presentations are especially interesting. Tours of the historic champagne cellars last a little under an hour and are offered daily every hour on the hour between 10 am and 3 pm—to be safe, call to double-check the schedule. There is also a tour of the pretty rose garden nestled on the slope to the left of the winery. The winery is open daily between 9 am and 4:30 pm and offers complimentary tasting. (707-824-7000, *www.korbel.com*)

Sampling champagne at Korbel will whet your appetite for more local wines. Leaving the winery, continue for a short distance along River Road, watching for a left-hand turn for Westside Road (if you go over the bridge, you have gone too far). Westside Road winds its way to Healdsburg, past vineyards, meadows with cows grazing, pretty apple orchards, and several wineries, including **Hop Kiln Winery** (6050 Westside Road, Healdsburg), which is open for tasting until 5 pm. The architecture at Hop Kiln (which, unsurprisingly, was originally built for drying beer hops) is very interesting, with whimsical chimneys jutting into the sky (707-433-6491, *www.hopkilnwinery.com*). The nearby **Rochioli Winery**, (6192 Westside Road, Healdsburg) offers tasting and tours by appointment (707-433-2305). Nearby **Healdsburg** has an attractive main square lined with quaint shops and restaurants.

Leaving Healdsburg, follow Hwy 101 north for the half-hour drive to Cloverdale where you take Hwy 128 heading northwest toward the coast. At first the road twists slowly up and over a rather steep pass. After the summit, the way becomes more gentle as you head down into the beautiful **Anderson Valley**, well-known for its delicious wines. Wherever the hills spread away from the road, the gentle meadows are filled with vineyards. If time permits, stop at the **Navarro Winery**, housed in an attractive contemporary building where complimentary wine tasting is offered (707-895-3686, *www.navarrowine.com*). As the road leaves the sunny open fields of grapes, the sun almost disappears as you enter a majestic redwood forest, so dense that only slanting rays of light filter through the trees. Upon leaving the forest, Hwy 128 soon merges with the coastal Hwy 1 (about a 60-mile drive from where you left Hwy 101). Here you join Hwy 1 going north through Albion and Little River, and then on to Mendocino.

Mendocino is an absolute jewel: a New-England-style town built upon headlands that jut out to the ocean. It is not surprising that the town looks as if it were transported from the East Coast because its heritage goes back to adventurous fishermen who settled here from New England, and, upon arrival, built houses like those they had left behind. (In fact, the "New England" setting, seen in the popular television series *Murder She Wrote*, was filmed here.) Tucked into the many colorful wood-frame buildings you find a wealth of art galleries, gift shops, inns, and restaurants. (Mendocino Coast Chamber of Commerce, 707-961-6300, *www.mendocinocoast.com*.)

Do not let your explorations stop at the quaint town, but venture out onto the barren, windswept headlands—a visit to Mendocino would not be complete without a walk along the bluffs. In late fall or spring there is an added bonus: spouts of water off the shoreline are an indication that gray whales are present.

Mendocino makes a most convenient base for exploring the coast. However, if breathtaking views are more important to you than quaint shops and restaurants, then stay overnight instead 16 miles south of Mendocino in **Elk**, a tiny old lumber town hugging the bluffs along one of the most spectacularly beautiful stretches of the sensational Mendocino coastline. Elk has several places to stay that are described in detail in the inn section of this guide—each has its own personality, each has a magnificent ocean view. Note: If you choose to overnight in Elk instead of the town of Mendocino, when Hwy 128 merges with Hwy 1, go south to Elk instead of north to Mendocino.

Staying in this area, you could most successfully be entertained by doing absolutely nothing other than soaking in the natural, rugged beauty of the coast. However, there are some sightseeing possibilities:

Whale watching is a must if you are here between Christmas and April when the gray whales migrate along the coast. We thoroughly enjoyed the two-hour whale-watching trip that we took from **Noyo Harbor** with **Telstar Charters**, owned and operated by Randy and Charan Thornton (Charan handles the reservations and Randy pilots the boat). Randy also takes people deep-sea fishing for crab, salmon, cod, and albacore year-round. (707-964-8770, *www.gooceanfishing.com*)

Fort Bragg. This is a sprawling town that, when compared to the quaintness of Mendocino, has little to offer architecturally except for an extremely colorful fishing harbor. At 18220 N. Hwy One you find the 47 acres of the **Mendocino Coast Botanical Gardens**. The mild, rainy winters and cool summers here provide ideal growing conditions for the collections in the gardens, which are sheltered by a native pine forest. The gardens include a fern-covered canyon, coastal bluffs, a rocky inter-tidal habitat, and

wheelchair-accessible trails that connect everything together. There are lots of places to picnic including the sheltered Cliff House with its spectacular views of the ocean. Two electric carts are available for those with special needs. The gardens are open daily between 9 am and 5 pm. Admission is $6. (707-964-4352, *www.gardenbythesea.org*)

The most popular attraction in Fort Bragg is the **Skunk Railroad**, which runs between Fort Bragg and Willits (*www.skunktrain.com*). During the summer months you can take either the all-day trip, which makes the complete round trip to **Willits**, or a half-day trip leaving in the morning or the afternoon. The train follows the old logging route through the redwood forests. Frankly, you will have already seen lovelier glens of redwood trees than those you will view on the ride, but the outing is fun, especially if you are traveling with children. The train station is in the center of town just after you pass over the rail tracks. Call ahead for reservations: 800-777-5865.

Leaving the Mendocino area, continue to follow the coast north and enjoy a treasury of memorable views: sometimes the bluffs drop into the sea, other times sand dunes almost hide the ocean, and at one point the beach sweeps right up to the road. At Rockport, Hwy 1 turns inland and twists and turns its way through forests and over the coastal range on 20 miles of narrow winding road. Arriving at **Leggett** (just before the junction with Hwy 101), look for a sign to your right indicating a small, privately owned redwood park where you can drive through a hole in a redwood tree.

From Leggett continue north along Hwy 101 signposted for Eureka. However, rather than rushing all the way up Hwy 101, follow the old highway, called the **Avenue of the Giants**, that weaves through the **Humboldt Redwoods State Park**. This is a 33-mile-long drive, but we suggest you select the most beautiful section by skipping the first part and joining the Avenue of the Giants at Myers Flat. As you exit at Myers Flat, the two-lane road passes a few stores and then glides into a spectacular glen of redwoods. A lovely section of the forest is at **Williams Grove**. Stop at the nearby park headquarters and obtain a map that directs you off the Avenue of the Giants to **Rockefeller Forest**, the oldest glen of redwoods left in the world—some date back over 2,000 years. The trees are labeled and a well-marked footpath guides you through the forest to the Big Tree, an astounding giant measuring 17 feet in diameter and soaring endlessly into the sky, and to the Flat Iron Tree (another biggie with a somewhat flattened-out trunk) located nearby in an especially serene grove of trees.

About ten minutes after rejoining Hwy 101, exit to **Scotia**. Established in 1869, the entire town—homes, shops, school, hotel—is owned by the largest lumber company in the world. The picturesque little redwood homes are dominated by the **Pacific Lumber Company**. You will find the small shopping center worth visiting just for the sake of seeing the redwood building constructed from pillars made from whole tree trunks.

Drive to the museum—an all-redwood building resembling a Grecian temple with redwood-tree pillars (bark and all) instead of marble. The museum displays photos, artifacts, and machinery used in the logging camps. It is here you obtain your redwood shingle giving directions for the self-guided mill tour. Pass in hand, you follow the "yellow brick road," a well-marked trail, highlighted with yellow arrows, which guides you throughout the factory. Your first stop is at the hydraulic de-barker where you watch through windows the bark stripped from the logs by high-pressure water, which sweeps back and forth over each log like a broom. Bits of bark and sprays of water cover the windows while the entire building rumbles as the giant logs are stripped naked. The next stop is the saw mill where logs are pulled back and forth beneath a giant-sized rotary saw that slices them into large boards. Walking along the overhead ramp, you watch the entire process from the first touch of the saw until the various-sized boards are neatly wrapped and bound tightly with straps. The Pacific Lumber Company mill is closed on weekends and holidays. Passes are given out for tours Monday through Friday, 8 am to 1:30 pm. It is best to check times in advance of your arrival by calling 707-764-2222.

Returning to Hwy 101, about a 10-mile drive brings you to the Ferndale exit. Founded in 1852, **Ferndale** is the westernmost town (more of a village than a town) in the continental United States. Its downtown with its gaily painted Victorian buildings has changed very little since the 1890s.

Ferndale

Main Street is a gem, lined with delightful little galleries and stores—a favorite being the irresistible candy shop where you view, through the window, hand-dipping of delectable chocolates. Many visitors enjoy the **Repertory Theater** on Main Street where some excellent plays are produced (707-786-5483). Epitomizing the colorful character of the town is the **Gingerbread Mansion**. Stop at Ferndale's **Museum** to learn more about her past as you tour Victorian rooms and see displays of old dairy and smithying equipment. (Shaw and 3rd Street, open Tuesday through Saturday 11 am to 4 pm and Sunday 1 to 4 pm, 707-786-4466.)

Centerville Beach is 5 miles west of Ferndale on Centerville Road (turn right on Ocean Avenue at the end of Ferndale). Here you have 9 miles of beaches backed by dairy farms to the north and steep cliffs to the south. Watch for harbor seals in the breakers and tundra swans, which congregate in the Eel River bottoms north of Centerville Road from mid-November to February.

Leaving Ferndale, retrace your way to Hwy 101 and continue north for the 10-mile drive to **Eureka**. The area surrounding the 101 is full of fast-food chains, gas stations, and commercial establishments, but a small portion of this large town, the **Old Town**, is worth a visit (G and D between 1st and 3rd). On the northwestern edge of this restored project lies the ornate **Carson Mansion** (2nd and M), the most photographed, ornate, Victorian mansion in northern California.

About 20 miles beyond Eureka, exit the 101 for the coastal hamlet of **Trinidad**. Although its houses are now mostly of modern architecture, Trinidad Bay has an interesting history. It was discovered by the Portuguese in 1595, claimed by the Spaniards in 1775, flourished in the 1850s Gold Rush as a supply port for the miners, and was later kept on the map by logging. Now Trinidad is a sleepy little cluster of homes nestled on the bluffs overlooking a sheltered cove where an untouristy wharf stretches out into the bay. Next to the wharf is the **Seascape Restaurant** where you can dine on fish straight from the little fishing boats. Stroll the mile-long path along the headlands enjoying the views and in winter the crashing rollers.

Wandering through the Wine Country

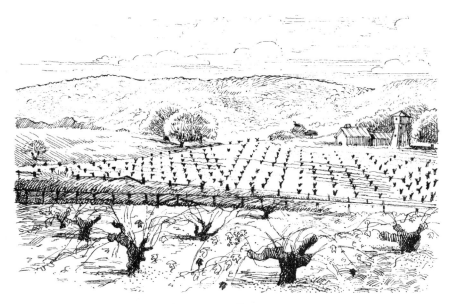

The Napa Valley

The Napa and Sonoma Valleys, just north of San Francisco, have earned a well-merited reputation for the excellence of their wines and many of the wineries are open to the public for tours and tasting. But there is so much more to lure you here than sampling wines—informative tours, exquisite artwork, historic buildings, movie memorabilia, and beautiful scenery abound. A visit to the wine country makes a pleasant excursion any time of year. In summer the days are long and warm, perfect for bike rides, picnics, music festivals, concerts, and art shows. As summer days give way to the cooler afternoons and crisp evenings of fall, the lush foliage on the thousands of acres of grapevines turns to red, gold, and yellow—a colorful reminder that it is time for harvest.

You can sense the energy of the crush as vintners work against the clock and weather to pick grapes at their prime. In winter, cool days are often washed by rain, but this is also an excellent time to visit since this is "off season" and the winery tours will be almost private as you travel from one vineyard to the next. Spring is glorious: mustard blossoms paint the valleys yellow, contrasting dramatically with the dark bark of the vines laced with the delicate green of new leaves.

Recommended Pacing: You cannot follow this complete itinerary in a day trip from San Francisco but you certainly can visit both the Napa and Sonoma wine regions in a day—it takes about an hour to drive from San Francisco to the southern boundary of either valley and a day trip would allow you to visit a winery or two and get the flavor of the region. However, since the valleys are so beautiful and to allow adequate time for leisurely tastings, we suggest that you select a base (because of their close proximity you can select either valley) and stay for a minimum of two nights. Please do not try to follow this itinerary just as we have described it—it encompasses more wineries than you can possibly do justice to in a week. Instead, use it as a framework to plan your own trip: select those wineries that appeal to you (you can check out the wines they produce on their websites) and plot your route on a detailed map. **The itinerary route is outlined on Map 4 at the back of the book.**

Weather Wise: The Napa and Sonoma Valleys have very similar climates. Summer days can be scorching hot and roads are often clogged with visitors. Autumn gives way to mild, sunny days, cooler afternoons, and crisp evenings. From autumn to spring you can expect some rain although many days will be sunny. In winter, temperatures are mild yet several degrees cooler than in the nearby San Francisco Bay Area.

Note: We have tried to be as accurate as possible when giving information about touring wineries, but things change, so be certain to give each winery a call in advance to see whether or not they are open and whether you need an appointment for a tour or tasting.

This itinerary wends up the Napa Valley and back down the Sonoma Valley. In the Napa Valley there are two parallel roads that stretch along its length—Hwy 29 and the

Silverado Trail. Hwy 29 is the busier and wider of the two. The Silverado Trail, more scenic, less commercial, hugs the eastern hills, offering a welcome escape from traffic. Our suggested route crisscrosses back and forth between Hwy 29 and the Silverado Trail, and then travels west to follow a path south through the Sonoma Valley.

From San Francisco, travel east on Hwy 80 across the San Francisco-Oakland Bay Bridge. After crossing the bridge, stay in the left-hand lane and follow Hwy 80 in the direction of Sacramento for 30 miles. Four miles after crossing the Carquinez Bridge, take Hwy 37 (the Marine World Parkway exit) for 2½ miles to Hwy 29 (Sonoma Blvd). Turn right towards Napa and stay on Hwy 29 into the town.

Napa sprawls for several miles. Ignore its unappealing outskirts and head for downtown, which has really improved in recent years (though not perfect yet), with some delightful restaurants and an attractive shopping precinct. If you have a passionate interest in food, its history and origins, head for **Copia** (500 First Street, Napa, CA 94559), dedicated to the celebration of food, wine, and the arts in US culture (take a right on First Street off Hwy 29). In our opinion, it's a rather overrated venue. The entrance fee is $14. Open 10 am to 5 pm. 707-259-1600, *www.copia.org*.

Returning to Hwy 29 (in the direction of Calistoga), turn left at the traffic lights on Redwood Road for the 6-mile drive to the **Hess Collection** winery (4411 Redwood Road Napa, CA 94558). Leaving the town behind, travel ever higher up Mount Veeder though pretty wooded scenery with glimpses of distant vineyards. Watch for the sharp left-hand turn in the road after 4 miles. You emerge from the trees at the winery surrounded by rolling vineyards. Visiting here gives you the opportunity to enjoy a lovely garden with lily pond, wisteria-covered walkway, and wildflower garden, laid out in front of an early-20th-century winery. When Mr. Hess purchased the winery in 1986 he set apart a portion of the historic ivy-covered stone structure to showcase a selection of his distinguished collection of paintings and sculptures. The production of wine and Mr. Hess's collection have been cleverly woven together and the visitors' tour encompasses wine production—fermentation vats, wooden barrels where the wine ages, and the bottling process—as well as the art housed in two large galleries. Tasting costs $3 for three wines. Open 10 am to 4 pm. 707-255-1144, *www.hesscollection.com.*

Return to Hwy 29 and cross it onto Trancas, which after 1½ miles becomes Hwy 121 (signposted for Lake Berryessa). Follow this road for 4 miles as it climbs into the wooded hills. Watch for a gate on the left marking the **Jarvis Winery** entrance (2970 Monticello Road, Napa, CA 94559). The gates automatically open after you give your name and tour information (book well in advance—tour groups are limited to a very small number). The tour is fun and the structure of the Jarvis Winery is different from that of any other you will see on this itinerary. It also produces excellent wines (Cabernet Franc, Cabernet Sauvignon, Chardonnay, and Merlot). All you see as you approach are two massive doors built into the hillside—it looks like an entrance into a bunker. But inside, another world opens up as you find yourself in a giant cave. You follow a path that forms a loop around the cavern, passing by an underground stream and a waterfall, and visit the Crystal Chamber, a grand reception hall. At the conclusion of the tour you sample fine wines at a small table surrounded by gilded chairs with blue velvet upholstery. Tours are offered at 10 am and 1:30 pm. Based on demand, extra tours are sometimes added. 707-255-5280 or 800-255-5280, *www.jarviswines.com.*

Leaving the Jarvis Winery, retrace your route back down the hill to the Silverado Trail. Turn right (north) on the Silverado Trail and follow it to Oak Knoll Avenue, a left-hand turn down a road bounded by walnut trees and vineyards. Watch for a small signpost and large gates marking the right-hand turn for **Trefethen Vineyards** (1160 Oak Knoll Avenue, Napa, CA 94558). Trefethen Vineyards is housed in a wooden building dating back to 1886 and surrounded by towering oaks. This handsome complex is family-owned and -operated, proving that size is not a prerequisite for excellence. Open 10 am to 4:30 pm, tours are by appointment. 707-255-7700, *www.trefethen.com.*

Continue west on Oak Knoll Avenue for the very short distance to Hwy 29, which you cross, turning right on Solano Avenue, a quiet country road that parallels the busy Hwy 29.

Solano Avenue ends on the outskirts of Yountville and ahead of you lies **Domaine Chandon** (1 California Drive, Yountville, CA 94559) where sparkling wine is made following the principles and rigid process dictated by the French *methode champenoise*. A wooden footbridge spans the creek-fed ponds and huge oak trees lead to the winery tucked back into the hillside. Complimentary tours are offered on the hour between 10 am and 6 pm. First you see the fermentation process in polished stainless-steel tanks and then continue on to observe the additional steps involved in making sparkling wine. In the cellar, bottles of sparkling wine are aged and riddled (turned). In the bottling room you see the process of freezing then disgorging the sediment, corking, cleaning, and labeling the bottles. A visit here shows French and Californian vintners sharing expertise and working side by side. After the tour enjoy a tasting of three to five wines for $8 to $12. Select your favorite and purchase a glass to enjoy on the adjacent terrace. There's an elegant restaurant that tiers down the hillside and in sunny weather lunch is served on the patio. 707-944-2280, *www.dchandon.com.*

Leaving Domaine Chandon, turn left, go under Hwy 29, and turn left on Washington Street into the small town of **Yountville**. As the road divides (Washington left, Yount right) take the left-hand turn if you are in a shopping mood and turn immediately left into the car park of **Vintage 1870**, a complex of little shops and galleries housed in a charming old brick winery.

Return to Yount Street and follow it past the town's quaint houses, turning left onto Yountville Cross Road. After a mile turn left on State Lane for the half-mile drive to **Goosecross Cellars** (1119 State Lane, Yountville, CA 94559). This micro winery is a small family-run and -owned operation—Geoff Gorsuch and college roommate David Topper purchased it from Geoff's parents, who live in the cute house in front of the winery. Walk through the aging vats into the tasting room to sample red varietals and a superb Chardonnay for a dollar each. Colleen Topper offers a very popular complimentary class in wine basics at 11 am every Saturday. Open 10 am to 4 pm. 707-944-1986, *www.goosecross.com.*

Retrace your steps to Yountville Cross Road and turn left for the short drive up the Silverado Trail to Oakville Cross Road where you turn left. The first winery on your right is your destination, **Plumpjack** (620 Oakville Cross Road, Oakville, CA 94562). The fanciful theater-set style of the complex is a clue that this is a winery that flaunts tradition—as an example, they have got rid of the cork in some of their reserve Cabernets and replaced it with a screw cap. Plumpjack derives its name from Shakespeare's portly character Jack Falstaff. Open for tasting 10 am to 4 pm, $5 per person. 707-945-1220, *www.plumpjack.com.*

Leave Plumpjack to your right and Oakville Cross Road takes you into the little town of **Oakville** where, as you turn right on Hwy 29, you see **Oakville Grocery** (on your right). If you plan to picnic, stop here for supplies and gourmet treats to accompany your winery purchases.

Just to the north of Oakville, on the right of Hwy 29, you soon come to **Opus One** (7900 Saint Helena Hwy, Hwy 29, Oakville, CA 94562) on your right. The winery is an exquisite showplace for the California Robert Mondavi family and the French Rothschild family. The gleaming white, circular structure looks a bit like a luxurious, futuristic coliseum. It certainly makes an impressive statement. As you enter this remarkable building, it is immediately obvious that no expense was spared. Visitors are treated as honored guests and wait in an elegant lounge before the tour begins (complimentary—you must sign up two to four weeks in advance). The optional tasting of their current vintage is $25, and the tasting room is open from 10 am to 4 pm. 707-944-9442, *www.opusonewinery.com.*

Almost opposite Opus One you find the **Robert Mondavi** winery (7801 Saint Helena Hwy, Hwy 29, Oakville, CA 94562). This modern winery, with a statue of Saint Francis at its entrance, was styled after the Franciscan missions, with an open-arched entry framing an idyllic view of vineyards. Nine different tours are offered, varying in length and cost. The hour-and-a-half vineyard and winery tour is extremely informative and provides a good general introduction to the essentials of winemaking. By special arrangement, you can also make reservations for the three- to four-hour advanced winegrowing tour ($30 per person), offered Wednesdays at 10 am, touring the fields and studying the grapes as well as the winery. After each tour guests are invited into the tasting room to sample the wines. The spacious lawn at the back is the site of popular summer concerts. Reservations are recommended. Open 9 am to 5 pm. 707-968-2000 or 888-766-6328, *www.robertmondaviwinery.com*.

Niebaum-Coppola Estate

Continue north into Rutherford and just as you enter the town turn left into the **Niebaum-Coppola Estate** (1991 Saint Helena Hwy, Hwy 29, Rutherford, CA 94573). In the late 1870s a Finnish sea captain, Gustave Niebaum, retired from shipping to invest his fortune in the Napa Valley, envisioning a winery that would produce magnificent wines, even surpassing the finest French wines. After his death, Niebaum's property was divided, but in 1995 the Francis Ford Coppola family (owners of the Niebaum-Coppola Estate since 1975) purchased the adjacent Inglenook château and its vineyards, thus reuniting the original historic estate. All the wine produced here is grown and bottled on the estate—a rare occurrence in today's viticultural world. Movie buffs will not want to miss this winery for upstairs, above the historic cellars, Mr. Coppola showcases an impressive collection of awards, memorabilia, and artifacts from his movies: the desk used in *The Godfather*, a Tucker car from the movie of the same name, the bamboo river cage from *The Deerhunter*, and costumes from *Dracula*. On the ground floor a display traces the history of the winery. You stroll through cool cellars into tasting rooms and gift shops. For $20 you can enjoy a château tour through the original stone aging cellar, which contains some magnificent large German oak casks, and taste four wines in the cellar room. Tours operate seven days a week at 10:30 am and 2:30 pm, and on Saturday also at 12:30 pm. A vineyard tour is also offered, weather permitting, on Fridays and Saturdays at 11 am at a cost of $20, including tasting. All tours are on a first-come, first-served basis, no reservations required. On a more informal basis, the tasting rooms are open to the public from 10 am to 5 pm and there is a $7.50 charge for the tasting of four wines. 707-968-1161, *www.niebaum-coppola.com*.

Across Hwy 29 you find **Beaulieu Vineyards,** commonly known as BV (1960 Saint Helena Hwy, Hwy 29, Rutherford, CA 94573). Half-hour tours covering the history and production of their wines are complimentary. There's a small fee for tasting. Open 10 am to 5 pm. 707-967-5200, *www.beaulieuvineyards.com*.

Leaving BV, turn south (left) and then immediately left again onto Rutherford Cross Road for the scenic drive across the valley (following Hwy 128 towards Lake Berryessa). At the Silverado Trail, go right and immediately right again on Hwy 128 for the scenic 15-mile drive to **Nichelini** (2950 Sage Canyon Rd, Hwy 128, Saint Helena, CA 94574). This winery was founded by the Nichelini family in 1884 and is still in the same family today, making it the oldest family-operated winery in the Napa Valley. The building itself is of historical interest: showing off founder Anton Nichelini's stonemasonry, the hand-hewn stone wine cellar takes you back to the Ticino region of Switzerland. The old Roman-type press, constructed by Anton himself and in use until 1956, is the centerpiece of the visitor area. It is believed to be the only one of its kind still standing at a California winery. Open Saturdays and Sundays, 10 am to 6 pm, for wine tasting, picnicking, and bocci ball. 707-963-0717, *www.nicheliniwinery.com*.

Returning to the Silverado Trail, head north (right) for a short distance, taking the first right-hand turn on Rutherford Hill Road, which winds up past Auberge du Soleil, to the **Rutherford Hill** winery (200 Rutherford Hill Road, Rutherford, CA 94573), housed in a weathered redwood barn draped with Virginia creeper and wisteria and surrounded by olive groves and shady woodlands. This is THE place to head for if you want to enjoy a picnic (bring your own food) for surrounding the winery are three shady picnic areas with fabulous views and lots of tables. Rutherford Hill winery is considered the leading producer of Merlot in the Napa Valley. The complimentary half-hour tour, offered at 11:30 am, 1:30 pm, and 3:30 pm, includes a visit to the vast wine caves. Guides at Rutherford Hill are friendly and proud of (as well as knowledgeable about) the winery and visitors are encouraged to ask questions. Wine tasting is $5 per tasting of five wines, reserve tasting is $10. Open 10 am to 5 pm. 707-963-1871, *www.rutherfordhill.com*.

From Rutherford Hill travel north on the Silverado Trail, cross over to Hwy 29 on Zinfandel Lane, and then jog north on Hwy 29 (approaching the town of Saint Helena) to visit the **V. Sattui** winery found on your right (111 White Lane Street, Saint Helena, CA 94574). Sattui winemaking history dates back to 1885 when Vittorio Sattui founded the winery in the North Beach district of San Francisco. Great-grandson Daryl Sattui revived the family tradition in 1973 by moving the winery to Saint Helena. Currently 15 vintage-dated wines are produced, all of which are sold exclusively at the winery or by mail order. With a lovely garden setting, this is an attractive winery with an excellent gift shop where you can also purchase picnic supplies, selecting from over 200 different kinds of cheeses, homemade salads, pâtés, breads, and desserts. There is also a wonderful picnic spot, with tables set on the lawn beneath shady trees. You are welcome to look into the cellars or, when wine is being bottled, watch the bottling line in action—there are no formal tours. Tasting is complimentary. Open 9 am to 6 pm in summer, 9 am to 5 pm in winter. 707-963-7774, *www.vsattui.com*.

Opposite V. Sattui you find **Dean and Deluca**, an up-market store for purchasing kitchenware, wine, cheese, and all manner of picnic supplies.

In **Saint Helena** Hwy 29 becomes the town's Main Street, lined with elegant stores, boutiques, and restaurants. Detour east two blocks off Main Street via Adams Street to the **Silverado Museum**, housed in a wing of the town's library. Dedicated to Robert Louis Stevenson, the little museum chronicles his life and contains books, paintings, and Stephenson memorabilia. Open 10 am to 4 pm, closed Mondays.

As Hwy 29 leaves the northern residential area of Saint Helena, turn left into **Beringer Vineyards** (2000 Main Street, Hwy 29, Saint Helena, CA 94574). Set on a knoll, surrounded by landscaped grounds, the magnificent Rhine House was built as a replica of the German home that Frederick and his brother Jacob left behind when they emigrated. A 45-minute guided tour is offered every half hour, Monday through Friday between 10 am and 5 pm (from November to March the last tour is at 4 pm), Saturday and Sunday starting at 9:30 am (availability is on a first-come, first-served basis). Tours emphasize the historical aspect of the winery and include a visit through the tunnels and caverns where the wine is aged in barrels. Tours are $5 per person and tickets can be purchased from 9:30 am for any tour time that same day. The tasting fee is $5 for three wines or $2 to $10 for reserve wines. 707-963-4812, *www.beringer.com*.

Four miles north, turn right off Hwy 29 onto Larkmead Lane to visit the **Frank Family Vineyards** (1091 Larkmead Lane, Calistoga, CA 94515). A vineyard has been on this spot since 1884. The main building was refurbished with local sandstone in 1906 and the resulting sturdy edifice is considered an archetype of the local wine country. Owners Richard Frank and Koemer Rombauer purchased the property from the Hans Kornell company, which is famous for its sparkling wines, and five types are still crafted in the champagne style, though nowadays the focus of the winery has shifted to the production of a superb range of still red and white wines. Take the light-hearted complimentary tour with Dennis and learn the importance of bra size and vibrators to the industry today. Bring a picnic to enjoy with your purchases in this pretty spot. Tasting is free of charge. Open 10 am to 4 pm. 800-574-9463 or 707-942-0859.

Returning to Hwy 29, take the first left, signposted Peterson Lane, and turn immediately up a driveway for the 1-mile drive up through woodlands to **Schramsberg Vineyards** (1400 Schramsberg Road, Calistoga, CA 94515). Built in 1862, Schrambsberg is the first hillside winery built in the Napa Valley and was featured by Robert Louis Stevenson in his chronicles of the wine country. Over 2 miles of tunnels are devoted to the production of sparkling wine and tours are by appointment only. In conjunction with the tour, wine tasting is offered at a charge of $10 for three current releases and $10 to $20 per glass for library selections. Open 10 am to 4 pm. 707-942-2414, *www.schramsberg.com*.

Back on the 29, you soon see your next destination, **Sterling Vineyards** (1111 Dunaweal Lane, Calistoga, CA 94515), a complex of low, white buildings crowning the hill to your right. Turn right on Dunaweal Lane to reach them. From the winery you can savor panoramic views looking down through tall pines to a checkerboard of vineyards. Access to Sterling is possible only by an aerial tramway (the first tram is at 10:30 am, the last at 4:30 pm). A fee of $6 is charged for the tram and a tasting; children under 18 are $4. A self-guided tour leads you through the maze of rooms that comprise the winery and concludes with the tasting. A very pleasant feature here is the melodic sound of bells from a bombed London church that ring out every half hour. 800-726-6136, *www.sterlingvineyards.com*.

Across the street, **Clos Pegase** (1060 Dunaweal Lane, Calistoga, CA 94515) is a joy for those who love stunning architecture, sculpture, and fine wine. When owner Jan Isaac Shrem, a Paris-based businessman and art collector, turned 50, he decided to move to Napa Valley and take up viticulture. Shrem enlisted the help of Michael Graves, who designed the structure with influences that range from ancient Rome to art deco. The result is an exquisite building that the *Washington Post* called "America's first monument to wine as art." Sculptures are placed on the edge of the vineyards, on the lawns, and in the winery. Tours are complimentary (11 am and 2 pm) and reservations are not required, but be aware that the afternoon weekend tour tends to be crowded. Several tasting options are offered for a nominal fee. Open 10:30 am to 5 pm. 707-942-4981, *www.clospegase.com*.

Our favorite Napa Valley town, **Calistoga**, bounded by rugged foothills and vineyards, is just a few miles north at the intersection of Hwy 29 and Hwy 128. Its main street, Lincoln Avenue, is lined on both sides by attractive shops and numerous restaurants. This charming town has been famous ever since Spanish explorers arrived in 1823 and observed Indians taking mud baths in steamy marshes. Sam Brannan, who purchased a square mile of land at the foot of Mount Saint Helena, gave the town its name: he wanted the place to be the "Saratoga of California" and so called it Calistoga. He bought the land in the early 1860s and by 1866 was ready to open his resort of a few cottages and palm trees. The oldest surviving railroad depot in California, now shops, received its first trainload of passengers when they came to Calistoga for the much-publicized opening of Sam Brannan's resort. For more than a hundred years, Calistoga has attracted visitors from all over the world, primarily for its hot springs and spas. People came in search of its glorious, healing waters long before the region became a popular destination for its wineries.

There are many excellent spa facilities and two kinds to choose from: with "heavy" mud and without. Among other places, traditional mud tubs are available at **Dr. Wilkinson's Hot Springs**, 707-942-4102, *www.drwilkinson.com,* and **Indian Springs**, 707-942-4913, *www.indianspringscalistoga.com.* Excellent spas include **Lavender Hill** (small and cute, great for couples and friends), 707-942-4495, *www.lavenderhillspa.com,* and **Mount View Spa** (a beautiful facility in the Mount View Hotel), 707-942 5789, *www.mountviewspa.com.*

Whenever we go to Calistoga, we always make a point of visiting **Old Faithful Geyser**, one of only three such regularly erupting geysers in the world. It erupts at intervals varying between 15 and 50 minutes, throwing a spume of about 4,000 gallons of water over 60 feet into the air. This is certainly an interesting phenomenon, although the staging is a bit honky-tonk. Old Faithful can be viewed from 9 am to 5 pm (9 am to 6 pm during daylight savings time). To reach the geyser, travel north from Calistoga on Hwy 128 to Tubbs Lane, turn right onto Tubbs Lane, and in half a mile you see the entrance to the geyser on your left. Cost $6, 707-942-6463, *www.oldfaithfulgeyser.com.*

Just beyond the geyser is the very interesting **Château Montelena** winery (1429 Tubbs Lane, Calistoga, CA 94515), founded in 1882 by Alfred Tubbs who brought over a French architect to build an "authentic" French château (you'll see that the architect took a little artistic license with this instruction). Tours lasting an hour and a half are offered at 9:30 am and 1:30 pm by appointment—you watch a film, visit the cellar in the château, tour the gardens and vineyards, and conclude with a tasting. If you are not able to secure a tour, you can still enjoy a tasting ($10), see the exterior of the château, enjoy a game of bocci ball, and wander round the lake, resplendent with swans and a bridge leading to a tea house on an island. 707-942-5105, *www.montelena.com.*

Another very personal wine-tasting experience is offered by the nearby **Vincent Arroyo** winery (2361 Greenwood Avenue, Calistoga, CA 94515). To reach it, proceed to the end of Tubbs Lane, turn right and first right on Greenwood Avenue, and the winery is on your right. This small, friendly, seven-employee micro winery offers you the chance to taste wine from the barrel and secure purchases from future bottlings. "JJ", the resident black lab, offers an amusing addition to your visit, for once she observes a barrel tasting in progress, she drops a golf ball (or two) at your feet and climbs high on the barrel stacks waiting for you to throw the ball for her to retrieve. You can also sample and purchase estate-produced olive oil. Hours vary so call ahead. 707-942-6995, *www. vincentarroyowinery.com.*

Leaving Calistoga, take the Petrified Forest Road (which becomes Calistoga Road) west to the outskirts of Santa Rosa, forsaking the Napa Valley for the neighboring Sonoma Valley. The road climbs and winds a scenic 12 miles through forest and past meadows where cattle graze next to orchards. You may wish to stop at the rather commercial **California Petrified Forest**, a grove of redwoods that was petrified by ash from the volcanic eruption of Mount Saint Helena over 6,000,000 years ago.

On the residential outskirts of Santa Rosa, turn left on Hwy 12 in the direction of Sonoma. This road travels down the center of Sonoma Valley, often referred to as the "Valley of the Moon" after Jack London's famous novel of the same name.

Your first destination in this lovely valley, **Landmark Vineyards**, lies 6½ miles to the south (101 Adobe Canyon Road, Hwy 12, Kenwood, CA 95452). Tucked up against the hillside, the winery enjoys spectacular views of towering Sugarloaf Ridge from its beautifully landscaped courtyard, lakeside picnic grounds (bring your own picnic), and vineyards, which you tour in a wagon pulled by massive Belgian dray horses (Saturdays only, April to October, 11:30 am to 3 pm). As an accompaniment to wine tasting, you enjoy beautiful gardens and the opportunity to play bocci ball. Tasting is complimentary except for a $10 charge for four reserve wines. Open 10 am to 4:30 pm. 707-833-0053 or 800-452-6365, *www.landmarkwine.com*.

The neighboring **Château St. Jean** (8555 Sonoma Hwy, Hwy 12, Kenwood, CA 95452) lies snug against the hillside. An extremely pretty road winds up through vineyards to the strikingly beautiful winery and main house surrounded by lush lawns. With the exception of its mock tower, Château St. Jean is Mediterranean-French in its architecture. Be careful to pronounce its name as the English "Jean" since the winery is named after the founder's wife, Jean Sheffield. A booklet outlines a self-guided tour of the courtyard garden, which leads to the Visitors' Center, a combination tasting room and gift shop. Tastings are $5 to $10 for a selection of five wines. Luxury wine tastings are available in the château. Open 10 am to 5 pm. 707-833-4134, *www.chateaustjean.com*.

Your next winery is the nearby **Kunde Winery** (10155 Sonoma Hwy, Kenwood, CA 95452) whose founder, Louis Kunde, settled in the Sonoma Valley in 1904. The present-day winery, which re-creates an 1883 barn that previously stood on the same site, houses a reception area with wine tasting and a small gift shop. Complimentary wine tasting is available between 10:30 am and 4:30 pm. Complimentary tours of the barrel-aging caves, which feature half a mile of interconnecting tunnels, are available approximately every half hour on Fridays, Saturdays, and Sundays. 707-833-5501, *www.kunde.com.*

Travel south on Hwy 12 for several miles before taking a turnoff to the right to **Glen Ellen**. In the center of this small, quaint, wooded town turn right for Jack London State Park. Before you reach the park, stop to visit the Benziger Winery found on the right.

Trolley at Benziger Winery

The **Benziger Winery** (1883 London Ranch Road, Glen Ellen, CA 95442), set on a wooded knoll, is a fun, family-run winery. If it's close to lunchtime, take advantage of picnic tables set under redwood trees (bring your own food). Before you walk up to the tasting room, follow the informative self-guided vine tour next to the parking lot. Benziger offers five or six tours a day starting at 11:30 am. You climb aboard a trolley pulled by a bright-red tractor for a tour of the vineyards, which lasts approximately 45 minutes. The day we took the tour the Benziger's dog climbed aboard and sat on the bench next to the other guests, happily wagging his tail as the tram moved through the fields. After the tour taste some of their excellent wines. 707-935-3000, *www.benziger.com.*

Continue on up the hill to **Jack London State Park** where Jack London is buried. This lovely wooded park was established as a tribute to the famous author who had such an impact on the Sonoma Valley. This strikingly handsome man lived a life of rugged adventure and wrote passionately about life's struggles and how to survive them with integrity. In the 16 years prior to his death at age 40 he wrote 50 novels, which were immensely popular and are today considered classics. Two of his more renowned novels are *Call of the Wild* and *Sea Wolf.* This park offers a fitting tribute to Jack London, a courageous, dynamic man, full of life and concern for others. Open all year 9:30 am to 5 pm (7 pm in summer), admission is $3 per vehicle. *www.parks.sonoma.net/jlpark.html.*

In the park you can visit the ruins of Wolf House (London's dream house, which mysteriously burned to the ground the night of its completion), Beauty Cottage (the cottage where London wrote much of his later work is staffed from noon to 4 pm on weekends), and the House of Happy Walls (the home that Charmian London built after her husband's death, open 10 am to 5 pm). This last building is now an interesting museum depicting London's life through numerous photographs, writings, and furnishings that belonged to the author. From the museum, paths lead to the other homes and the gravesite. After visiting the park, return on Arnold Drive into Glen Ellen, turn right, and travel south (past the Sonoma State Home) to Madrone where you turn left, crossing over to Hwy 12, which takes you into Sonoma.

Sonoma is a gem of a town. By simply exploring the boundaries of its main square you will glimpse some of California's most important periods in history. (A small admission fee is charged to tour Sonoma's historic buildings.) On the square's northern edge sits the **Sonoma Barracks**, a two-story adobe building that was the Mexican provincial headquarters for the Northern Frontier under the command of General Vallejo. The adjacent wood-frame **Toscano Hotel** has been restored and on weekends guides lead interesting tours through the rooms. The nearby **Mission San Francisco Solano de Sonoma**, the last Franciscan mission built in California, was restored in the early 1900s. If you visit during the week, you may see elementary-school children, dressed as missionaries with their simple cloaks and rope ties, experiencing history "hands on" as they work with crafts and tools from the days of the missionaries. One hall of the mission houses an unusually beautiful collection of watercolor paintings depicting several of California's missions. The long, low adobe building across the way, the Blue Wig Inn, originally built to house soldiers assigned to the mission, enjoyed a more colorful existence as a saloon and gambling room during the Gold Rush days. *www.parks.sonoma.net/sonoma.html.*

Mission San Francisco Solano de Sonoma

In addition to the historic sites on Sonoma's plaza, there are numerous shops and boutiques to investigate, including some wonderful specialty food stores where you can purchase picnic supplies. The **Sonoma Cheese Factory** on Spain Street is interesting to visit. The front of the shop has a deli and at the back, behind a glass partition, you can observe the making of cheese. Open daily 8:30 am to 5 pm, 707-996-1000.

Leaving the square, go east on Napa Street for 2 miles to Old Winery Road where you turn left to visit the region's oldest winery, **Buena Vista** (18000 Old Winery Road, Sonoma, CA 95476), built in 1857. Nestled in a wooded glen, the old ivy-covered buildings are very picturesque with arched caverns and stone walls. Picnic tables are set under the trees (bring your own food and be prepared for quite a crowd in the summer). Purchase a wine glass and enjoy four tastes for $5. At 2 pm a tour guide gives a presentation of the historical founding of the winery. Open 10 am to 5 pm. 800-926-1266 or 707-938-1266, *www.buenavistawinery.com.*

General Vallejo, the military commander and director of colonization of the Northern Frontier (until the Bear Flag Revolution established California as a free and independent republic), lived nearby with his wife and their 12 children. Vallejo's Home, "**Lachryma Montis**" (translated to mean mountain tear, an adaptation of the Indian name given to a free-flowing spring that surrounds the property), is well signposted on the outskirts of town on Spain Street. In its day this lovely Victorian-style house was considered one of the most elegant and lavishly decorated homes in the area, and is still attractively furnished. *www.parks.sonoma.net/sonoma.html.*

Leave Sonoma south on Broadway (Hwy 12), continuing on to Hwy 121 towards San Francisco.

A short drive brings you to the **Gloria Ferrer Winery** (23555 Hwy 121, Sonoma, CA 95476). The Ferrer family, who brought expertise in making Spanish sparkling and table wines, hails from Catalonia, Spain and, consequently, the winery resembles a small Catalonian village. A wide road sweeps up to the winery through the vineyards. Tours begin at 11 am but vary, so call ahead. They start from the spacious tasting room whose windows look out over the vineyards and valley. Most of the narrative is given in a room decorated with winemaking instruments from the Ferrers' winery in Spain. The riddling of the bottles to capture the sediment is explained, and then you go to the observation room to see the process of freezing then disgorging the sediment, corking, cleaning, and labeling the bottles of sparkling wine. The tour then descends into a maze of interconnected wine-storage tunnels. It is awesome to stand next to towering heights of stacked bottles. The tour concludes back in the tasting room. Wine tasting is $4 to $7 per glass. 707-933-1917, *www.gloriaferrer.com.*

One more winery awaits you before you return to San Francisco. Just a short drive from the Gloria Ferrer Winery you come to the **Viansa Winery** and Italian marketplace (25200 Hwy 121, Sonoma, CA 95476). Founded in 1990 by Vicki and Sam Sebastiani, Sam being a third-generation Sonoma Valley winemaker, this lovely winery produces Italian varietals, all of which are sold exclusively at the winery or by mail order. The hilltop location is especially inviting with its shaded picnic tables (for food bought on site) overlooking acres of vineyards and wetland. In the marketplace you can purchase gifts, wine, and delicious food items prepared daily in the Viansa kitchen, or sample one of the many pantry foods set out for tasting. You can enjoy four complimentary wine tastings. Tours of the cellars (11 am and 2 pm) cost $5. Open 10 am to 5 pm. 707-935-4700, *www.viansa.com.*

From the Viansa Winery it is less than an hour's drive back to San Francisco by continuing along Hwy 121 to Hwy 37 and onto Hwy 101, which takes you over the Golden Gate Bridge into the city.

Ballooning over the Napa Valley

Wandering through the Wine Country

Yosemite, the Gold Country & Lake Tahoe

Half Dome, Yosemite

This itinerary features two of California's most spectacular natural attractions, majestic Yosemite National Park and beautiful Lake Tahoe, and links them together by one of California's best-kept secrets—the spirited, nostalgic, Gold Rush towns, which string along the Sierra foothills. These colorful towns date back to 1848 when the cry went up that gold had been found at Sutter Creek, precipitating the rush to California by men eager to make their fortunes. Overnight, boom towns sprang up around every mining camp, with a cluster of similar-style saloons, restaurants, hotels, dance halls, and homes. Gold Rush fever quickly cooled and many of the towns were left, quietly forgotten, until tourists rediscovered their charm. Today these benignly neglected towns have been spruced up and bustle with activity: antique shops, art galleries, nifty boutiques, attractive restaurants, and appealing inns are tucked into old Victorian houses lining sleepy streets. The highway that runs through the mother lode country is numbered 49 after the gold-seeking miners who were known as the Forty-Niners.

Recommended Pacing: We recommend a minimum of two nights in Yosemite and suggest that you try to stay at accommodation in the park (see following page). Either before or after visiting Yosemite, you have a perfect opportunity to explore California's Gold Rush Country. Rather than backtracking, plan to progress through the region, spending at least one night in the south and one night in the north. From the northern region of the Gold Country it is a logical continuation on to Lake Tahoe. Many people enjoy Lake Tahoe as a resort and will spend at least a week here, basking on its sandy beaches in the summer and skiing down the snow-covered peaks that ring its waters in the winter. If you are visiting Lake Tahoe as a tourist, we recommend a two-night visit. **The itinerary route is outlined on Map 5 at the back of the book.**

Weather Wise: Heavy snow is the norm at Tahoe and Yosemite during the winter, while most of the Gold Rush towns are beneath the snow line and experience heavy winter rains. During summer months the days are hot in Yosemite and Tahoe, and several degrees warmer in the Gold Country.

As you read through this itinerary, please be aware that each of the areas featured could well be a destination in itself. Yosemite and Lake Tahoe are especially popular resorts and an entire vacation could easily be dedicated to either one. If that is your desire, just extract from the itinerary the portion that suits your interests. However, the Gold Country is not as well known and makes a super link between Yosemite and Tahoe—or, for that matter, a great destination in its own right.

Since Yosemite makes a most convenient first-night stop from either San Francisco or Los Angeles, driving directions are given from both so that you can tailor the trip to your own needs. Much of the first day of this itinerary is spent driving to Yosemite National Park, about a four- to five-hour drive from San Francisco or a six- to seven-hour drive from the Greater Los Angeles area. A brief description of what to see and do during your stay in San Francisco is included in *San Francisco to Los Angeles via the Coast*, while the list of attractions of the much larger, more sprawling Los Angeles are included in *Leisurely Loop of Southern California.*

Leave San Francisco east over the Bay Bridge, in the direction of Oakland. Once across the bridge, stay in the middle lane and follow signs for Hwy 580, heading east, signposted Stockton. Stay on Hwy 580 for about 48 miles until you come to Livermore where Hwy 580 meets Hwy 205, which you take, continuing east, following signs for Manteca. Near Manteca, take Hwy 120 east, directly to the northern gate of Yosemite National Park. Total driving distance is about 200 miles.

Leave Los Angeles heading north on Hwy 5 until you come to the junction of Hwy 99, which you take north (signposted Bakersfield). Continue on Hwy 99 to the north edge of Fresno where you take Hwy 41 north, directly to the southern gate of Yosemite National Park. Total driving distance is about 300 miles.

The main attractions of the over 1,000 square miles of **Yosemite National Park** lie within the narrow 7-mile-long **Yosemite Valley**, which is where you should try to stay if at all possible. A two- or three-night stay in the park is recommended. From hotels through tented cabins, all accommodations in Yosemite are controlled by the **Yosemite Concessions Services (YCS)**—for information call 209-372-0200. It is necessary year-round to make reservations well in advance by phoning 559-252-4848. Visit their homepage on the National Park Service website at *www.nps.gov.*

From the stately and very expensive **Ahwahnee Hotel**, through lodges, cabins, tented camps, and regular campsites, Yosemite has accommodations to suit every pocketbook. If your taste in hotels runs to grand, stay at The Ahwahnee. **Yosemite Lodge** provides more moderately priced accommodations in both cabins and motel/hotel-type rooms. Still less expensive are the tented camps that provide canvas tents on wooden board floors (you do not need sleeping bags since beds and linens are provided). The budget choice is regular camping. But please remember—space is very limited in every category and reservations are essential.

While the attractions of staying in the valley cannot be denied, a more relaxed, serene, country atmosphere pervades the **Wawona Hotel**, located within the park, but about a 30-mile drive south of the valley on Hwy 41. With its shaded verandahs overlooking broad rolling lawns, the hotel presents a welcoming picture. Bedrooms with private bathrooms are at a premium—most rooms use communal men's and women's bathrooms (sometimes situated quite a distance from your bedroom).

Yosemite Valley, an awe-inspiring monument to the forces of nature, is bounded by magnificent scraped granite formations—**Half Dome**, **El Capitan**, **Cathedral Rock**, **Clouds Rest**—beckoning rock climbers from around the world. And over the rocks, cascading to the valley far below, are numerous high waterfalls with descriptive names such as Bridalveil, Ribbon, Staircase, and Silver Strand. Below the giant walls of rock the crystal-clear River Merced wends its way through woodlands and meadows of flowers. Undeniably, this is one of the most beautiful valleys anywhere in the world.

Your first stop should be the information center to obtain pamphlets, books, and schedules. The park service offers a remarkable number of guided walks, slide shows, and educational programs—look over the possibilities and select the ones that most appeal to you.

Once you are in the valley, park your car and restrict yourself to travel aboard the free shuttle buses as you can do most of your sightseeing by combining pleasant walks with shuttle-bus rides. Alternative modes of transportation are on horseback on guided trips and by bike (bicycles can be rented in the park). Because the valley is flat, it has miles of paths for biking—a very unstrenuous, efficient way of getting around.

Be warned that during the summer months Yosemite Valley is jammed with cars and people—spring and fall are much more civilized times to visit.

Within the park, but beyond the valley floor, are many areas of great natural beauty. Situated just inside the park's southern perimeter is the **Mariposa Grove** of giant sequoias. It was here that John Muir, the great naturalist who fathered the idea of the national park system, persuaded President Theodore Roosevelt to add the 250-acre grove of trees to the Yosemite park system. A tram winds through the grove of sequoias as the driver tells the stories of these giant trees—some of the largest in the world.

To the south of the valley Hwy 41 climbs for about 10 miles (stop at the viewing point just before the tunnel) to the Glacier Point turnoff. It is a 15-mile drive to the spectacular **Glacier Point**—a vista point over 3,000 feet above the valley floor. From Glacier Point everything in the valley below takes on Lilliputian proportions: the ribbon-like River Merced, the forest, meadows, and waterfalls all dwarfed by huge granite cliffs. Beyond the valley a giant panorama of undulating granite presents itself. The ideal time to visit for taking photographs is early in the morning or evening. Rangers at Glacier Point offer evening interpretive programs.

Leave Yosemite by the northern gate on Hwy 120 to **Groveland**, a handsome old town shaded by pines. The nearby town of Big Oak Flat is little more than a couple of houses strung along the road. As Hwy 120 drops steeply down 5 miles of twisting road to Hwy 49, the shady pine forests of the mountains give way to rolling, oak-studded foothills, the typical scenery of the Gold Country.

Heading north on Hwy 49, detour into **Chinese Camp**, home to over 5,000 Chinese miners in the 1850s and now almost a ghost town sleeping under a profusion of delicate Chinese Trees of Heaven.

The main street of **Jamestown** is off Hwy 49 and therefore free of thoroughfare traffic. With its wooden boardwalks, balconies, and storefronts, Jamestown has managed to retain much of the feel of the Gold Rush days. Inviting shops, particularly the emporium, merit a browse, the western-style saloons are full of local color, and the **1859 Historic National Hotel** as well as the **Jamestown Hotel** have been restored to a beauty such as the Gold Rush days never witnessed. Just above Main Street on Fifth Avenue is the **Railtown 1897 State Historic Park** where visitors can see old freight and passenger cars, steam trains, and the roundhouse. Rides on an old steam train are offered on summer weekends. (209 984-3953, *www.csrmf.org/railtown*)

Leaving town, continue up the main street and cross Hwy 49 onto a peaceful little road that takes you through the countryside to Columbia. Follow signs for Columbia or, wherever a junction is unmarked, continue straight. A 15-minute drive brings you to Parrot Ferry Road on the outskirts of the town.

City Hotel, Columbia

In the 1850s **Columbia** was one of the largest towns in California, with many saloons, gaming halls, and stores. Today the main street is closed to car traffic and has been restored as a state park to reflect the dusty, raucous days when Columbia was the "gem of the southern mines." The renovated buildings of Main Street are like exhibits that make learning fun. Be sure to visit the Wells Fargo office, fire station, candy store, mining museum, and concession shops where costumed citizens sell goods appropriate to the period. You can enjoy a cold sarsaparilla at the saloon, munch candy rocks at the Candy Kitchen, and pan for gold at the mining shack. It is great fun to climb aboard a stagecoach for a ride through the town or take a tour to the Hidden Treasure Mine.

Both the **Fallon** and **City Hotel** have been restored (at vast expense) by the State of California to mirror the look of two of Columbia's hotels in Gold Rush days. The City Hotel on Main Street has a less ornate Victorian decor, reflecting the Columbia of the 1860s.

Parrot Ferry Road leads north from Columbia, crosses the dam and continues through hilly countryside in the direction of Murphys. If you would like to try your hand at rappelling into the largest cavern in California, you have the opportunity at **Moaning Cavern**. (You can, of course, take the saner descent down a spiral staircase into a room capable of holding the Statue of Liberty.) The rappel is exciting, and with outfitting, instruction, and a boost of confidence, you descend through a small opening into the well-lit cavern—a most exhilarating experience.

From the caves a short drive brings you to Hwy 4 where you turn east (right) for about a 20-mile drive to **Calaveras Big Trees State Park**, a 6,000-acre preserve of forest including two magnificent stands of sequoia trees. A 45-minute self-guided tour takes you through the North Grove and the nearby visitors center provides information and history on these mammoth trees. If you have time and interest, you can visit the more distant South Grove of giant sequoias.

Leaving the park, retrace your route down Hwy 4 and detour into **Murphys**, a sleepy Gold Rush town sheltered under locust and elm trees where several old buildings and an **Old Timers' Museum** reflect its Gold Rush heritage. Well signposted from the center of town is another cavern complex, **Mercer Caverns**, with rooms of stalactites, stalagmites, and other interesting limestone formations. You might also want to detour to a beautiful winery, **Ironstone Vineyards,** set on the hill outside Murphys. (Turn off Main Street up the road to the side of Murphy's Hotel, then at the stop sign turn right on Six Mile Road and travel 1 mile.) The grounds are absolutely gorgeous in their landscaping and at the end of an extremely informative tour it is a memorable experience to taste wine while listening to the winery's magnificent organ from the old Alhambra Theater. Complimentary tours are offered daily at 11:30 am, 1:30 pm, and 3:30 pm (no 11:30 am tour during winter months). The winery is open daily between 10 am and 5 pm (closed at Christmas and Thanksgiving) for complimentary tasting. Ironstone Vineyards is located at 1894 Six Mile Road, Murphys. (209-728-1251, *www.ironstonevineyards.com*)

At the junction of Hwys 4 and 49 sits **Angels Camp**, a pleasant town with high sidewalks and wooden-fronted buildings. Today Angels Camp's fame results not from mining, but from the frog-jumping contests held every May. There is even a monument to a frog taking the place of honor on the main street along which almost all the shops sell items carrying a frog motif.

Leave Angels Camp traveling north on Hwy 49 through San Andreas where nearly all evidence of Gold Rush days has been obliterated by modern shopping centers and commercial businesses. On the outskirts of the town Hwy 49 makes a sharp turn to the east (right), which is signposted Jackson. A 7-mile drive brings you to **Mukulumne Hill**, which in its heyday was one of the more raucous mining towns, though now it seems to be quietly fading away. Turn off Hwy 49 and loop through town past the impressive (though genteelly shabby) Hotel Leger and turn left in front of the crumbling I.O.O.F building, then through the residential area and back onto the main road.

Jackson still supports roughly the same population as it had during the Gold Rush—consequently, modern shopping centers and sprawling suburbs are the order of the day. Turn right at the first stop sign in town and almost immediately left to the main street. Set above the old town in an impressive Victorian home is the **Amador County Museum**, 225 Church Street (open Wednesday to Sunday 10 am to 4 pm). The various rooms have rather eclectic exhibits from the Gold Rush era: for example, the kitchen is full of 19th-century cookware while a small upstairs bedroom displays Indian baskets. Set in an adjacent building is a scale working model of the North Star Stamp Mill, which crushes tiny stones.

Retrace your route to where you turned off Hwy 49 and turn left on Hwy 88 signposted for Lake Tahoe and Pine Grove. Just outside Pine Grove turn left (signposted for your next two destinations, Indian Grinding Rock State Park and Volcano) and follow one of the Gold Country's prettiest back roads to **Chaw'se Indian Grinding Rock State Park**. A giant slab of limestone has over 1,000 grinding mortars worn into it by Indian women grinding acorn meal. A typical Miwok village has been built nearby with a ceremonial roundhouse and various tree-bark dwellings. The adjacent cultural center, built in the style of an Indian roundhouse, has interesting displays from several local Indian tribes.

Just a short drive takes you past the turnoff for Sutter Creek and into **Volcano**, one of the smallest (population 100), prettiest Gold Country towns, which boasted the first lending library and theater group in the state. Now it is a tiny one-street town whose most impressive building is the three-storied, balconied **Saint George Hotel**. Several weathered building fronts give an impression of what the town looked like in more prosperous days. Three miles beyond the town lies **Daffodil Hill** where over 25,000 daffodils provide a colorful spring display.

Follow the narrow wooded ravine alongside Sutter Creek as it twists down to the town of the same name. **Sutter Creek** rivals Nevada City as the loveliest of the Gold Rush towns. Its main street is strung out along busy Hwy 49 but somehow the noisy logging trucks and commercial and car traffic do not detract from its beauty. False wooden storefronts support big balconies, which hang over the high sidewalks of the town. Today many of the quaint wooden buildings are home to antique, craft, and gift shops.

Amador City and **Drytown**, the first two towns you encounter after leaving Sutter Creek as you head towards Placerville on Hwy 49, have an old-world charm and are worth exploring. However, following them is a string of commercial towns that offer nothing of attraction to the tourist although the intervening countryside is still most attractive. Follow Hwy 49 as it weaves through the commercial sprawl of **Placerville**, crosses Hwy 50, and climbs out of town.

It is an 8-mile drive along Hwy 49, through apple orchards and woodlands, to Coloma where the Gold Rush began. Or you can make it a 25-mile drive by taking a right turn east just after leaving Placerville onto Hwy 193, a narrow road that twists down a thickly forested canyon to Chili Bar (a popular spot for rafters to launch) and then does a spectacular weaving climb out of the valley through Kelsey and into **Georgetown**. Stop to explore Georgetown's shaded streets and then pick up Marshall Road (turn left behind the gas station), which takes you down to Hwy 49 where you turn south into Coloma.

Set on the banks of the American River, the scant remains of the boom town of **Coloma** are preserved as **Marshall Gold Discovery State Historic Park**. It all began in 1848 when James Marshall discovered gold at **Sutter's Sawmill**. The remaining historic buildings are scattered over a large area, each separated by expanses of green lawn and picnic places along the banks of the river. The residential part of town is a sleepy little cluster of attractive houses set back from the river—it is hard to believe that there was once a population of over 10,000 here. The museum shows a short film on gold discovery and provides information for a self-guided tour. A duplicate of Sutter's original sawmill, looking like a big shed, sits on the bank of the river. For a change of transportation, a number of companies offer one-day rafting trips down the most famous section of the South Fork of the American River. We thoroughly enjoyed the trip that we took with

Beyond Limits Adventures. It's a class 3 (intermediate) section of river that combines pretty scenery and whitewater as your raft plunges into Satan's Cesspool, Hospital Bar, and Ambulance Driver. Minimum age seven, season April to October. (800-234-7238, *www.rivertrip.com*)

Auburn lies 20 miles farther north along Hwy 49, which weaves through its suburbs, crosses Hwy 80, and continues as a fast, wide road for approximately 24 miles into Grass Valley. An alternative, far more attractive, and just a few miles longer route, is to take Hwy 80 north to the Colfax-Grass Valley exit and follow Hwy 174 through pretty woodlands and orchards into Grass Valley. (The following sightseeing suggestion, Empire Mine State Park, is signposted on your left as you near town.)

Grass Valley has a booming economy and sprawls far beyond its historic boundary. Its old downtown buildings housing everyday stores attest to its prosperity. Save town explorations for adjacent Nevada City and concentrate on Grass Valley's **Empire Mine State Park** at the southern end of town. This hard-rock mine produced $100,000,000-worth of gold before it closed. An exhibition depicts the mining methods used by miners who came here from the Cornish tin mines in England. Park personnel offer tours of the mine buildings, the most interesting of which is the opulent home of William Bourne, the mine's original owner. (530-273-8522)

The adjacent town of **Nevada City** is as handsome as Grass Valley is functional. The old mining stores and saloons have been cleverly converted into eateries ranging from family-style cafés to gourmet restaurants, antique stores, boutiques, bookstores, and the like. Old-fashioned gas lamps light the streets at night, providing a perfect backdrop for a horse-drawn-carriage ride. Many settlers came here from the east bringing with them the deciduous trees of their home states, so Nevada City is one of the few places in California that has the glorious fall foliage.

A great many events occur in Nevada City including the popular Victorian Christmas (Thanksgiving to Christmas—roast chestnuts and carolers), Summer Nights, and the

Teddy Bear Convention (April). The town also hosts parades such as the Joe Cain Parade (Mardi Gras), markets, festivals, and tours that give you plenty of excuses to visit this delightful spot at all times of the year.

Nevada City

As a conclusion to your Gold Country explorations, take a 45-mile round trip to **Malakoff Diggins** where high-powered jets of water were blasted at a mountainside to extract gold. The method was very successful, but it clogged waterways for miles and left a lunar landscape where there had once been a forested mountainside. This is a very pleasant summer-evening trip, but rather than run the risk of returning down narrow country roads in the dark, make the loop as you leave Nevada City for Lake Tahoe. The route is quite well signposted, but it gives you reassurance to have in hand the map from Nevada City Chamber of Commerce. (530-265-2692, *www.nevadacitychamber.com*)

Leave Nevada City going north on Hwy 49, following it through wooded countryside for 11 miles to the marker directing you right to Malakoff Diggins (signposted Tyler Foote Crossing Road). The narrow paved road leads you through the forest and, just as you are beginning to wonder quite where you are going, a signpost directs you right down a dirt road into **North Bloomfield**, a town of white-painted houses and buildings set behind picket fences under forest shade. (The town is being restored by the park service and the museum/ranger station is a useful informational stop.) The road through town leads to the diggins proper, a vast lunar landscape of awesome scars. If the weather is inclement, turn back at this point and return to Nevada City by way of the paved highway. Otherwise, continue along the well-maintained dirt road (forking left and downhill at junctions), which leads you down through some lovely scenery to a narrow wood-and-metal bridge spanning a rocky canyon of the South Yuba River where you pick up the paved road that brings you back to Hwy 49 on the outskirts of Nevada City.

Leave Nevada City on Hwy 20 east, a freeway which soon becomes a two-lane highway passing through forests and along a high ridge giving vistas of the Sierras. As Hwy 20 ends, take Hwy 80 towards Truckee, a fast freeway that climbs into the Sierra mountains through ever-more-dramatic rugged scenery.

The freeway climbs over **Donner Pass** and by **Donner Lake**, both named in honor of the group of settlers led by George Donner who in 1846 became snowbound while trying to cross the Sierra Nevada in late fall. Harsh conditions and lack of food took many lives and resulted in the survivors resorting to cannibalism.

Take Hwy 89, the Tahoe City exit, and follow it alongside the rushing **Truckee River** to **River Ranch Lodge**, an inn where in summertime it is great sport to sit on the patio and watch the river tumbling by.

Follow the Truckee River to its source, **Lake Tahoe**. Tucked in a high valley, Lake Tahoe is a vast, blue, icy-cold lake ringed by pine forests and backed by high mountains. The lake has about 70 miles of shoreline, a maximum depth of 1,645 feet, and a summer temperature of about 65 degrees. When people from the San Francisco Bay Area say they are "going to the mountains," Tahoe is usually where they're heading. While certain enclaves have their share of hot dog stands, McDonald's restaurants, and glitzy gambling casinos, there are many unspoilt areas where you can enjoy the exquisite beauty of the lake and its surrounding stunning scenery. For bikers and joggers, a marvelous, seemingly endless trail traces a path along the lakefront and down the Truckee River.

Tahoe City combines rustic, folksy shops, restaurants, and everyday stores with two quite interesting tourist attractions: Fanny Bridge and the Gatekeeper's Cabin. **Fanny Bridge** is very close: just turn right at the supermarket, and there it is. You will see immediately the derivation of "Fanny" when you see the tourists leaning over the railing to watch the trout gobble up the food tossed to them. On the same side of the bridge where the fish feed, outlet gates are opened and shut to control the level of the lake—the entire flow of water exiting from Lake Tahoe is regulated here as the water runs into the Truckee River. The other attraction of Tahoe City, the **Gatekeeper's Cabin**, sits on the bank of the Truckee. The rustic old cabin, once home to the man who controlled the river level, is now an attractive small museum operated by the local historical society.

Hugging the shoreline, Hwy 89 opens up to ever-more-lovely vistas as the road travels south. Nine miles south of Tahoe City brings you to **Sugar Pine State Park** with its many miles of hiking trails, and camping and picnic sites. In summer you can tour the nicely furnished Ehrman Mansion, once the vast lakeside summer home of a wealthy San Francisco family.

You will know by the sheer beauty of your surroundings when you are at **Emerald Bay**. The road sits hundreds of feet above a sparkling, blue-green bay and miles of Lake Tahoe stretch beyond its entrance. Center stage is a small wooded island crowned by a stone tea house. A 1½-mile trail winds down to the lake—it seems a lot farther walking up—and in summer you can tour **Vikingsholm**, the 38-room lakeside mansion built in 1929 and patterned after a 9th-century Norse fortress. It is the finest example of Scandinavian architecture in America and is filled with Norwegian furniture. (*www.vikingsholm.com*)

Just below Emerald Bay a trail leads from the parking lot up a ¼-mile steep trail to a bridge above the cascading cataract of **Eagle Falls**, which offers fantastic views of Lake Tahoe. A mile farther up the trail is **Eagle Lake**, in an isolated, picture-perfect setting.

Emerald Bay

A memorable outing from Tahoe is a day trip to Nevada's silver towns, Virginia City and Carson City. Leaving Tahoe City, follow the northernmost shore of the lake across the Nevada state line and take Hwy 431 from Incline Village over Mount Rose to the stoplight at Hwy 395. Cross the highway and go straight ahead up the winding Geiger Grade, Hwy 341, to **Virginia City**. Built over a honeycomb of silver mines, in its heyday Virginia City had a population of over 30,000. Its wooden sidewalks, colorful saloons (you must visit the Bucket of Blood Saloon), and false-front buildings with their broad balconies make it a town straight out of a John Wayne movie. The stores sell everything from homemade candy to western boots and several have been reconstructed as museums. You can walk up to the old cemetery, take a steam-train ride, or tour a mine.

Leaving town, travel on through Gold Hill and Silver Hill to Hwy 50 where you turn south for the 7-mile drive to **Carson City**, the state capital. The town itself has little of interest except for the **Nevada State Museum**, just across the street from the Nugget Casino on the main road (open 8:30 am to 4:30 pm daily). The highlight of the museum is the re-created silver mine in the basement. You walk along rail car lines in semi-darkness, past exhibits of miners at work and mine machinery—a lot safer than going down a working mine. (775-687-4810)

To return to Tahoe, go south on Hwy 395, the main street of town, to Hwy 50 west. Turn right and when you come to Lake Tahoe turn right, following the lake to Tahoe City.

Leaving Lake Tahoe, it is a fast four- to five-hour freeway drive, via Hwy 80, to the San Francisco Bay Area. If you are going to Los Angeles, take Hwy 80 to Sacramento and Hwy 5 south to Los Angeles—a fast eight- to nine-hour drive.

Places to Stay

The location of the Albion River Inn is impressive—right on the bluff overlooking the handsome bay formed by the estuary of the River Albion. The architecture creates the ambiance of a New England village: softly hued clusters of cottages perch on the cliffs surrounded by a meadow where long grass waves in the wind. Gardens filled with brightly colored flowers line the walkways along the bluff and the quiet is broken only by the deep-throated call of the foghorn. Each of the bedrooms offers a sweeping view of the inlet where the fishing boats bob about in the ever-changing tides. All of the rooms are spacious, romantic, beautifully decorated, and very private and all have fireplaces and binoculars for whale watching. Other extras include complimentary wine, newspapers, and coffee makers. Rooms are priced by size and location—with those having the most dramatic views both from the bedroom and the bathtub commanding the highest price. The acclaimed Albion River Inn Restaurant with its award-winning wine list is adjacent to the inn with picture windows overlooking the sea. A hearty breakfast is served including fresh fruits, juices, homemade breads, and other specialties of the house. *Directions:* From Cloverdale drive west on Hwy 128 to Hwy 1, and north 3 miles to Albion. The inn is on the northwest side of the Albion bridge.

ALBION RIVER INN
Owners: Flurry Healy & Peter Wells
Manager: Karen Malone Deitz
3790 N. Hwy 1
P.O. Box 100, Albion, CA 95410, USA
Tel: (707) 937-1919, (800) 479-7944
Fax: (707) 937-2604
20 rooms
Double: $160–$310
Open: all year, Credit cards: all major
karenbrown.com/california/albionriverinn.html

Amador City with its quaint old west-style houses was a bustle of activity during the Gold Rush days. Now it's a peaceful place (except for the logging trucks that rumble through town periodically), with its old wooden stores full of craft and antique shops and the Imperial Hotel, looking as though it belongs in a cowboy movie. There is immediate charm as soon as you walk into this renovated western hotel where you wouldn't be surprised to see prospectors leaning at the bar. Beyond the bar lies a spacious, high-ceilinged dining room, its red-brick walls hung with fanciful Victorian art. Dining is casual and the menu is short: usually three appetizers, seven entrees, five or six desserts. Upstairs, the six bedrooms are a delight—nothing fancy or frilly, but each thoughtfully appointed and accompanied by a small, sparkling bathroom with tub or shower and heated towel bar. Room 6, decorated warmly in tans and navy, is a real winner with an elaborate art-deco bed. The whimsical hand-painted headboard in room 5 is echoed in the paintings of clothes on the closet in room 3. Rooms 1 and 2 share the large balcony at the front of the hotel. There are two sets of adjoining rooms. Guests help themselves to early-morning coffee and tea before going in for breakfast. *Directions:* Amador City straddles Hwy 49, 6 miles north of Jackson. The Imperial Hotel is on your right at the bend in the main street.

IMPERIAL HOTEL
Owner: Rhonda Uhlman
14202 Hwy 49
P.O. Box 195, Amador City, CA 95601, USA
Tel: (209) 267-9172, (800) 242-5594
Fax: (209) 267-9249
6 rooms
Double: $90–$130
Open: all year, Credit cards: all major
karenbrown.com/california/imperialhotel.html

We don't often include resorts in our book, but the stunning location of the Seascape Resort prompted us to make an exception. This sprawling complex of seven buildings rests on the bluffs overlooking the Monterey Bay—you can't get much closer without being on the beach. On a stretch of residential street, the resort is quiet and low key. The beach is a short walk down a private paved path (or take the golf-cart shuttle if you prefer) and there are three pools with outdoor Jacuzzis. Guests can choose from studios, one-bedroom suites, or two-bedroom villas. Each suite is handsomely furnished in light colors and offers a private balcony with ocean view, fireplace, full kitchen, and television. Families are easily accommodated in the larger villas (averaging 1200 square feet). Children are quite welcome here: in fact, there is a "kids' club" during the summer months, featuring planned activities for children between five and ten years old. Sanderlings Restaurant, set on two levels of the main building and offering spectacular vistas, is named after the scurrying shorebirds on the beach. The resort makes a good home base for visiting the Monterey Bay Aquarium, taking children to the Santa Cruz Beach Boardwalk, and golfing on nearby courses. *Directions:* About 9 miles south of Santa Cruz, take the Larkin Valley Road exit off Hwy 1 and go west on San Andreas Road. Turn right on Seascape Boulevard.

SEASCAPE RESORT–MONTEREY BAY
Manager: Jim Maggio
One Seascape Resort Drive
Aptos, CA 95003, USA
Tel: (831) 688-6800, (800) 929-7727
Fax: (831) 685-0615
285 rooms
Double: $250–$550*
 *Breakfast not included: $12–$15
Open: all year, Credit cards: all major
karenbrown.com/california/seascaperesort.html

In a quiet rural setting just outside the town of Atascadero you find Oak Hill Manor, a large, modern home built in the Californian Tudor style on acres of gently undulating land overlooking the Santa Lucia Mountains. This welcoming inn reflects the owners' love of Europe, with rooms named for European cities or themes such as the St. Andrews or Alpine Suites. You can even enjoy a game of pool, cards, or darts in the common Pub Room. The luxurious guestrooms are decorated with rich colors and fabrics and many have large Jacuzzi tubs and fireplaces for utter relaxation and comfort. Three of the rooms are in the main house and the remaining five in the Carriage House just across the garden. Settle on the patio of the Parisienne Suite with a glass of wine and views of the mountains or splurge and reserve the Alpine Suite if you would like to be quite undisturbed, as it is the only accommodation on the second floor of the Carriage House. With the Edna Valley to the south and Paso Robles to the north, Atascadero is perfectly located for wine-tasting getaways. Hearst Castle is a 45-minute drive away, while the beach towns of Cambria, Morro Bay, and Cayucos are even closer. *Directions:* Halfway between San Francisco and Los Angeles. Take Hwy 101 to the Santa Barbara Road exit, turn east and drive ½ mile, turning right on Hampton Court.

OAK HILL MANOR
Owners: Risë & Maurice Macaré
12345 Hampton Court
Atascadero, CA 93422 , USA
Tel: (805) 462-9317, (866) 625-6267
Fax: (805) 462-0331
8 rooms
Double: $170–$235
Open: all year, Credit cards: all major
karenbrown.com/california/oakhillmanor.html

The lovely Ballard Inn is located in the Santa Ynez Valley, a lush region of rolling hills planted with vineyards or sectioned off with white picket fences. Set just off the road, the Ballard was built as an inn but carries the appearance of a gracious sprawling residence. White picket fences enclose its narrow front garden and a wide porch winds round it. The dining room, serving bountiful breakfasts and gourmet dinners (Wednesday through Sunday evenings), is located just off the entry to the right. To the left, another cozy room invites you to linger over afternoon hors d'oeuvres or venture on into the sitting room where large, deep sofas steal you away for lazy conversations in front of an open fireplace. Guestrooms are located upstairs or in a neighboring wing just off the graveled driveway. Rooms are comfortable and attractively decorated, each with a small, functional private bathroom. Although, at first, rooms overlooking the front garden seem preferable to those overlooking the parking area, rooms at the back are quieter. If you like horses, ask about the neighboring miniature horse farm. We visited in spring when every mother was matched with a tiny foal—adorable. *Directions:* From Hwy 101, take the Solvang exit, following Route 246E through Solvang to Alamo Pintado. Turn left, drive 3 miles to Baseline Avenue, then turn right. The inn is on the right side.

BALLARD INN
Owners: Steve Hyslop & Larry Stone
2436 Baseline Avenue
Ballard, CA 93463, USA
Tel: (805) 688-7770, (800) 638-2466
Fax: (805) 688-9560
15 rooms
Double: $195–$275
Closed: Christmas, Credit cards: all major
Select Registry
karenbrown.com/california/theballardinn.html

Deetjen's Big Sur Inn, a cluster of rustic, weathered redwood houses, trimmed in white and topped by green roofs, was built in the early 1930s by Helmuth Deetjen, who crafted the cabins in the style of his native Norway. If you are looking for the amenities of a modern hotel, Deetjen's will definitely not be your cup of tea. However, those who appreciate old-fashioned charm and the splendor of nature will be enthralled by this very special property—it exemplifies the lifestyle of those who first came to the magnificent Big Sur area to enjoy a gentle life, uncluttered by possessions. Guestrooms are nestled in amongst the redwoods in buildings with individual names and characters. Old hand-hewn doors (without locks) open to a medley of varying room configurations, all warmed by fireplaces, wood-burning stoves, or electric heaters. The rooms, decorated with antique accents and rustic fabrics, are charming in their utter simplicity. Walls are paper-thin— whispering becomes second nature so that everyone can enjoy the surrounding peace and quiet. There are four romantic dining rooms with a cozy fireplace, low, beamed ceilings, soft lighting, country antiques, painted furniture, and tables dressed with linens. *Directions:* Located on the east side of Hwy 1, 30 miles south of Carmel and about 3 miles south of Big Sur.

DEETJEN'S BIG SUR INN
Innkeeper: Laura Moran
Hwy 1
Big Sur, CA 93920, USA
Tel: (831) 667-2377, Fax: (831) 667-0466
20 rooms
Double: $75–$195*
 *Breakfast not included
Open: all year, Credit cards: MC, VS
karenbrown.com/california/deetjensbigsurinn.html

Ventana, surrounded by 240 acres of meadows and forests, is nestled in Big Sur, a gorgeous stretch of coast where the hills plunge down to meet the crashing sea. In contrast to the coastline, there is nothing rugged about Ventana Inn and Spa—it is the most sophisticated, deluxe resort where guests are pampered and provided with every luxury. After check-in a golf cart takes you and your luggage to your room, found in one of 12 natural-wood buildings. The decor varies (depending upon which section you are in) but each guestroom has the same ambiance with natural-wood paneling, luxurious fabrics, and leather chairs. All rooms have a large terrace with a latticed wood screen and a fireplace (be sure to request real logs if this is important to you)—some have private spas. All have a pretty view to the hills and forest or to the sea on the horizon. Wine and cheese are served in the afternoon and a Continental breakfast of pastries and fruit is set out each morning. There are two 75-foot swimming pools with adjacent Japanese bath (some areas are designated as clothing-optional), and a luxurious spa with facials and massages. Massages are also available in the privacy of your room. Walk the forest path (or arrange for a van) to take you to dinner at Cielo's restaurant. *Directions:* Thirty miles south of Carmel on the east side of Hwy 1, just south of the Big Sur State Park.

❄ ⏫ ☕ 💳 ⛷ 🥾 🍷 P 🍴 🚭 ≈ 🎿

VENTANA INN & SPA
Manager: Sal Abaunza
Hwy 1
Big Sur, CA 93920, USA
(800) 628-6500, Fax: (831) 667-2419
60 rooms
Double: $340–$1000
Open: all year, Credit cards: all major
karenbrown.com/california/ventana.html

The Chateau de Vie is an intimate bed and breakfast, sweetly tucked away behind a white lattice fence in lush gardens of beautiful roses, exotic flowers, and mature fruit trees. Built in 1981, it was designed to resemble a small French country château. The decor is elegant, and the use of dark, rich wall colors gives an air of masculinity. The comfortable living room is done in soothing tones of olive and taupe, with linen window coverings and French doors leading to a deck with umbrella-covered tables—a perfect place to relax with a glass of wine and to enjoy cheese and hors d'oeuvres. After waking up to the coffee or tea that arrives outside your door in the morning, mosey down to the handsome dining room with its forest-green walls and large window seat or to the back deck for a gourmet repast of fresh-baked scones and fruit followed by a cooked breakfast that will equip you for a full day of sightseeing. All of the guestrooms overlook the pretty garden and are appealingly decorated in bold colors and textures. We loved the spaciousness and privacy of our top-floor room. Relax in the secluded Jacuzzi tub that sits on the edge of the vineyard. If you are feeling energetic take Jake, the friendly golden retriever, for a walk through the surrounding vineyards. *Directions:* From Calistoga take Hwy 128 north. When you reach Tubbs Lane, go ¼ mile farther, turn right along a small lane and the Chateau de Vie is the first house on your right.

CHATEAU DE VIE
Owners: Felipe Barragan & Peter Weatherman
3250 Hwy 128
Calistoga, CA 94515, USA
Tel: (707) 942-6446, Fax: (707) 942-6456
4 rooms
Double: $189–$249
Open: all year, Credit cards: all major
karenbrown.com/california/chateaudevie.html

Christopher's Inn is located in an easy-to-find, walk-to-everything spot in the quaint town of Calistoga with its boutiques and delightful restaurants. Owner Christopher Layton has employed his considerable architectural talents in developing this charming and secluded haven right next to Hwy 29. Guestrooms come in a wide range of types and sizes and are priced accordingly, so be sure to specify exactly what you want. The oh-so-cozy queen-bedded rooms have private entrances and are very nicely decorated. At the other end of the spectrum are the splendid French suites, sumptuously attired in the manner of a luxurious château, with decadent bathrooms where you can soak in two-person Jacuzzi tubs before flickering firelight. The quietest accommodation is found in a pair of two-bedroom cottages, each with a trundle bed in the sitting room—these face a peaceful suburban street and are perfect for family reunions or small groups of friends. In the morning a basket is delivered to your room with a bounty of delicious breakfast treats. The Laytons are personable, helpful innkeepers who nevertheless enforce their cancellation policy—contact the inn for details. *Directions:* Coming north on Hwy 29, the inn is 500 yards past the John Deer tractor sales barn, on the right side of the road before the blinking intersection light.

CHRISTOPHER'S INN
Owners: Adele & Christopher Layton
1010 Foothill Boulevard
Calistoga, CA 94515, USA
Tel: (707) 942-5755, Fax: (707) 942-6895
21 rooms
Double: $175–$425
Open: all year, Credit cards: all major
karenbrown.com/california/christophersinn.html

In the 1970s Monica Bootcheck, Tom Stimpert, and Bob Beck shared a three-apartment houseboat in Sausalito. Their friendship endured and 20 years later, along with their spouses, they pooled their talents of architecture, contracting, interior design, and marketing and built the Cottage Grove Inn. The inn is a complex of 16 individual cottages tucked into a beautiful grove of century-old Siberian Elm trees. The property reflects the nostalgic charm of yesteryear. From the outside each of the sweet, doll-house-like cottages has a similar appearance, with a clapboard exterior painted a warm dove gray, accented by deep-coral-colored shutters and crisp white trim. A romantic porch stretches across the front of each cottage with two white wicker rockers just begging you to relax with a good book. Inside, each cottage has its own personality, achieved through decorative accessories, beautiful wall colors, fine fabrics, lovely linens, and high-quality furnishings. Another bonus: each has a wood-burning fireplace and an enormous bathroom featuring a wonderful, deep Jacuzzi tub big enough for two (and cozy bathrobes). A romantic place to hide away with someone you love. *Directions:* From Hwy 29, turn east on Lincoln. Just before the road curves left as it leaves town, you will see the inn on your left.

COTTAGE GROVE INN
Owner: Valerie Beck
1711 Lincoln Avenue
Calistoga, CA 94515, USA
Tel: (707) 942-8400, (800) 799-2284
Fax: (707) 942-2653
16 cottages
Double: $250–$325
Open: all year, Credit cards: all major
karenbrown.com/california/cottagegrove.html

Privately tucked away on a gently sloping 20 acres just one mile from Calistoga's shopping and dining, you find Meadowlark, an elegant Napa valley retreat. Cross the white covered bridge and enter the restful haven created by Kurt Stevens and Richard Flynn. Seven, air-conditioned, rooms are your home from home. All are tastefully furnished, with some with four-poster pencil beds and french doors leading to their own deck or terrace. All are equipped with TV, VCR and ensuite marble tile bathrooms featuring whirlpool tubs for two. The two suites have sitting rooms equipped with sleeper sofas for an extra guest. The (clothing optional) mineral pool, hot tub and sauna have spacious flagstone terraces to soak up the California sunshine in secluded privacy. Licensed therapists provide in house massage. A modern cottage, adjacent to the pool area, complete with marble bathroom, its own kitchen and dining area, with fireplace and French doors to views across the meadow makes a perfect weekend (or longer!) hideaway for parties of up to five persons. A gourmet breakfast is served in the central farmhouse, circa 1880, overlooking the horse pasture. Well behaved dogs are welcome. Meadowlark is gay friendly. *Directions:* From Hwy 101, take the River Road/Guerneville exit and turn right onto Mark West Springs Road. Follow it to the end and turn left towards Calistoga onto Petrified Forest Road, the inn is on your right.

MEADOWLARK COUNTRY INN
Owners: Kurt Stevens & Richard Flynn
601 Petrified Forest Road
Calistoga, CA 94515, USA
Tel: (800) 942-5651, Fax: (707) 942-5023
7 rooms, 1 cottage ($325–$395)
Double: $165–$265
Open: all year, Credit cards: all major
karenbrown.com/california/meadowlark.html

As an alternative to the bed and breakfasts near Cambria's shops and galleries, the Blue Whale Inn offers guests more privacy and the opportunity to stroll for miles along Moonstone Beach. The front room and parlor enjoy expansive ocean views through picture windows. It is here that guests are served a delicious breakfast and wine, cheese, and cookies are set out in the afternoon. Stretching out behind the main building are the guestrooms, buffered from the parking area by a border of flowers and opening at an angle to capture a distant ocean view. Country in their decor, the rooms are attractive with light-pine furnishings, chintz and floral fabrics, and canopy beds. Each of the spacious mini suites has a fireplace, television, telephone, refrigerator, and a top-of-the-line bathroom with Jacuzzi tub. Motels line the beach frontage and without a doubt the Blue Whale Inn is the best of the bunch. The resident innkeepers are friendly and helpful, extending a warm welcome to both new and their many returning guests. *Directions:* Turn west off Hwy 1 north at the exit sign for Moonstone Beach. Follow Moonstone Beach Drive past the hotels that line this coastal frontage to the Blue Whale Inn.

BLUE WHALE INN
Owners: Jan Crowther & Kate McGill
Innkeepers: Jay & Karen Peavler
6736 Moonstone Beach Drive
Cambria, CA 93428, USA
Tel: (805) 927-4647, (800) 753-9000
Fax: (805) 927-3852
6 rooms
Double: $210–$260
Open: all year, Credit cards: MC, VS
karenbrown.com/california/bluewhaleinn.html

Nestled in the pines on a quiet suburban street above the town of Cambria the J. Patrick House, centers on a rustic log cabin whose open-plan layout and country-cozy decor create an inviting atmosphere, with guests gathering round the fire in the late afternoon for appetizers and wine. A full breakfast is served in a cheerful room overlooking the little garden. In the evening this adorable cabin can be your private retreat if you are lucky enough to snag the upstairs bedroom, Clare. The other bedrooms are found in the "carriage house" across the back garden. Named for counties in Ireland, each room has a wood-burning fireplace or stove, window seat, and country antiques. Each room has its own personality and all have a private bath and shower except one, which has a shower. There's also a tiny parlor where you can wait for friends and it's here that the inn's famous "killer" chocolate-chip cookies are set out in the evening. It's a short drive into town for dinner and shopping. This is a perfect base for exploring the Paso Robles wine region, visiting Hearst Castle, and soaking up coastal vistas. *Directions:* Exit off Hwy 1 east on Burton Drive and travel half a mile. The house is on the right.

J. PATRICK HOUSE
Owners: John Arnott & Ann O'Connor
2990 Burton Drive
Cambria, CA 93428, USA
Tel: (805) 927-3812, (800) 341-5258
Fax: (805) 927-6759
8 rooms
Double: $159–$210
Open: all year, Credit cards: MC, VS
Select Registry
karenbrown.com/california/jpatrick.html

This pretty little Victorian is suspended in a time warp at the heart of historic Cambria with its galleries, shops, and restaurants. A gate in the picket fence opens to a brick walkway leading through the garden to the small porch and entry. Inside, the decor is refreshing, clean, light, and minimalist, with whitewashed walls and the warm patina of natural pine floors, and there's a remarkable collection of photos and memorabilia of all the house's occupants. The five simple and extremely tasteful guestrooms have snug en-suite shower rooms. Request my favorite, the Garden Room, for then you can sit out on your balcony and enjoy your own private access to the winding little paths of the garden. At the front of the inn, the Parlor Room, once used as a school classroom, is now a pretty bedroom with a bay window and bird's-eye-maple furnishings. A Continental breakfast is set in the parlor and trays provided so that you can take your breakfast back to your room. Take your room key across the road to Fermentation and enjoy a complimentary tasting of wines from small private vineyards. If you arrive early, check in at the Shop Next Door, an excellent excuse to purchase some of Bruce's well-chosen antiques. Cambria with all its shops and restaurants is on your doorstep. *Directions:* From Hwy 1 turn east on Burton Drive to Cambria Village.

SQUIBB HOUSE
Owner: Bruce Black
Innkeeper: Kory Rusco
4063 Burton Drive
Cambria, CA 93428, USA
Tel: (805) 927-9600, (866) 927-9600
Fax: (805) 927-9606
5 rooms
Double: $105–$185
Open: all year, Credit cards: all major
karenbrown.com/california/thesquibbhouse.html

The Inn at Depot Hill, just two blocks up the hill from the beach and picturesque village of Capitola-by-the-Sea, dates back to 1901 when it was built as a Southern Pacific railroad station. The property does not sit on a large lot, so the grounds are minimal. Inside, the inn's imaginative decor reflects the theme of first-class train travel at the turn of the century: the bedrooms are handsomely decorated and named after different parts of the world—as if a guest were taking a railway journey and stopping at different destinations. My favorite is the unexpectedly Oriental Kyoto room, tucked away in a secluded corner complete with Buddha, reflecting pool, Asian antiques, and a huge soaking tub. The rooms feature many caring touches such as cutwork lace sheets and pillowcases, and sumptuous feather beds. There is a wealth of other amenities including televisions and VCRs, luxurious marble bathrooms, some Jacuzzi tubs on private outdoor patios, and even mini televisions in all of the bathrooms. An elegant full breakfast is served either in the dining room, the romantic walled garden, or your room. Complimentary early-evening wine and hors d'oeuvres and late-evening desserts and port are served from the dining-room buffet. *Directions:* South on Hwy 1 from Santa Cruz. Take the Park Avenue exit, turn right and go 1 mile. Turn left onto Monterey, then immediately left into the inn's driveway.

INN AT DEPOT HILL
Manager: Tom Cole
250 Monterey Avenue
Capitola, CA 95010, USA
Tel: (831) 462-3597, (800) 572-2632
Fax: (831) 462-3697
12 rooms
Double: $260–$385
Open: all year, Credit cards: all major
Select Registry
karenbrown.com/california/innatdepothill.html

A short walk off Ocean Avenue and central Carmel with its shops, galleries, and restaurants (48 at last count—leave that diet behind!), the Cobblestone Inn is a wonderful example of California cute. Wrapped around a central courtyard replete with trees, flowers, and creepers, where a sheltered brick patio is set with tables and chairs, the inn has been attractively decorated and furnished in an appealing California country style. Rooms come in a range of sizes but all have similar amenities including refrigerator, phone, television, and fireplace. Ample, functional bathrooms are finished in a mix of tile and painted wood paneling and have a generous supply of fluffy white towels. We appreciated the value of the "cozy queens" and enjoyed the ambiance of "standard queens" but really fell for the spaciousness of the "single-room king" suites (rooms 6 and 18) and especially liked room 27 with its four poster bed and spa tub. Families traveling with children should request the two-room suites (11 and 23), each equipped with a king-sized bed and a separate sitting room. In the evening hors d'oeuvres and wine are served in the lounge with its comfy sofas and fieldstone fireplace. A full buffet breakfast is provided, to be enjoyed indoors or out on the patio in the sunshine of a Carmel morning. *Directions:* From Hwy 1, take the Ocean Avenue exit then turn left on Junipero. The Cobblestone is on your right on the corner of 8th Street.

COBBLESTONE INN
Innkeeper: Sharon Carey
Junipero between 7th & 8th Streets
P.O. Box 3185, Carmel, CA 93921, USA
Tel: (831) 625-5222, (800) 833-8836
Fax: (831) 625-0478
24 rooms
Double: $125–$275
Open: all year, Credit cards: all major
karenbrown.com/california/cobblestoneinn.html

The Mission Ranch, which in days long past was a working farm, was bought and renovated with great sensitivity for its heritage by Clint Eastwood. The inn is located on 22 acres, quite a long walk from the center of Carmel, yet a world away in tranquillity (in fact, sheep still graze in the meadow in front of the hotel). The ranch offers a wide range of accommodations in terms of setting, views, and price. The least expensive guestrooms are found in the old barn, while more deluxe rooms are located in small meadow-front cottages. The latter have fireplaces and private porches with old-fashioned rocking chairs that beckon you to watch the sun set over the sea. There are also six bedrooms in the charming old farmhouse, which has an ornate Victorian-style living room with heavy oak furniture and a grand piano. Whichever room you choose, you cannot help being captivated by the peaceful beauty of the property and its well-maintained gardens. For exercise, there are six tennis courts and a workout room, plus, of course, a lovely beach within a 15-minute walk. A Continental buffet breakfast is served in the clubhouse next to the tennis courts. The Restaurant at Mission Ranch has an attractive terrace where guests can dine outside on warm evenings. *Directions:* From Hwy 1, turn west onto Rio Road, then left at the Mission and wind round the Mission to the ranch.

MISSION RANCH
Manager: Theresa Jung
26270 Dolores
Carmel, CA 93923, USA
Tel: (831) 624-6436, (800) 538-8221
Fax: (831) 626-4163
31 rooms
Double: $100–$280
Open: all year, Credit cards: all major
karenbrown.com/california/missionranch.html

The Normandy Inn exudes the charm and storybook quality that make this town so famous. As you walk down the main street toward the ocean, you cannot help stopping and smiling at this whimsical inn, which stretches for almost two blocks in the heart of town. Over the years it has grown to include not only the two-story building where the reception parlor, breakfast room, and many of the bedrooms are located, but also several cozy cottages and three houses—each house has three bedrooms, two bathrooms, and a kitchen. If you want to splurge, ask for one of the adorable cottages. Happily, although the buildings vary architecturally, there is a pleasing continuity of style that blends them harmoniously. The gardens too are absolutely stunning. Carmel is famous for its flowers—shops and hotels all vie to outdo their neighbors with the finest floral displays, but the Normandy Inn wins the prize. Like the exterior, the guestrooms have a similarity of feel. Each exudes a country-French ambiance and is attractively decorated in a color scheme of blue and white. This is an extremely well-run, friendly small hotel (with a swimming pool!) where guests are warmly greeted, a Continental breakfast is included, sherry is offered in the afternoon, and free parking is available. *Directions:* Leave Hwy 1 at Ocean Avenue. The Normandy Inn is on your left, just past Monte Verde.

NORMANDY INN
Owner: Max Hoseit
Innkeeper: Sandra Backinger
Ocean Avenue & Monte Verde
P.O. Box 1706, Carmel, CA 93921, USA
Tel: (831) 624-3825, (800) 343-3825
Fax: (831) 624-4614
48 rooms
Double: $99–$500
Open: all year, Credit cards: all major
karenbrown.com/california/normandy.html

With the ocean three blocks away, Sea View Inn is within easy walking distance of the much-photographed Carmel beach and you can catch the tiniest glimpse of the ocean through the trees from the inn's third floor. This large Victorian house looks as though it were once a large home, when in fact it has always been an inn. Deep-red-colored board-and-batten wainscoting accented by a plate rail displaying antiques and interesting bric-a-brac sets the welcoming mood for the living room and adjacent parlor where Continental breakfast, afternoon tea and coffee, and evening wine and sherry are served. Both rooms are warmed by cozy fireplaces, with games, books, and magazines scattered about, which add a comfortable, lived-in feel. The largest bedrooms are found on the second floor. Room 6 has an elegant decor with an Oriental rug, Ralph Lauren prints, and white window shutters, while Room 7 has a dramatic Oriental-style four-poster bed draped with blue-and-white Chinese-motif fabric. The four tiny bedrooms tucked under the steeply slanting attic ceilings on the third floor provide the very snuggest of accommodation. Each is lavishly decorated in a Provence floral print gathered into canopies and covering huge bed pillows. *Directions:* Take the Ocean Avenue exit from Hwy 1 to Camino Real and turn left—Sea View Inn is just after 11th Street on the left.

SEA VIEW INN
Owners: Diane & Marshall Hydorn
Innkeeper: Margo Thomas
Camino Real between 11th & 12th Streets
P.O. Box 4138, Carmel, CA 93921, USA
Tel: (831) 624-8778, Fax: (831) 625-5901
8 rooms
Double: $100–$175
Open: all year, Credit cards: all major
karenbrown.com/california/seaviewinn.html

Carmel's quaint gingerbread architecture, profusion of colorful flowers, and tall, shady trees are all happily combined at the Vagabond's House Inn. Set around a flagstone courtyard shaded by a giant oak tree and surrounded by fuchsias, azaleas, camellias, and rhododendrons, the inn is made up of a group of attached storybook English cottages, brick and half-timbered, topped by a thick shake roof, making this one of Carmel's most appealing-looking inns. Most of the guestrooms open directly onto the courtyard with its fountain and abundance of flowers including colorful fuchsias cascading from hanging boxes set in the oak tree. All of the bedrooms have been refurbished and are very inviting, with pretty coordinating fabrics on the comforters, cushions, and window coverings. Every bedroom has at least two antique clocks and many have their own cozy sitting nook and fireplace (be sure to request a room with a wood-burning as opposed to a gas fireplace). In the morning you phone reception to let them know when you would like a breakfast tray brought to your room. When you check in, be sure not to miss the antique toy collection in the lounge. *Directions:* Take the Ocean Avenue West exit from Hwy 1, turn right on Dolores Street, and go three blocks to 4th Street. The Vagabond's House Inn is on the corner of 4th Street and Dolores.

VAGABOND'S HOUSE INN
Owner: Dennis LeVett
Innkeeper: Dawn Dull
Dolores & 4th Street
P.O. Box 2747, Carmel, CA 93921, USA
Tel: (831) 624-7738, (800) 262-1262
Fax: (831) 626-1243
11 rooms, Double: $125–$250
Open: all year, Credit cards: all major
Select Registry
karenbrown.com/california/vagabonds.html

Set high above the shore just south of Carmel, at the northern gateway to Big Sur, sits the little coastal community of Carmel Highlands. Coastal views are the name of the game at the Tickle Pink Inn and the reservations folks are particularly helpful and happy to discuss each and every vista. Whether spotting whales while sipping wine on the terrace (there is an excellent cheese and wine hour), soaking in views from your Jacuzzi tub, or gazing at coastal vistas from in front of your crackling log fire, there is a view for you. The utilitarian-like structure belies an absolutely charming interior with quality decor in restful, muted colors. Relax by the fire, borrow a movie, soak up the view from your private deck, and be "tickled pink" by the sugar-pink sheets. Newspapers are delivered to your door—request breakfast to accompany them or make your own selections from the extensive breakfast buffet. As the inn's motto says, "Rest a bit for 'tis a rare place to rest at." Just up the road are the 1,250 acres of our favorite state reserve, Point Lobos, known as the "greatest meeting of land and water in the world"— be sure to visit. *Directions:* Take Hwy 1 south from Carmel for 4 miles. Highland Inn and the Tickle Pink Inn share the same driveway, Highland Drive, on the east side of the highway.

TICKLE PINK INN
Manager: Mark Watson
155 Highland Drive
Carmel Highlands, CA 93923 , USA
Tel: (831) 624-1244, (800) 635-4774
Fax: (831) 626-9516
34 rooms, 1 cottage
Double: $249–$479
Open: all year, Credit cards: all major
karenbrown.com/california/ticklepink.html

Threading into the hills east of Carmel is the beautiful Carmel Valley where, unlike Carmel, which tends to be foggy, almost every day is blessed with sunshine. Here, tucked into its own 330-acre oasis, is Stonepine, built by the Crockers, an early California dynasty of great wealth. Anticipation of the very special treat waiting builds as impressive, wrought-iron gates open magically for you to enter. The road crosses a small bridge then winds through the trees, ending in the courtyard of the impressive château. Inside, a quiet elegance emanates from every niche and corner. You definitely feel like a guest in a private mansion as you roam from library to sitting room to dining room, each decorated to perfection. Upstairs are beautiful guestrooms of which Chanel and Tattinger, a two-story suite, are favorites. Four additional bedrooms are found in the paddock house and two more in the Briar Rose Cottage. If you want complete privacy, opt for Hermés House, a French-styled two-bedroom cottage just outside the walled gates, perched above the racetrack. Although it has a swimming pool and a tennis court, Stonepine was built as a ranch, and horses are the main attraction—there is a superb equestrian center and guests often bring their own horses. *Directions:* From Hwy 1 travel east on Carmel Valley Road (G16) for 13 miles and Stonepine is on your right after Carmel Valley village.

STONEPINE ESTATE
Owner: Gordon Hentschel
Manager: Rosie Bonilla
150 E. Carmel Valley Road
Carmel Valley, CA 93924, USA
Tel: (831) 659-2245, Fax: (831) 659-5160
16 rooms, 3 cottages
Double: $375–$1250
Open: all year, Credit cards: all major
karenbrown.com/california/stonepine.html

Staying at the Inn on Mt. Ada is like stepping into a fairy tale—suddenly you are "king of the mountain." This is not too far from reality, since the inn is the beautiful Wrigley family mansion (chewing gum, you know), their vacation "cottage" built high on the hill overlooking Avalon harbor. If you arrive by ferry at Catalina Island, you cannot miss the house: the mansion appears like a white wedding cake to your left above the harbor. The inn is expensive, but money seems almost immaterial, because, once through the door, you have bought a dream. You are truly like a pampered guest in a millionaire's home, with hardly a hint of commercialism (until you pay the bill) to put a damper on the illusion. The lounges and dining room have been redecorated with soft, pretty colors and traditional furniture and fabrics appropriate to the era when the house was built. Upstairs are six individually decorated bedrooms, the grandest having a fireplace, sitting area, and a terrace with breathtaking views of the harbor. Rates include all the extras such as complimentary use of your own golf cart, a full scrumptious breakfast, and lunch. Coffee, tea, soft drinks, fruit juice, and freshly baked cookies are always available in the den and sun porch. Rates include breakfast & lunch. *Directions:* By boat from Long Beach, San Pedro, and Newport Beach. By helicopter from Long Beach and San Pedro.

INN ON MT. ADA
Owners: Susan Griffin & Marlene McAdam
398 Wrigley Road
P.O Box 2560, Avalon, Catalina Island, CA 90704, USA
Tel: (310) 510-2030, Fax: (310) 510-2237
6 rooms
Double: $340–$640*
 *Includes breakfast & lunch
Open: all year, Credit cards: all major
karenbrown.com/california/innonmtada.html

The Coloma Country Inn, a handsome early-American farmhouse, was built in 1852, four years after gold was discovered at Sutter's Mill, just down the street. Today Coloma is a sleepy little village where the scant remains of the heady Gold Rush days are separated by wide green lawns sloping up from the American River, giving it the air of being a well-kept park. The Coloma Country Inn sits in the middle of the park, its wraparound porch inviting guests to relax and sip a glass of wine while soaking in the beauty of the surrounding tranquil countryside. Inside, the decor is very appealing, American-country style, with handmade quilts, fresh flowers, and other country accents. Your room might feature a balcony or brick patio with a rose garden. An 1898 carriage house offers a suite with its own flowering courtyard, sitting room, and kitchenette—perfect for families. Behind the inn is a cheerful pond with a colorful collection of wild ducks begging to be fed from the dock. The surrounding Gold Country holds many great attractions and in addition to exploring the historic sites, or hiking or biking on the many mountain and river trails, outdoor activity abounds. The South Fork of the American River offers Class III rapids for exciting but safe whitewater rafting. *Directions:* Take Hwy 50 from Sacramento to Placerville and exit on Hwy 49, going north for 8 miles to Coloma.

COLOMA COUNTRY INN
Owners: Candie & Kerry Bliss
345 High Street
P.O. Box 502, Coloma, CA 95613, USA
Tel: (530) 622-6919, Fax: (530) 626-4959
6 rooms
Double: $110–$240
Open: all year
karenbrown.com/california/colomacountryinn.html

Columbia is a state-preserved town whose shops and stores have been re-created to show life in the heyday of the California Gold Rush. On Main Street is the exquisitely restored City Hotel. Prior to 1874 the building was a gold assay office, the state company headquarters, an opera house, and a newspaper office. Now it is owned by the State of California and partially staffed by students from Columbia College's hotel management program (consequently the staff, dressed in their period costumes, are exceedingly young and wonderfully friendly). The excellent restaurant and the conviviality of the adjacent What Cheer bar provide an especially pleasant way to spend an evening. The high-ceilinged bedrooms have Victorian or early-American furniture. The very nicest rooms open directly onto the parlor, rooms 1 and 2 having the added attraction of balconies overlooking Main Street. All the bedrooms have private en-suite toilets and washbasins. It is not a problem to have showers down the hallway when slippers, robes, and little wicker baskets to carry soap, shampoo, and towels are provided. A bountiful Continental breakfast is served on the buffet in the dining room. Ask about the possibility of taking part in a murder mystery weekend. *Directions:* From Hwy 99 take Hwy 108 east to Sonora, then Hwy 49 north for the 4-mile drive to Columbia.

COLUMBIA CITY HOTEL
Manager: Tom Bender
Columbia State Historic Park
Columbia, CA 95310, USA
Tel: (209) 532-1479, (800) 532-1479
Fax: (209) 532-7027
10 rooms
Double: $105–$125
Open: all year, Credit cards: MC, VS
karenbrown.com/california/cityhotel.html

The Fallon Hotel is owned and operated in the same way as the nearby City Hotel in this gem of a Gold Rush town. The hotel opened in 1986 after receiving a $4,000,000 refurbishment from the State of California. The bedrooms are perfect reflections of the opulent 1880s, with patterned ceilings, colorful, ornate wallpaper, and grand antique furniture. Front rooms have shaded balconies. All have en-suite pull-chain toilets and ornate washbasins. Like the nearby City Hotel, showers are down the hall and slippers, bathrobes, and baskets of toiletries are handily provided. One downstairs room has wider doors for wheelchair access. A simple buffet-style Continental breakfast is served in the adjoining ice-cream parlor. In the Fallon Hotel building is the Fallon Theater, offering a year-round schedule of contemporary dramas, musicals, and melodramas. When making reservations at either the City or Fallon hotels, ask about their excellent-value-for-money theater and dinner packages. Ask about the possibility of taking part in a murder mystery weekend. *Directions:* From Hwy 99 take Hwy 108 east to Sonora, then Hwy 49 north to Columbia.

FALLON HOTEL
Manager: Tom Bender
Columbia State Historic Park
Columbia, CA 95310, USA
Tel: (209) 532-1470, (800) 532-1479
Fax: (209) 532-7027
14 rooms
Double: $75–$125
Closed: Mon to Wed in winter, Credit cards: MC, VS
karenbrown.com/california/fallonhotel.html

Barbara Gage's lovely old two-story home with its weathered brick exterior, a restored former stage stop, sits just a garden's distance from the Middle Fork of the Feather River. You enter into the coolness of the house into the front room with a lovely old trestle table set before a large open fireplace. Stools are drawn up to a counter in front of the open country kitchen. Of the four guestrooms in the house, the Parlor Room is for the romantic—a warm, paneled, library room with a fireplace and double Victorian brass bed—while the larger Trading Post Room has a seating area and one single and one queen bed. The two charming School rooms are upstairs. Cross the bridge and follow a forested footpath to the two-bedroom cottage with its inviting porch, little kitchen, small central sitting area with wood-burning pot-bellied stove, and small back bedroom with private bath. In the larger Creekside Cabin you will find the dramatic bedroom cantilevered directly over Jackson Creek. The Northfield Cabin has three bedrooms and a large deck overlooking the creek. The inn has a 1-mile frontage on the Feather River long known as an excellent trout fishery. *Directions:* From Cromberg on Hwy 89/70 take the Old Cromberg Road and follow it past the old cemetery to the bottom of the hill and Twenty Mile House.

TWENTY MILE HOUSE
Owner: Barbara Gage
Old Cromberg Road
P.O. Box 30001, Cromberg, CA 96103, USA
Tel: (530) 836-0375, Fax: (530) 836-2128
4 rooms, 3 cottages
Double: $125–$175
Open: all year
karenbrown.com/california/twentymilehouse.html

The Blue Lantern Inn, perched on a bluff offering unparalleled views of the fascinating harbor of Dana Point and the blue Pacific, is an outstanding inn on southern California's Riviera. The inn is designed in a Cape Code style—a most appealing building whose many gables, towers, and jutting rooflines create a whimsical look. The façade is painted a soft gray made even prettier by its crisp white trim. Each of the 29 guestrooms is individually decorated—some with light-pine, some with wicker, others with dark-mahogany furniture. The traditional-style furnishings are mostly reproductions and are of excellent quality. Each room has a gas log fireplace and spacious bathroom with Jacuzzi tub. Many of the rooms capture magnificent views of the sea. A full signature breakfast is served buffet style each morning in the sun room, a cheerful room where sunlight streams through the wall of windows or outside on the view terrace. Wine and hors d'oeuvres are served every afternoon, often in the book lined library. Other amenities include 3 conference rooms and a well-equipped exercise room. The Blue Lantern is more of a sophisticated small hotel than a cozy bed and breakfast, but the management is superb and the warmth of welcome cannot be surpassed. *Directions:* From the Pacific Coast Hwy 1, turn west on Street of the Blue Lantern and go one block.

BLUE LANTERN INN
Innkeeper: Lin McMahon
34343 Street of the Blue Lantern
Dana Point, CA 92629, USA
Tel: (949) 661-1304, (800) 950-1236
Fax: (949) 496-1483
29 rooms
Double: $155–$500
Open: all year, Credit cards: all major
karenbrown.com/california/bluelanterninn.html

Deep within Lassen National Park lies Drakesbad Guest Ranch, set in an idyllic high mountain valley. A broad sweep of grassy meadow cut by a tumbling river gives way to towering pines rising to rocky peaks. There's no electricity at Drakesbad—the warm glow of a kerosene lamp lights your cozy paneled bedroom. Furnishings are simple: polished pine-log chairs and beds topped by quilts, simple country curtains, and a pine dresser and bedside table. Our favorite rooms are in the little cabins that nestle at the very edge of the meadow with their smart modern bathrooms and French doors opening to a tiny deck where you can sit and watch the deer grazing at twilight. Other cabins nestle in the pines. Rooms upstairs in the main lodge have half baths. Evenings are for books, games, and conviviality by the fireplace in the lodge, conversation around the campfire, or stargazing from the soothing warmth of the swimming pool, which is fed by the natural warmth of a hot spring. Days are for walks, horseback riding, and swimming. A bell is rung to announce meals, which are served in the rustic pine dining room whose tables are topped with flowery mats and napkins. It's a family place full of people who came as children returning year after year with children and grandchildren. Some even remember when guests slept in tents on the meadow. Rates include all meals. *Directions:* Take Hwy 36 to Chester. Turn left at the fire station and go 17 miles.

DRAKESBAD GUEST RANCH
Innkeepers: Billie & Ed Fiebiger
End of Warner Valley Road
Drakesbad, CA 96020, USA
Tel: (530) 529-1512 ext 120, Fax: (530) 529-4511
19 rooms
Double: $252–$308*
 *Includes all meals
Open: Jun to Oct, Credit cards: MC, VS
karenbrown.com/california/drakesbadguestranch.html

The Elk Cove Inn is one of the town's cutest Victorian houses, with perky gables and a million-dollar view of cove and towering rock weathered by the crashing sea. In the main house, the gathering room is set with breakfast tables in front of two walls of windows looking out to the spectacular coastline. The extensive breakfast buffet is set on baker's racks with lots of choices of fruit and a variety of cooked dishes. Before heading out for dinner in the evening you can enjoy a drink in the cozy oceanfront bar. When I stayed in March 2002, owner David Lieberman was enthusiastically embarking on a complete revamp of the bedroom decor and plans were moving ahead to add a sitting room beside the gazebo. There are several guestrooms in the main house but the most deluxe accommodations are four suites built on a bluff overlooking the sea, each with a large living room with a spectacular view, a spacious bedroom, a private deck, and a large bath equipped with Jacuzzi. Four tiny cottages also enjoy ocean views through large picture windows. You can book the hot tub for a private soaking. A little walkway leads down to the coastal path and from here you can walk into town or down to the beach. *Directions:* Elk is 15 miles south of Mendocino, 6½ miles south of the junction of Hwy 128 on Hwy 1. The inn is on the south edge of Elk as the road winds down the hill.

ELK COVE INN
Owner: David Lieberman
6300 South Hwy 1
P.O. Box 367, Elk, CA 95432, USA
Tel: (707) 877-3321, (800) 275-2967
Fax: (707) 877-1808
15 rooms
Double: $130–$350
Open: all year, Credit cards: all major
karenbrown.com/california/elkcoveinn.html

The Griffin House, a pretty little clapboard house painted gray with white trim and with a white picket fence, dates back to the late 1800s when it served as the local doctor's office and pharmacy. Later, five cottages were added behind the office to house some of the lumbermen coming to the growing town of Elk. The garden cottages are pleasant and very good value for money, but truly outstanding are the doll-house-like cottages on the edge of the bluff. In fact, these three separate little houses offer the most sensational views anywhere on the California coast. Each of these cottages, named after one of the early settlers of Elk, has a wood-burning stove, a sitting area, a wall of windows overlooking the coast, and a private redwood deck with chairs and table. These tiny cottages are cleanly simple in their decor, with nothing contrived or quaintly cute, just providing old-fashioned, basic comfort but with a vista so spectacular it fairly takes your breath away. The pub here offers evening meals and good cheer (hours vary). *Directions:* Off the west side of Hwy 1, at the center of Elk.

GRIFFIN HOUSE
Owner: Patty Sarb
Innkeepers: Terry Smith & Lynda Aubrey
5910 South Hwy 1
P.O. Box 190, Elk, CA 95432, USA
Tel: (707) 877-3422, Fax: (707) 877-1853
4 rooms, 3 cottages
Double: $100–$250
Pub
Open: all year, Credit cards: all major
karenbrown.com/california/griffinhouse.html

The Harbor House has a fantastic location on one of the most spectacular bluffs along the Mendocino coast. There is even a little path, with benches along the way, winding down the cliff to a secluded private beach. The home was built in 1916 as the home of the president of Goodyear Redwood Lumber Company, so it is no wonder that everything inside and outside is built of redwood. The inn is appealing, with the ambiance of a beautiful, elegant country lodge. You enter into a redwood-paneled living room dominated by a large fireplace, also made of redwood. An Oriental carpet, comfortable sofas, beamed ceiling, soft lighting, and a grand piano add to the inviting warmth. Doors lead from the lounge to the verandah-like dining room, stretching the length of the building, with picture windows looking out to the sea. A delicious set-price four-course dinner is served each evening at 7 pm and such is the reputation of the food that guests from other inns often dine here. A broad wooden staircase leads upstairs to spacious, sophisticated, beautifully furnished bedrooms that make you feel as if you are a guest in a private home. Four appealing little cottages set in the trees beside the main house have been refurbished—try to book one with an ocean view. *Directions:* From Hwy 101 take Hwy 128 west. At Hwy 1 turn left and drive south for 5 miles.

♨ ■ CREDIT 🏊 🏃 🏇 @ P 🍴 🚭 ♨ 🐕 🍷

HARBOR HOUSE INN
Owners: Elle & Sam Haynes
5600 South Hwy 1
P.O. Box 369, Elk, CA 95432, USA
Tel: (707) 877-3203, (800) 720-7474
Fax: (707) 877-3452
10 rooms, Double: $300–$475*
*Includes breakfast & dinner
Open: all year, Credit cards: all major
Select Registry
karenbrown.com/california/harborhouseinn.html

Carter House Inns are made up of four buildings: the majestic Carter House, the adorable Bell Cottage and the Carter Cottage next door, and the adjacent Hotel Carter. The inns are the dream of Mark Carter who, after restoring several Victorian homes, chose to build his own (the Carter House), using the original plans for a Victorian house designed by the architect who built the Carson Mansion, a Victorian showplace in Eureka. All of their bedrooms are generously appointed with antique furniture, original artwork, and cozy flannel robes. While the Carter House offers the most delightful antique-filled rooms, if you are in the mood for something more sensuous, opt for a suite. The suites at the Hotel Carter offer large whirlpool tubs (in the bedroom) with marina views, fireplaces, king beds, large showers with two heads, entertainment centers, and well-stocked refrigerators (not complimentary). The Hotel Carter's lobby and dining room are the center for socializing—guests enjoy hors d'oeuvres and wine in the early evening, a nightcap of homemade cookies and tea before bed, outstanding dinners, and bountiful breakfasts. The inn's Restaurant 301 is among 81 dining establishments worldwide to hold a Wine Spectator Grand Award. *Directions:* Take Hwy 101 north to Eureka, where it turns into 5th Street. From 5th Street, turn left on L Street and go two blocks.

CARTER HOUSE INNS
Owners: Christi & Mark Carter
301 L Street
Eureka, CA 95501, USA
Tel: (707) 444-8062, (800) 404-1390
Fax: (707) 444-8067
31 rooms
Double: $155–$1,400
Open: all year, Credit cards: all major
Select Registry
karenbrown.com/california/carterhousevictorians.html

Brothers Cornelius and John Daly came from Ireland to Eureka and in 1895 founded a successful chain of northern California clothing shops. When their business flourished, the brothers returned to Ireland in search of wives, married sisters Annie and Eileen, and returned to Eureka to build them impressive homes next door to each other. Now Annie and Con's home is a delightful bed and breakfast run with warm enthusiasm by Donna and Bob Gafford. Enjoy wine and hors d'oeuvres in the living room with its wood-burning fireplace, grand mahogany trim and wallpaper that conveys the charm and grace of the Victorian era. Then relax in the cozy parlor to watch television, view a movie or read a book from the Inn's library of mystery novels, or perhaps a game of 8-ball on the Inn's beautiful billiard table is more to your liking. I particularly enjoyed the Garden View and Victorian Rose suites with their spacious bedrooms, sitting rooms (in what were once sleeping porches), and modern bathrooms. A short walk takes you through Eureka's more commercial district to its handsome historic old town (between D and G and 1st and 3rd streets) where attractive shops and restaurants occupy restored buildings. *Directions:* From San Francisco take Hwy 101 275 miles north to Eureka. The highway turns into 5th Street. From 5th Street turn right into H Street—The Cornelius Daly Inn is on your left.

CORNELIUS DALY INN
Owners: Donna & Bob Gafford
1125 H Street
Eureka, CA 95501, USA
Tel: (707) 445-3638, (800) 321-9656
Fax: (707) 444-3636
5 rooms
Double: $95–$170
Open: all year, Credit cards: all major
karenbrown.com/california/thedalyinn.html

Ferndale is a jewel—a wonderfully preserved Victorian town 5 miles from the northern California coast. Happily, the town's most beautiful Victorian, a fantasy of ornate turrets and gables, is an inn: the Gingerbread Mansion. Walking through the parlors and breakfast room is like taking a step back into Victorian times. While the bedrooms continue the Victorian theme, I feel certain that the prude Victorians would be quite aghast at several of the more sensuous rooms. If money is no object, request the Empire Suite, an open-plan bedroom and bathroom combination where you can soak in a claw-foot tub in front of one of the two fireplaces, relish the complexity of operating a shower with eight heads, and sleep in a king-size bed where towering Ionic columns (pillars) soar to the rafters. Alternatively, request your room according to whether you want a tub in the room (Lilac), his-and-her tubs in the room (Gingerbread), fireplaces (five rooms), or a sleeping loft for a child (Hideaway). I particularly enjoyed the Garden Room with its fireplace, old-style bathroom, and French windows opening onto a private balcony overlooking the clipped hedges and colorful flowerbeds of the garden. *Directions:* From Hwy 101 north, take the Fernbridge/Ferndale exit, following signs to Ferndale. When you reach Main Street, turn left at Six Rivers and go one block.

GINGERBREAD MANSION
Owners: Maggie Dowd & Tom Amato
400 Berding Street
Ferndale, CA 95536, USA
Tel: (707) 786-4000, (800) 952-4136
Fax: (707) 786-4381
11 rooms
Double: $150–$400
Open: all year, Credit cards: all major
Select Registry
karenbrown.com/california/thegingerbreadmansion.html

Set back just off the busy River Road in the heart of the Russian River wine valley, the Farmhouse Inn is the brainchild of sister-and-brother team Catherine and Joe Bartolomei, who have completely renovated the property. The main house, circa 1876, resplendent in new yellow and white trim with black shutters, is home to the restaurant, which serves breakfast daily and is also open for dinner Thursday through Sunday. A hand-painted frieze of family members around the large dining area attests to the fact that this is a fourth-generation Forestville family. Eight nicely appointed guestrooms are found in a row of attached cottages across the gravel driveway. Dating back to 1899, these former workers' cottages have been transformed into havens of sumptuous modernity with feather beds, luxurious European linens, and immaculate white-tiled bathrooms (double jetted tubs are the order of the day), with clever touches such as garden windows that bring the wildflowers outside up close and personal. Most rooms have saunas and fireplaces, and the two suites each have a sizeable sitting area. Relax by the pool, and pamper yourself with a relaxing massage. This is a great base for exploring the Russian River vineyards. *Directions:* From Hwy 101 take the River Road exit north of Santa Rosa and head west for a little over 7 miles. The Farmhouse Inn is on your left at the junction with Wohler Road.

❋ ⚓ 🅿 💳 ☎ 🏹 👫 🐎 🍸 P 🍴 ≈ 🛶 🐾 ⛷ 🏌

FARMHOUSE INN
Owners: Catherine & Joe Bartolomei
7871 River Road
Forestville, CA 95436, USA
Tel: (707) 887-3300, (800) 464-6642
Fax: (707) 887 3311
8 rooms
Double: $175–$299
Open: all year, Credit cards: all major
karenbrown.com/california/farmhouse.html

You would think you were in England instead of northern California when you first see the large Tudor-style Benbow Inn. The English theme continues as you step inside the lounge with its large antique fireplace flanked by comfortable sofas, antique chests, paintings, needlepoint, cherry-wood wainscoting, two grandfather clocks, potted green plants, and a splendid Oriental carpet. At tea time complimentary English tea and scones are served. The dining room, too, is very English: a beautiful, sunny room with beamed ceiling and dark-oak Windsor chairs. Both the reception hall and the dining room open out to a pretty courtyard overlooking the river. The traditionally decorated bedrooms vary in size—all the way up from small bedrooms located both in the main hotel and in an annex, which also opens onto the courtyard. The one disadvantage of the Benbow Inn is its proximity to the freeway, but loyal guests do not seem to mind. A wonderful feature here is the very special Christmas celebration with wondrous decorations, music, and dining (the whole month of December). The Benbow Inn is also justifiably proud to share the news of their award of excellence by the Wine Spectator. *Directions:* Drive north on Hwy 101. Just south of Garberville, take the Benbow exit—the hotel is on the west side of the freeway.

BENBOW INN
Owners: Teresa & John Porter
445 Lake Benbow Drive
Garberville, CA 95442 , USA
Tel: (707) 923-2124, (800) 355-3301
Fax: (707) 923-2122
55 rooms
Double: $99–$365*
*Breakfast not included: $10
Open: Apr 14 to Jan 4, Credit cards: all major
karenbrown.com/california/benbowinn.html

It is hard not to notice Beltane Ranch, a pale-yellow board-and-batten house encircled on both stories by broad verandahs, set on the hillside off the Valley of the Moon Road. Check in at the cozy country kitchen when you arrive: if no one is around, you will find a welcome note on the chalkboard hung by the back door. The house has no internal staircase, so each room has a private entrance off the verandah—which was probably very handy when this was the weekend retreat of a San Francisco madam. Incidentally, this also explains the southern architecture of the house as "madam" hailed from Louisiana. The bedrooms, decorated in family antiques, have a very comfortable ambiance. Chairs and hammocks are placed on the verandah outside each room and offer a wonderful spot to settle and enjoy peaceful countryside views beyond the well-tended garden. A small yellow cottage behind the main house with more contemporary decor enjoys a snug sitting room opening to a private patio and has breakfast delivered into its "silent butler." Beltane produces five varieties of wine grapes as well as its own olive oil. For the energetic, there are miles of private walking trails and a tennis court. Beltane Ranch continues to remain a personal favorite. *Directions:* Beltane Ranch is on your right 1½ miles after passing the turnoff to Glen Ellen.

BELTANE RANCH
Owner: Alexa Wood
Innkeeper: Anne Soulier
11775 Hwy 12 (Sonoma Hwy)
P.O. Box 395, Glen Ellen, CA 95442, USA
Tel: (707) 996-6501, Fax: none
6 rooms
Double: $140–$220
Open: all year
karenbrown.com/california/beltaneranch.html

On the main road that weaves through the quaint town of Glen Ellen, the Gaige House Inn is an elegant Victorian with a luxurious, contemporary interior. More Architectural Digest than Country Home, its crisp lines and Indonesian/Japanese details are the brainchild of your hosts, Ken Burnet and Greg Nemrow. They take great pride in their home and pay special attention to every little detail, from the bountiful gourmet breakfasts to the hand-ironed quality linens. I felt love at first sight for the Gaige Suite, an oh-so-spacious room with huge four-poster bed, massive deck, and decadent bathroom the size of my first apartment. Then we were swayed by the complete seclusion of the Creekside Suite with its private deck overlooking the creek and lavish bathroom. Although being bowled over by the luxury of these premier rooms, we were also very impressed with the distinct personalities of all the other bedrooms. The inn prides itself on its gourmet breakfasts. Languish by the pool or treat yourself to a spa treatment or massage on the secluded creekside deck or in the privacy of your room. *Directions:* Driving north on Hwy 12 from Sonoma, turn left on Arnold Drive, which is signposted to Glen Ellen. The inn is on the right, just before you arrive in town.

GAIGE HOUSE INN
Owners: Ken Burnet & Greg Nemrow
Innkeeper: Susan Burnet
13540 Arnold Drive
Glen Ellen, CA 95442, USA
Tel: (707) 935-0237, (800) 935-0237
Fax: (707) 935-6411
17 rooms, Double: $150–$600
Open: all year, Credit cards: all major
Select Registry
karenbrown.com/california/gaigehouseinn.html

Groveland is a quaint Gold Rush town just half an hour from the west entrance to Yosemite, with Hwy 120 forming its one main street. It is a great place to stop for either breakfast or lunch at the corner PJ's Café, and for those who choose to overnight here and just take a day trip into the park, the Groveland Hotel offers very comfortable and attractive accommodation. Fronting Main Street, the hotel is actually two buildings dating from 1849 and 1914 joined by a wraparound verandah. One building dates from the Gold Rush and the other was built as a boarding house to accommodate the executives from San Francisco here to oversee the building of the massive Hetch Hetchy water project. No two rooms are alike and yet each is pleasing in its decor, decorated with a blend of antiques and attractive fabrics. Although opening onto the street, some rooms on the main floor and upstairs at the front enjoy lovely bay windows. There are two rooms, one with a queen, the other with twin beds, which each have only one window and therefore no views, but they are a great value for their price. An extensive buffet breakfast and evening glass of wine are included in the room rate. We have received rave reviews on the dinners served in the Victorian Room restaurant. *Directions:* Groveland is two hours from Sacramento along the historic stretch of Hwy 120.

❄ ☕ 🏊 CREDIT ☎ 🎿 🚶 🏇 P 🍴 ⚓ ♿ 🍇

GROVELAND HOTEL
Owner: Peggy Mosley
18767 Main Street
P.O. Box 481, Groveland, CA 95321, USA
Tel: (209) 962-4000, (800) 273-3314
Fax: (209) 962-6674
17 rooms
*Double: $145–$165**
 Service charge: $3/room night Energy Surcharge
Open: all year, Credit cards: all major
karenbrown.com/california/groveland.html

With a backdrop of towering redwood and pine trees, the weathered, wood-sided cottages of the North Coast Country Inn step up the hillside just off the east side of Hwy 1. Although it does not have ocean views, the inn's wooded setting is lovely and the accommodation is some of the best in the area. Maureen and Bill Shupe use the original old farmhouse as their private residence and patterned the neighboring cottages after its rustic and appealing design. Each spacious guestroom cottage is attractive in its individual, country decor, enjoys its own private entrance off a porch or surrounding deck, and is equipped with a dining area (four guestrooms have kitchenettes), a wood-burning fireplace, and an en-suite bathroom. I especially liked Aquitaine with its handsome four-poster bed, beamed ceiling, and large windows, though for the best view and complete privacy I would select either Southwind or Evergreen. Set aside time for the secluded hot tub set into a two-level redwood deck, magical at night under the beauty of the stars. A maze of pathways weaves upwards from the front lawn with its fruit trees into the redwoods to emerge at a sheltered meadow with a gazebo. *Directions:* Located at Hwy 1 and Fish Rock Road, 4 miles north of Gualala and ¼ mile north of Anchor Bay.

NORTH COAST COUNTRY INN
Owners: Maureen & Bill Shupe
34591 South Hwy 1
Gualala, CA 95445, USA
Tel: (707) 884-4537, (800) 959-4537
Fax: (707) 884-1833
6 rooms
Double: $175–$215
Open: all year, Credit cards: all major
karenbrown.com/california/northcoastinn.html

Beach House, 3½ miles from the town of Half Moon Bay, offers stunning views of the ocean and the boats of Princeton Harbor. Welcoming guests since 1997, the Beach House has 54 lofts, each with a patio or balcony, most boasting spectacular vistas of the entire 7-mile stretch of crescent-shaped coastline aptly named Half Moon Bay. Although the hotel fronts a highway, double-paned windows on the street-facing rooms block the noise. Each loft is a tastefully decorated two-tiered suite with a king-size bed and sleeper-sofa. Designed with the guest's comfort in mind, every loft enjoys a wood-burning fireplace, wet bar, refrigerator, CD/stereo system, robes, and bathroom with double sinks and deep tub. If you are traveling with children, ask about their "family accommodation"—two neighboring lofts that share a common main door. Those on a budget might opt for a non-view room. For extra space and comfort, the 625-square-foot Half Moon Suite has two decks, vaulted ceilings, and a sitting area in the bedroom. Guests enjoy a Continental breakfast buffet of croissants, muffins, scones, and fruit either on the outdoor patio or in their rooms. Beach House combines breathtaking views of the ocean with the comforts of a quality hotel. *Directions:* From San Francisco take Hwy 1 south (about 25 miles). Beach House is on the right just after Pilar Point Harbor.

BEACH HOUSE
Manager: Charlie Dyke
4100 North Cabrillo Hwy
P.O. Box 129, Half Moon Bay, CA 94019-0129, USA
Tel: (650) 712-0220, (800) 315-9366
Fax: (650) 712-0693
54 rooms
Double: $165–$335
Open: all year, Credit cards: all major
karenbrown.com/california/beachhouse.html

For those who love to be lulled to sleep by the rhythmic sound of crashing waves, the Cypress Inn, positioned directly across the road from the 5-mile-long sandy stretch of Miramar Beach, will be just your cup of tea. The Cypress Inn is a contemporary building with a weathered-wood façade with turquoise trim. Giving credence to the inn's name, a windswept cypress tree towers by the entrance. Inside, a native-folk-art theme prevails. As you enter, there is a snug sitting area to your left with wicker chairs and sofa grouped around a fireplace. Bedrooms in the main building tend to be on the cozy size and are delightfully decorated in inviting, bright colors. The large top-floor suite offers million-dollar ocean views and a rooftop patio. Each of the rooms has a television, gas-log fireplace, built-in bed with reading lamps, wicker chairs, writing desk, and glass doors opening onto private balconies overlooking the ocean. Our favorite rooms are the upstairs king-bedded rooms (Point Reyes and Mavericks) with magnificent ocean views in the adjacent Lighthouse building. We especially enjoyed Mavericks—named for the huge waves—with a surfboard hung over the bed and photos of Jeff Clark riding the waves. *Directions:* Take Hwy 1 south from San Francisco. Turn right on Medio Avenue (1½ miles beyond the stoplight at Pilar Point Harbor). Cypress Inn is at the end of the street.

CYPRESS INN ON MIRAMAR BEACH
Innkeeper: Kelly Barba
407 Mirada Road
Half Moon Bay, CA 94019, USA
Tel: (650) 726-6002, (800) 832 3224
Fax: (650) 712-0380
18 rooms
Double: $215–$385
Open: all year, Credit cards: all major
Select Registry
karenbrown.com/california/cypressinn.html

Half Moon Bay is a delightful little beachside town just 45 minutes south of San Francisco, packed with interesting shops, galleries, and restaurants. One of the most attractive of several lovely Victorians along Main Street is the 1890s Old Thyme Inn, bordered by a white picket fence and named for the herb found in the inn's fragrant cottage garden. The seven bedrooms also take their names from the garden: Mint is decorated in shades of restful green, its queen four-poster decked with crisp white linens before a fireplace. For the most spacious of quarters, opt for the Garden Room, which has a queen four-poster bed, a Jacuzzi tub for two tucked into a corner of the room, and its own private garden entrance. Rick and Kathy really focus on a full breakfast served at the large round table in the parlor/dining area. The parlor is the center of activity at the inn though on sunny evenings guest often enjoy sherry and hors d'oeuvres on the patio. The beach is six blocks away and it's an easy stroll to places to eat that range from the adjacent Cetrella restaurant with its good food and jazz music to an excellent pizza parlor. San Francisco and the many nearby beaches are huge attractions. *Directions:* Take Hwy 1 south from San Francisco to Half Moon Bay (30 miles). Turn left at the first stoplight onto Main Street and drive through town—Old Thyme Inn is on the left.

OLD THYME INN
Owners: Kathy & Rick Ellis
779 Main Street
Half Moon Bay, CA 94019, USA
Tel: (650) 726-1616, (800) 720-4277
Fax: (650) 726-6394
7 rooms
Double: $130–$300
Open: all year, Credit cards: all major
karenbrown.com/california/oldthyme.html

The Belle de Jour Inn, a complex of farm cottages built in 1873, has a rural, hillside setting just to the north of historic Healdsburg. The impeccably maintained complex has five cottages with guestrooms plus a single-story farmhouse, the home of Brenda and Tom, who run their small inn with a professional eye to detail. The Caretaker's Suite has French doors opening onto a trellised deck and a pine four-poster, king-size canopy bed topped with Battenberg lace. The Terrace Room is charming, with a fireplace and a whirlpool tub for two, overlooking the terrace and valley. The Morning Hill Room is cozy with a fireplace and a shuttered window seat. The Atelier, with sitting room, is large and lovely. The Carriage House accommodates a magnificent deluxe, second-floor country suite with vaulted ceilings, plank-wood floors, antique pine furniture, fireplace, and a whirlpool tub for two in its own stained-glass alcove—very romantic. All rooms have gas fireplaces, refrigerators, CD players, robes, and hairdryers—several have DVD players and direct satellite TV. A full country breakfast is served in the owners' breakfast room. For a memorable wine-tasting experience, Tom will take you in his 1925 vintage auto along the backroads of the wine country. *Directions:* From Hwy 101 exit at Dry Creek Road then go east to Healdsburg Avenue. Turn left at the lights and go north for 1 mile. The entrance is directly across from the Simi Winery.

BELLE DE JOUR INN
Owners: Brenda & Tom Hearn
16276 Healdsburg Avenue
Healdsburg, CA 95448, USA
Tel: (707) 431-9777, Fax: (707) 431-7412
5 cottages
Double: $195–$335
Open: all year, Credit cards: all major
karenbrown.com/california/belledejourinn.html

Haydon Street Inn is set in a quiet neighborhood four blocks from Healdsburg's main plaza. The inn is most attractive: a soft-blue Victorian with a crisp, white trim, fronted by a white picket fence heavily laden with pink roses. The main house has a lovely country living room, sitting room, and dining area for guests' use. The six bedrooms, one downstairs and five upstairs, are decorated with homey, Victorian-style furnishings. The Turret Room, a smaller room, has a fireplace and lovely claw-foot soaking tub. The Rose Room on the first floor has a queen and single bed, plus a Jacuzzi tub, and comfortably accommodates three people. At the rear of the garden is a Victorian-style cottage with two large guestrooms upstairs. Each cottage room has a private entrance and beautiful pine floors. As an added touch of luxury, the bathrooms have double whirlpool bathtubs. When we visited, the four people staying in the cottage for a family reunion were relaxing under the umbrellas on the lawn and enjoying a glass of the wine that is served every day at 6 pm. The Bertapelles prepare a full country breakfast served on Luneville French or Spode china. *Directions:* From Hwy 101 take the Central Healdsburg exit. Turn right on Matheson to Fitch, right on Fitch to Haydon, and left on Haydon.

HAYDON STREET INN
Owners: Pat & Dick Bertapelle
321 Haydon Street
Healdsburg, CA 94558, USA
Tel: (707) 433-5228, (800) 528-3703
Fax: (707) 433-6637
8 rooms
Double: $120–$210
Open: all year, Credit cards: all major
karenbrown.com/california/haydonstreet.html

Healdsburg has some delightful shops and delectable restaurants within strolling distance of the main square and the Healdsburg Inn on the Plaza. The entrance to the inn is through double doors into a high-ceilinged reception area that serves both as an art gallery and gift shop. A wide flight of stairs winds up to a central lounge and the sunny solarium where wine and snacks are set out in the evening and the breakfast buffet is laid in the morning. A fridge is well stocked with soft drinks and snacks are always available for those in search of a little something. Off the lounge the bedrooms are decorated in a traditional Victorian style, and either overlook the plaza through bay windows (our favorite) or open onto balconies in the rear of the building. All rooms enjoy air conditioning, a TV with VCR (lots of good movies are available), and telephone. Most have fireplaces and some have whirlpool tubs for two. The Carriage House behind the main building enjoys total seclusion, has a cozy fireplace in its living room, full kitchen, bedroom, bathroom, and private terrace—it's perfect for longer stays. This is a well-run, friendly inn with very hospitable owners and staff. *Directions:* Leave Hwy 101 north at the Central Healdsburg exit. Drive down Healdsburg Avenue north and make a right on Matheson Street.

HEALDSBURG INN ON THE PLAZA
Owners: Genny Jenkins & LeRoy Steck
Manager: Dyanne Celi
110 Matheson Street
Healdsburg, CA 95448, USA
Tel: (707) 433-6991, (800) 431-8663
Fax: (707) 433-9513
10 rooms, 1 cottage
Double: $155–$295
Open: all year, Credit cards: MC, VS
karenbrown.com/california/innontheplaza.html

The Honor Mansion, a soft-beige Victorian with white trim and a maroon door, sits behind a white picket fence on a residential street. Behind its formal Victorian façade lies a luxurious haven of tranquility. You are welcome to enjoy the parlors (one has a TV and VCR) and the soothing sound of water falling into the koi pond on the shady patio, or you can relax by the pool after a day's sightseeing. However, to my mind, a stay at the Honor Mansion is all about secluding yourself in your own romantic hideaway. I was particularly taken with the romance of staying in the old water tower with its snug upstairs sitting room, downstairs bedroom and shower room, and private deck with outdoor canopied Jacuzzi tub. However, I finally settled on the total seclusion of the Garden Suite with private driveway and outdoor canopied Jacuzzi tub on one of its private decks. Wherever you decide to stay, you will enjoy the very best, from lush robes to fine linens that make you want to just melt into bed. Enjoy wine and hors d' oeuvres in the evening and browse Steve and Cathi's personally rated list of nearby restaurants for dinner. *Directions:* From Hwy 101 exit at Dry Creek Road and turn right. At the first stoplight, Grove Street, turn right. The Honor Mansion is 1/2 mile down on your right.

※ ☕ ✄ 💳 ☎ 🏃 👫 🐎 ♈ P 🚭 ≋ ⚓ ♿ 🍇

HONOR MANSION
Owners: Cathi & Steve Fowler
14891 Grove Street
Healdsburg, CA 95448, USA
Tel: (800) 554-4667, Fax: (707) 431-7173
12 rooms, 1 cottage
Double: $200–$575
Open: all year, Credit cards: MC, VS
Select Registry
karenbrown.com/california/honormansion.html

Madrona Manor, just a few minutes by car from the heart of Healdsburg, is secluded in 8 acres of glorious grounds. This fantasy gingerbread mansion (on the National Register of Historic Places) was built in 1881 by John Alexander Paxton, a tycoon of great wealth. The main building houses the reception area, several lounges, and a spacious dining room opening onto a large covered terrace. Antiques abound, emphasizing the Victorian mood of the home. A flight of stairs leads up to our four favorite second-story rooms, which are decorated with handsome Victorian furniture original to the house. Other guestrooms are found in the Carriage House, the Meadow Wood Complex, and the Garden Cottage (with its own private garden and sheltered deck). The Schoolhouse Suites are located in the original schoolhouse for the ranch—two suites each with sitting room, Jacuzzi, private deck, and garden. Lush lawns, perfectly manicured gardens, towering trees, and secluded nooks provide a haven of beauty and tranquillity. A swimming pool offers a refreshing interlude after a day of visiting the nearby Sonoma vineyards. *Directions:* From Hwy 101 north take the Central Healdsburg exit, turn left at the second traffic light, and go under the freeway. You will be on Westside Road and will see the hotel entrance straight ahead as the road bends to the left.

MADRONA MANOR
Owners: Trudi & Bill Konrad
Manager: Joe Hadley
1001 Westside Road
Healdsburg, CA 95448, USA
Tel: (707) 433-4231, (800) 258-4003
Fax: (707) 433-0703
22 rooms
Double: $235–$475
Open: all year, Credit cards: MC, VS
karenbrown.com/california/madronamanor.html

The Beach House at Hermosa Beach occupies a spectacular location on the beach just steps from the heart of this lively southern California town. Even if you have no desire to join in all the fun on the sand or roller-blade, bike, run, walk, or stroll the path that separates the beach from the inn, you will relish the people watching that this location affords. The rooms are referred to as "lofts" and all have a patio or balcony. Each loft is a tastefully decorated two-tiered suite (separate living room and bedroom areas) with a king-size bed and sleeper sofa. Designed with the guest's comfort in mind, every loft enjoys a wood-burning fireplace, wet bar, refrigerator, CD/stereo system, robes, and bathroom with deep tub. If you are traveling with children, ask about their family accommodation—two neighboring lofts that have an interconnecting door. Those on a budget might opt for a non-view room. The Continental breakfast buffet of croissants, muffins, scones, and fruit is served either in the beachfront Strand Café or in the guestrooms. Room service is available from the adjacent Good Stuff restaurant. *Directions:* Going south on the 405, exit at Redondo Beach Blvd. Go right to the Pacific Coast Hwy, turn left, then right on Hermosa and left on 14th. Valet parking is $17 per day.

BEACH HOUSE
Manager: Kevin McCarthy
1300 The Strand
Hermosa Beach, CA 90254, USA
Tel: (310) 374-3001, (888)895-4559
Fax: (310) 372-2115
96 rooms
Double: $224–$359
Room service from neighboring restaurant
Open: all year, Credit cards: all major
karenbrown.com/california/hermosabeachhouse.html

We greatly appreciate the letters we often receive from readers sharing a particular favorite inn along with the unwritten implication that they are astounded that we could have missed such a gem. In the case of the Cedar Street Inn, I received a letter from the owner herself! My only defense is that I simply missed the inn, tucked just off North Circle Drive on a small, quiet street of the same name. Within walking distance of the cute shops and restaurants at the heart of Idyllwild, the Cedar Street Inn offers quiet accommodation in cottagey rooms opening onto a central patio. The guestrooms, some of which are housed in private cabins, are individual in decor and offer their own special appointments and appeal. To name just a few of the rooms: the Victorian Suite enjoys a large Roman tub and fireplace; the Attic is accessed by its own private spiral staircase to an outside deck and boasts a bathroom which overlooks the treetops; the Captain's Quarters is decorated in a nautical decor and is warmed by a river-rock fireplace; the Carriage House is a tri-level suite with fireplace and a bathroom equipped with both tub and shower. Patty and Gary Tompkins are your gracious innkeepers, intent on making your stay at the Cedar Street Inn a special and memorable one. *Directions:* Turn off Route 243, turn east on North Circle Drive, and then turn right on Cedar Street.

CEDAR STREET INN
Owners: Patty & Gary Tompkins
25880 Cedar Street
P.O. Box 627, Idyllwild, CA 92549, USA
Tel: (909) 659-4789, Fax: (909) 659-1049
8 rooms, 3 cabins
Double: $75–$205*
 *Breakfast not included
Open: all year, Credit cards: all major
karenbrown.com/california/thecedarstreetinn.html

Idyllwild is a mile-high village of some 3,500 residents and with its magnificent hiking trails affords a wonderful weekend getaway just two hours from the metropolitan areas of southern California. The Fern Valley Inn is a country inn of 11 charming cabins nestled in the pines. Each cabin features antiques and handmade quilts, with care taken to tastefully capture the beauty of the surroundings. The Fern Grotto cottage is attractive and spacious, with a large rock fireplace and a lush color scheme of whites and greens—ideal for honeymoons or special retreats. Warm cedar walls, quaint country decorations, and a kitchen make the Country Cottage a comfortable home-away-from-home. Fireplaces enhance the ambiance and make for a warm and cozy setting during the cooler fall and winter nights. Several of the cottages feature a fully stocked kitchen. The grounds are serene—pathways wind amongst the cottages, leading to the heated pool and herb and lilac gardens. Homemade tea breads incorporating seasonal fruits and vegetables are set in baskets in each cottage, allowing guests the convenience of a Continental breakfast at their leisure. Private cabins are also available for groups. *Directions:* Take Hwy 10 west from Los Angeles to Banning and Hwy 243 to Idyllwild. Turn left on North Circle, right on South Circle, and left on Fern Valley Road.

FERN VALLEY INN
Owners: Theo & Jamie Giannioses
25240 Fern Valley Road
P.O. Box 116, Idyllwild, CA 92549, USA
Tel: (909) 659-2205, (800) 659-7775
Fax: (909) 659-2630
11 cottages
Double: $95–$155
Open: all year, Credit cards: all major
karenbrown.com/california/fernvalleyinn.html

Brigadoon Castle is spectacular. Tucked away on a private oasis of 86 acres and bounded by national forest, it is a magnificent property and a wonderfully romantic hideaway. The turreted entrance to the castle is through a handsome arched wooden door framed by ivy and wisteria. Inside, although impressive with its vaulted archways, dramatic stair, lofty ceilings, wide passageways, and regal decor, the ambiance is also welcoming and intimate. The two-tiered living room is magnificent, with sofas set before a brick fireplace, which rises to the loft library, a lovely room looking out through towering windows to the surrounding greenery. Outside the living room a brick terrace stretches to the edge of the woods and a path beckons on up to the hot tub. Three guestrooms are found in the main castle. Fiona's Suite is especially attractive with its rich water-marked-taffeta wall coverings in beiges and creams, specially designed four-poster bed, fireplace, and sitting area whose windows frame the outdoor greenery. The gatekeeper's house, The Cottage, has its own living room, fireplace, loft bedroom, deck with hot tub, and a gorgeous setting next to the rushing creek. This is hostess Geri MacCallum's adventure of a lifetime, and she invites you to come to Brigadoon and let the magic stir your heart! *Directions:* Igo is located 15 miles southwest of Redding. Call for directions.

BRIGADOON CASTLE
Owner: Geri MacCallum
9036 Zogg Mine Road
P.O. Box 84, Igo, CA 96047, USA
Tel: (530) 396-2785, (888) 343-2836
Fax: (530) 396-2784
3 rooms, 1 cottage
Double: $215–$325
Open: all year, Credit cards: all major
karenbrown.com/california/brigadooncastle.html

The Blackthorne Inn is the whimsical creation of Susan and Bill Wigert. They have built a Hansel and Gretel house tucked among the treetops, loaded with peaked roofs, dormer windows, funny little turrets, bay windows, and an octagonal tower. Steps wind up through the trees to the main entry level, which is wrapped by an enormous wooden deck emphasizing the tree-house look. A dramatic floor-to-ceiling stone fireplace warms the soaring living room with its walls of windows looking out onto the trees. Open-tread spiral staircases lead up and down to the rustically decorated bedrooms. The favorite choice of many is the Eagle's Nest, located in the octagonal tower, where walls of glass give the impression that you are sleeping under the stars—camping at its best. And to add to that woodsy-outdoors experience, the bathroom is outside, in the dressing room opposite the hot tub. Each of the other guestrooms has its own personality, whether it is with stained-glass windows, a private entrance, a separate sitting room, or a bay window looking out into the trees. *Directions:* Take Sir Francis Drake Boulevard off Hwy 1 to Olema. Turn right, go 2 miles, then turn left toward Inverness. Go 1 mile, then turn left on Vallejo Avenue (at Debra's Bakery) for half a mile to the inn.

BLACKTHORNE INN
Owners: Susan & Bill Wigert
266 Vallejo Avenue
P.O. Box 712, Inverness, CA 94937, USA
Tel: (415) 663-8621, Fax: (415) 663-8635
5 rooms
Double: $275–$325
Open: all year, Credit cards: MC, VS
karenbrown.com/california/blackthorneinn.html

Built as a hunting lodge by the Empire Club in 1917, this dark-shingled building highlighted with a white trim porch hung with greenery is a magical retreat set in a wooded grove just up from Tomales Bay. It's the brainchild of owner Margaret Grade who orchestrates its decor (rustic fun with hunting-lodge overtones), cooks (a set menu with open-fire and woodstove cooking only), and selects the snippets of wisdom ("I do think best while holding a tomato") painted on the dining-room walls. It all adds up to the lighthearted, whimsical, totally escapist experience that we all need at times and it's only an hour and a half north of San Francisco. Select the accommodation that best suits you. Above the restaurant two of the guestrooms enjoy outdoor showers on private decks looking out through the trees to Tomales Bay. In the surrounding woodland you find rooms varying in size from snug quarters to large cottages. For complete seclusion, request the Boathouse on the waterfront, or one of the cabins hidden away atop the ridgeline. Whichever room you choose, you will find an escapist rustic decor and rough-hewn beds topped with flannel linens in checks and plaids and draped with heavy throw blankets. Note that breakfast is not included in the room rate. Point Reyes National Seashore with all its delights is on your doorstep. *Directions:* Manka's is at Argyle and Callendar Way.

MANKA'S INVERNESS LODGE
Owner: Margaret Grade
30 Callendar Way
P.O. Box 1110, Inverness, CA 94937, USA
Tel: (415) 669-1034, (800) 585-6343
Fax: (415) 669-1598
11 rooms, 4 cabins
Double: $185–$515*
 *Breakfast not included: $15
Open: all year, Credit cards: MC, VS
karenbrown.com/california/mankasinvernesslodge.html

Ten Inverness Way, a delightful shingled house built as a family home in 1904, sits in a quiet location at the center of Inverness, a short walk from the shore of Tomales Bay. The heart of the house is the oh-so-spacious living room with comfortable sofas drawn round the large stone fireplace and little tables and chairs attractively set for breakfast. The adjacent sunroom is stacked with books and information on the area. Teri Mowery makes guests feel very welcome, a sentiment echoed by her regal Siamese cats, Cassandra and Theodore. Upstairs are three very nice bedrooms, all freshly and prettily decorated. The most spacious and private quarters are offered by the ground-floor Garden Suite with its sitting room opening up to a private deck and its queen-sized bed set in an alcove decorated with a flower-filled mural. Settle in, relax, and make yourself at home—it's that kind of place—and don't forget to make a reservation for a private soak in the hot tub. For dinner, guests often walk the few blocks to Manka's. Teri is happy to pack a picnic and give advice on where to go and what to see in the adjacent Point Reyes National Seashore. *Directions:* Drive into Inverness on the main road, Sir Francis Drake Boulevard, and watch for the sign pointing to your left to Ten Inverness Way.

TEN INVERNESS WAY
Owner: Teri Mattson Mowery
Ten Inverness Way
P.O. Box 63, Inverness, CA 94937, USA
Tel: (415) 669-1648, Fax: (415) 669-7403
5 rooms
Double: $145–$180
Open: all year, Credit cards: MC, VS
karenbrown.com/california/teninvernessway.html

Built in 1859 and proudly claiming to be one of California's ten oldest hotels, the National Hotel is located on the main street of Jamestown, the gateway to the Gold Country. The first floor accommodates a wonderful restaurant where an extravagant breakfast buffet and morning newspapers are set out for resident guests and where lunch, dinner, and a Sunday champagne brunch are available to residents and non-residents. The handsome old redwood bar in the Gold Rush Saloon offers refreshment, possible entertainment, and local gossip. A steep stairway just off the entry leads to the nine guestrooms on the second floor. Wonderful old brass-and-iron beds decked with regal comforters, handsome trunks, lovely old armoires, antique washbasins, and lace curtains at the windows dominate the decor, which is pleasing and reminiscent of the Gold Rush era—but with modern comforts. All guestrooms enjoy private bathrooms and the hotel has a wonderful "soaking room" with an oversized claw-foot bathtub. This is available to all guests, who are supplied with bathrobe and slippers. The guestrooms are comfortable, air-conditioned, and all accessed off the one central hallway. The two front rooms overlook the balcony and the action of Main Street. *Directions:* Jamestown's Main Street intersects both Hwys 108 and 49 on the east and west ends of town.

NATIONAL HOTEL
Owner: Stephen Willey
18183 Main Street
P.O. Box 502, Jamestown, CA 95327, USA
Tel: (209) 984-3446, (800) 894-3446
Fax: (209) 984-5620
9 rooms
Double: $90–$140
Open: all year, Credit cards: all major
karenbrown.com/california/nationalhotel.html

Located in a residential area south of the old Gold Rush town of Julian is a miniature southern mansion, painted white with four stately columns accenting the front of the house. Inside, the home is lovely and inviting in its decor, with a definite sense of family and home. The living room opens onto a sunlit dining room with a wall of windows looking out to a sloping forest of trees. Guests gather in the dining room for a lavish, homemade breakfast served elegantly on family china and silver. Downstairs there are two bedrooms. The French Quarter room has a New Orleans theme and is wallpapered in muted shades of tan and dusty pink with a handsome Louis XVI antique bed. The Julian Suite is the largest room, with a king wrought-iron bed, gas-burning fireplace, whirlpool tub for two, and mountain view. Breakfast is served privately to this room in the dinette area. Upstairs, there are three guestrooms. The Honeymoon Suite is decorated in burgundy and tapestry; the East Room is decorated in blues and whites; the Cotton Baron's Room, in yellows and blues, has an arch over the bed and is furnished with white hand-painted antiques. A spa is available in the rose garden area. *Directions:* One mile southwest of town on Hwy 78/79. From Main Street make a left on Pine Hills Road. After 2-3/10 miles make a right on Blue Jay Drive.

THE JULIAN WHITE HOUSE
Owner: Alan Marvin
3014 Blue Jay Drive
P.O. Box 824, Julian, CA 92036, USA
Tel: (760) 765-1764, (800) 948-4687
Fax: none
5 rooms
Double: $130–$195
Open: all year, Credit cards: all major
karenbrown.com/california/julianwhitehouse.html

Just a block off Main Street on a Julian hillside sits a lovely property, which boasts a very loyal clientele. It is not surprising when you see the accommodation: guestrooms are lovely, with handsome country furnishings complemented by beautiful wallpapers and coordinating fabrics. The Yellow Bellflower, for example, is decorated in tones of soft blues and yellow, with a beautiful blue arch of faience hung on the wall over the bed, materials of a subtle pinstripe and blue check, and a multi-colored quilt draped at the foot of the bed. There is nothing country-cute in the decor—rather, rooms are spacious and subtle in their elegance. Cottage guestrooms, all with private entrances, are tucked in a garden setting along a wandering path and central courtyard. All rooms are equipped with TV and VCR (complimentary video library), all have fireplaces, and most have whirlpool tubs. Bathrooms are spacious, modern, and wonderfully appointed. At the top of the property, the handsome lodge offers more standard rooms in terms of size and price, a lovely large public room with high vaulted ceilings and river-stone fireplace, a dining room, and an upstairs common area with sofa, lounge chairs, and TV. Room prices include a full breakfast and evening hors d'oeuvres. Dinner is offered to guests only on selected evenings. *Directions:* Washington Street crosses Main Street at the north end of town.

※ ☛ ≋ 🗀 ☎ 🕏 🏃 🏇 ☿ P ⑪ 🐾 ⛷ 🍇

ORCHARD HILL COUNTRY INN
Owner: Straube Family
2502 Washington Street
P.O. Box 2410, Julian, CA 92036-0425, USA
Tel: (760) 765-1700, (800) 71-ORCHARD
Fax: (760) 765-0290
22 rooms, Double: $205–$285
Dinner Wed & Sat only
Open: all year, Credit cards: MC, VS
Select Registry
karenbrown.com/california/orchardhillcountryinn.html

Looking for a place to stay with vineyard views, wine tasting, and comfortable accommodations all in one spot? Look no further. Landmark Vineyards owners Mary and Michael Colhoun offer a choice of two self-catering facilities. The Guest Suite, which is actually housed in a quiet wing of the main winery building, offers a large, elegantly decorated twin-bedded room with fireplace and high, beamed ceiling, and a modern bathroom. The view across its private patio and the vineyard beyond is dominated by Sugarloaf Ridge and Hood Mountain. Farther afield in the vineyard you find the white clapboard Guest Cottage. Delightfully modernized and decorated in bright blues and white, this one-bedroom cottage has twin beds, a fully fitted kitchen, sitting room with comfortable sofa and chairs, bathroom, washer and dryer, and even its own wildflower garden with recliners on the lawn—everything you could need for a private getaway in the heart of Sonoma Valley. Select a favorite libation from the tasting room just a few steps away and take it back to sip on your patio while you drink in the views of vineyards and Sugarloaf Ridge. Breakfast muffins, tea, and coffee are provided on a hospitality tray in your room. *Directions:* From Sonoma, take Hwy 12 towards Santa Rosa. Landmark Vineyards is on your right after 15 miles.

LANDMARK
Owners: Mary & Michael Colhoun
101 Adobe Canyon Road
Kenwood, CA 95452, USA
Tel: (707) 833-0053, (800) 452-6365
Fax: (707) 833-1164
2 cottages
Double: $170–$195
Open: all year, Credit cards: all major
karenbrown.com/california/landmark.html

Just a block from the ocean and the hustle and bustle of La Jolla village, The Bed & Breakfast Inn at La Jolla sits on a quiet, stylish suburban street. Originally built for George Kautz in 1913, the home's most famous occupant was the composer John Phillip Sousa, who lived here during the '20s. Behind its street-front façade you enter a grassy, flower-filled courtyard where the only sound is that of a tinkling fountain. Guests often take a breakfast tray out here on balmy mornings—alternatively, you can eat with your fellow guests round the breakfast table. Bedrooms vary from snug upstairs rooms in the original house to a spacious suite with a sitting room offering distant views of the ocean horizon. Beautiful furnishings, lovely fabrics, and fabulous antiques have been carefully selected by the decorator, who also serves as the inn's PR person. It's an excellent location for walking to the beach, shops, and restaurants of La Jolla village and it is just 200 yards from the Museum of Contemporary Art. I was pleased with the availability of on-street parking. *Directions:* From San Diego take I-5 and exit right on La Jolla Village Drive. Turn left on Torrey Pines Road and proceed 2½ miles to Prospect Street. Turn right, drive through downtown La Jolla, and opposite the Museum of Contemporary Art turn right on Draper Avenue—the inn is the second building on the left.

※ ⛱ ☕ 💳 ☎ 🚶 👫 🐴 P 🚶 🛶 ♿

THE BED & BREAKFAST INN AT LA JOLLA
Owner: Mary Louise Micuda
7753 Draper Avenue
La Jolla, CA 92037, USA
Tel: (858) 456-2066, (800) 582-2466
Fax: (858) 456-1510
15 rooms
Double: $179–$399
Open: all year, Credit cards: all major
Select Registry
karenbrown.com/california/lajollabandb.html

The Scripps Inn enjoys an absolutely magnificent setting just steps away from the white sand of La Jolla's gorgeous cove and beach and expanse of sparkling blue water. You can walk or bike for miles along the pedestrian trail that contours along the bluff and it is also just a few short blocks up the hill to the heart of the village with its elegant shops and delightful restaurants. Two wings of guestrooms wrap around the central car park, with upstairs rooms accessed off a covered walkway. The rooms are fresh and pretty—light and airy in their decor with tans, creams, and beiges in the fabrics complementing the light woods of the furnishings. All of the rooms have glimpses of the ocean, though for view none can rival suite 14 where large sitting-room windows frame a 180-degree vista of La Jolla Cove. The two-bedroom suites and room 14 have a kitchenette and two rooms have fireplaces. In the evening it's a short walk into the village where you are spoilt for choice of restaurants. Muffins and pastries and a variety of juices (there are in-room coffee makers) are set out in the reception niche in the morning along with trays to take breakfast back to your room or to the lanai. *Directions:* Drive through downtown La Jolla on Prospect Street, and just after the Museum of Contemporary Art turn right on Cuvier, left on Coast, and immediately left into the inn's car park.

SCRIPPS INN
Innkeeper: Omar Solorzano
555 Coast Boulevard South
La Jolla, CA 92037, USA
Tel: (858) 454-3391, (800) 439-7529
Fax: (858) 456-0389
14 rooms
Double: $225–$415
Open: all year, Credit cards: all major
karenbrown.com/california/scrippsinn.html

La Valencia with its subtle-pink adobe-like walls, thick Spanish-tiled roof, and tower domed with blue-and-gold mosaics is a captivating hotel with much old-world charm. The reception opens onto a dramatic long parlor whose soft-buff-colored walls, wrought-iron chandeliers, subdued lighting, blue-and-yellow tiled planter, luscious displays of fresh flowers, and painted ceiling are dramatized by a wall of glass framing the sea. Guests gather in the evening in the Whaling Bar with its collection of scrimshaw before enjoying dinner in the La Rue Restaurant, or on the most special of occasions at the 12-table Sky Room Restaurant, which sits atop the hotel with dramatic 180-degree ocean views. While all the bedrooms are beautifully decorated, the most luxurious are those in the Ocean Villas that terrace down behind the hotel toward La Jolla Cove—these spacious rooms and suites are exquisite. Within the main body of the hotel our favorite bedrooms are those with little balconies just large enough for a couple of chairs—some have ocean views while others overlook the bustle of the village. A tempting pool is set on an ocean-view terrace amidst the perfectly tended gardens. *Directions:* Exit I-5 north at Ardath Road (5 south at La Jolla Village), travel to Torrey Pines Road, and turn right on Prospect Street. Pull up in front of the hotel and the valet will park your car.

LA VALENCIA HOTEL
Director: Michael Ullman
1132 Prospect Street
La Jolla, CA 92037, USA
Tel: (858) 454-0771, (800) 451-0772
Fax: (858) 456-3921
115 rooms, 1 cottage
Double: $300–$3500*
*Breakfast not included
Open: all year, Credit cards: all major
karenbrown.com/california/lavalencia.html

Although Eagle's Landing is a bed and breakfast, it is run so professionally that guests have the feeling that they are in a miniature hotel. There are four guestrooms with private bathrooms and although each varies in decor, they all maintain a comfy-homey ambiance and are all meticulously kept. One of the bedrooms, Fireside Suite, is enormous, with its own wood-burning fireplace and a spacious private deck with a panoramic view. However, my favorite room is the cozy Woods Room, tucked amongst the trees with its own little terrace and entrance. The living room has a large fireplace in the corner and a splendid long wooden trestle table, big enough for all the guests to gather and share their day's adventures. Just off the dining room is a cozy nook where guests enjoy breakfast. Dorothy prides herself on treating her guests to a full breakfast every morning and a special brunch on Sunday mornings, a hearty start for exploring the lake, which is just a short walk from Eagle's Landing. Since this is a private lake, public access is available only in the town of Arrowhead (about a five-minute drive or a thirty-minute lakeside walk away). *Directions:* Turn north from Hwy 18 following signs for Blue Jay. Before you reach the lake, the road splits. Turn left on North Bay and watch for Cedarwood on your left—Eagle's Landing is on the corner of North Bay and Cedarwood.

EAGLE'S LANDING
Owners: Dorothy & Jack Stone
27406 Cedarwood
Lake Arrowhead, CA 92352, USA
(Mail: PO Box 1510, Blue Jay CA 92317)
(800) 835-5085, Fax: (909) 336-2642
4 rooms
Double: $95–$195
Open: all year, Credit cards: all major
karenbrown.com/california/eagleslanding.html

The Saddleback Inn is tucked into its own wooded oasis just a short stroll from Lake Arrowhead Village. Although the inn dates back about 70 years to when it was built in the style of an English tavern by two sisters from the Midwest, there is nothing "dated" about this intimate inn. Its present owners have completely renovated every nook and cranny, creating an elegant, yet charming hotel. Luckily, they have kept the old-world look with the use of a few antiques plus many reproductions in the decor. The reception area is located in the main lodge, which exudes a Victorian mood in its cozy bar and dining room. The original staircase leads off the lobby to ten guestrooms commemorating past guests like Howard Hughes, John Wayne, and Charles Lindburgh. Scattered throughout the 3½ acres are small cottages connected by pathways, which house the remaining guestrooms. All of the rooms are decorated with Laura Ashley fabrics and wallpapers, and most have double whirlpool tubs in the bathroom—a wonderful respite after a day of hiking or sightseeing. Enjoy fine dining in their award-winning restaurant. A pretty beach is within walking distance. *Directions:* From Hwy 18 take the Lake Arrowhead turnoff. Drive 2 miles and the hotel is on the left at the entrance to Lake Arrowhead Village.

SADDLEBACK INN
Owners: Kurt & Bonnie Campbell
300 S. State Hwy 173
P.O. Box 1890, Lake Arrowhead, CA 92352, USA
Tel: (800) 858-3334, Fax: (909) 336-6111
34 rooms, Double: $129–$218*
*Breakfast not included
Restaurant: lunch and dinner Tue–Sun
Open: all year, Credit cards: all major
karenbrown.com/california/saddlebackinn.html

Glendeven is a delightful New England-style farmhouse built in 1867 by Isaiah Stevens for his bride, Rebecca. Today, this beautiful clapboard home is absolutely decorator-perfect and continues to be one of our favorite places to stay. I'm certain you will echo our sentiments and whether you select a room in the main house or Stevenscroft, a stylish gabled annex in the garden, or choose the seclusion of the suite behind the art gallery, you will be as thrilled with the place as we are. Most rooms have superb, not-so-distant ocean views and fireplaces; all have immaculate decor and beautiful bathrooms. Breakfast is served in your room on a tray, or snugly in a picnic basket if you are away from the main house. We were reluctant to leave the confines of our room but just had to take the path across the highway that leads to the clifftops. In the evening we walked down the well-lit woodland pathway to a restaurant next door for dinner. If you are traveling with friends or family, consider renting La Bella Vista, a two-bedroom, two-bathroom house across the meadow from Glendeven. It has spectacular ocean views, a hot tub, and a kitchen. Glendeven is adjacent to Van Damme State Park with its scenic walking paths. *Directions:* From San Francisco take Hwy 101 north, Hwy 128 west, then Hwy 1 north for 8-2/10 miles.

GLENDEVEN
Owners: Sharon Williams & Higgins
8205 North Hwy 1
Little River, CA 95456 , USA
Tel: (707) 937-0083, (800) 822-4536
Fax: (707) 937-6108
10 rooms, 1 cottage
Double: $145–$250
Open: all year, Credit cards: all major
Select Registry
karenbrown.com/california/glendeven.html

The Inn at Schoolhouse Creek offers a range of comfortable, charming, and eclectic accommodations. An assorted collection of century-old cottages, lodges, the historic Ledford family home (circa 1860), and two modern suites nestles in 8 private acres set back across Hwy 1 from the ocean. All are individually decorated in a casual country-cottage style, liberally sprinkled with family antiques and curiosities, and offer a choice of views and varying degrees of spaciousness. Each has a fireplace (some wood, some gas), full bath (many with spa tubs), and private deck or garden sitting area. Some have self-catering kitchens. The focal point is the comfortable old Ledford farmhouse, with its redwood ceilings and paneled walls. Curl up with a book or game by the fire, enjoy breakfast on the sun porch. Owners Maureen Gilbert and Steven Musser go out of their way to stress that this is a family destination—children and pets are welcome, and well catered for. Sample the delights of nearby Mendocino but return in time to soak in the hot tub and reflect on the day's activities while you watch the sun set over the Pacific. *Directions:* From San Francisco take Hwy 101 north, Hwy 128 west, then Hwy 1 north for 7 miles and you will see the inn on your right before you reach the Van Damme State Park.

INN AT SCHOOLHOUSE CREEK
Owners: Maureen Gilbert & Steven Musser
7051 North Hwy 1
Little River, CA 95456, USA
Tel: (707) 937-5525, (800) 731-5525
Fax: (707) 937-2012
16 rooms
Double: $130–$250
Open: all year, Credit cards: all major
karenbrown.com/california/schoolhouse.html

Vineyards are beginning to dress the foothills of the Livermore Valley in the shadow of the windmills and the Purple Orchid Inn Resort and Spa offers a convenient and luxurious retreat for exploring the wineries. A beautiful, sprawling log structure set against a backdrop of its own olive orchards, the inn is intended to be a destination in its own right. Owner Karen Hughes describes the inn as a place of wellness where guests can visit, relax, and make healthy life choices. Enjoy the expanded spa, whose staff is extensively trained in various massage methods, special body wraps, salt glows, and skin care. Definitely ask about the spa and golf packages. For dining, there are lots of local restaurants and on Friday evenings at the inn a delicious fondue repast (cheese, chicken, beef, and chocolate) is available. In the mornings, the chef will prepare whatever you crave for breakfast. The guestrooms, all with fireplaces, are attractive and bathrooms enjoy nice fixtures and Jacuzzi tubs (some for two). The newest patio suites are equipped with refrigerator, microwave, and a stocked bar. Gorgeous hand-carved scenes on the guestroom doors depict the theme and decor for the rooms. *Directions:* Exit Hwy 580 at Vasco Road to the south. At its end turn left on Tesla Road and then take a left on Cross Road to the inn.

PURPLE ORCHID INN
Owner: Karen Hughes
4549 Cross Road
Livermore, CA 94550, USA
Tel: (925) 606-8855, (800) 353-4549
Fax: (925) 606-8880
10 rooms
Double: $179–$380
Open: all year, Credit cards: MC, VS
Select Registry
karenbrown.com/california/purpleorchid.html

Nestled in the Bel-Air hills of Los Angeles in a neighborhood of exclusive homes on a lush 12-acre plot transected by babbling streams, the Hotel Bel-Air is exceptional—elegant and sophisticated, yet unpretentious and extending a truly warm welcome, which includes a thoughtful tea service. Furnishings are gorgeous, with handsome antiques and dramatic flower arrangements. The one- or two-story buildings nestling in the greenery are painted in a soft pastel wash with white doors, creating a peaceful and soothing effect. There is an elegant interior restaurant and a terrace for dining under the shade of canopies and trees. Light meals are also available poolside as is a summertime grill. The setting is quiet, with the sound of fountains and a running stream breaking the natural silence. Most of the beautifully decorated guestrooms enjoy handsome tiled floors warmed by lovely needlepoint carpets. Service is ever-present but subtle, and nothing is too much of a problem or effort on the part of the staff. In my research I have seen some of the world's finest hotels and the Bel-Air made such an impression, I am determined to return to it as others do—on vacation instead of business! *Directions:* Take Sunset Boulevard west off Hwy 405 and then turn north on Stone Canyon Road for about 1 mile. The hotel is on the left just past the intersection of Tortuosa Way.

HOTEL BEL-AIR
Manager: Carlos Lopes
701 Stone Canyon Road
Los Angeles, CA 90077, USA
Tel: (310) 472-1211, (800) 648-4097
Fax: 310-476-5890
91 rooms
Double: $385–$3000*
 *Breakfast not included
Open: all year, Credit cards: all major
karenbrown.com/california/hotelbelair.html

Los Olivos was originally a stagecoach town; now its main street houses interesting stores, restaurants, and Fess Parker's inn and spa. (Hollywood aficionados will remember Fess playing Davy Crockett in the '50s.) Beautiful in decor and lavishly comfortable, this elegant inn is an excellent place to stay and sample the wines of the Santa Inez Valley—of course you must visit the Fess Parker Winery. Each of the guestrooms, whether upstairs in the main building or across the street, features wood moldings, brass fixtures, and French armoires, all of which combine to create a romantic, early-20th-century ambiance. Guestroom amenities include a mini refrigerator, television, fireplace, beds topped with plump down comforters, and, in several rooms, a Jacuzzi bathtub. The award-winning Vintage Room restaurant has an elegant, French-country ambiance and Le Saloon is an attractive full-service bar opening onto the sheltered patio. Summer travelers appreciate the lovely heated swimming pool and Jacuzzi. Pamper yourself with a massage or a treatment at Spa Vigne, located just up the road in a little cottage. *Directions:* From Los Angeles, take Hwy 101 north. Approximately 5 miles north of Buellton, exit onto Hwy 154. Proceed 2 miles and turn right on Grand.

FESS PARKER'S WINE COUNTRY INN & SPA
Manager: Bill Phelps
2860 Grand Avenue
P.O. Box 849, Los Olivos, CA 93441, USA
Tel: (805) 688-7788, (800) 446-2455
Fax: (805) 688-1942
21 rooms
Double: $250–$450
Open: all year, Credit cards: all major
karenbrown.com/california/fessinn.html

Behind Casa Malibu's bland '50s motel façade you find a simple, attractive entry dressed with fresh flowers opening onto the back central courtyard. The manicured back garden is beautifully landscaped and flows to a tiled patio, which extends out to a glass-enclosed bay-window alcove set with tables overlooking the ocean. A single-story wing of 7 lovely rooms sits right on the beach. These delightful high-ceilinged rooms are decorated in pale colors, furnished with wicker and open onto glass-walled decks. Several have jacuzzi tubs, fireplaces and connecting doors. Other rooms are found in the building that fronts the Pacific Coast Hwy, either on the first floor overlooking the lush interior courtyard or on the second floor enjoying views of the courtyard garden and glimpses of the distant blue water. Some rooms are equipped with kitchenettes, some with gas fireplaces, and others with a deck. Continental breakfast is offered each morning in the lobby and room service is available from local restaurants for lunch and dinner. Beach towels, umbrellas and chairs are on hand for you to take down to the beach which is freshly raked every morning. *Directions:* Located in the heart of Malibu 1/3 mile south of the pier.

CASA MALIBU
Owners: Joan & Richard Page
22752 Pacific Coast Hwy
Malibu, CA 90265, USA
Tel: (310) 456-2219, (800) 831-0858
Fax: (310) 456-5418
21 rooms
Double: $99–$379
Open: all year, Credit cards: all major
karenbrown.com/california/casamalibu.html

Constructed in 1989, the Malibu Beach Inn resembles the type of small hotel you would find on the Mediterranean, washed in a soft peach and detailed with green awnings and door trim, with white doors and tile roof. The entrance doors swing open automatically to reveal a spacious lobby and sitting area dressed with a fireplace, and an arched doorway opens out to a tiled deck set with tables. All the guestrooms at the back of the inn open up to magnificent ocean views and the sound of surf. All these rooms have a private oceanfront balcony, a queen-size bed, bamboo furniture, and full amenities such as a fully stocked wet bar and bathrobes. First-floor rooms have two-person Jacuzzis on double-wide balconies while all the other rooms have fireplaces. One suite is found on each floor and enjoys a larger deck, Jacuzzi, and fireplace. The largest rooms, "pier rooms", are located to the side of the hotel and are angled towards the ocean view rather than being oceanfront. What they lack in view they make up for by having king-size beds and more space. All third floor rooms have vaulted beamed ceilings. A substantial continental breakfast is set in the lobby and for lunch or dinner you can order from the 24 hour picnic menu or order room service from local restaurants. *Directions:* Located in the heart of Malibu just south of the pier.

❄ ⚓ ☕ 🏄 CREDIT ☎ 🚻 🤸 🚶 🏃 🐎 🍸 P 🎿 ⚓ ♿

MALIBU BEACH INN
Manager: Brian Bescoby
22878 Pacific Coast Hwy
Malibu, CA 90265, USA
Tel: (310) 456-6444, (800) 462-5428
Fax: (310) 456-1499
47 rooms
Double: $209–$379
Open: all year, Credit cards: all major
karenbrown.com/california/malibubeach.html

Set on 92 acres of meadow, woodland, and creek, Victorian Gardens is a lovely, two-story, classic Victorian. While decoration reflects the Victorian period, the house is filled with light and there is a refreshing absence of clutter or bric-a-brac. Furnishings are an artistic arrangement of both traditional and contemporary, with the Zambonis' family heirlooms and art treasures on display. Warmed by a large open fireplace, the huge kitchen is definitely the heart of the house. Elegant five-course dinners feature Italian regional dishes, incorporating not only fresh homegrown produce but also game birds and sheep raised on the property. While there are four guestrooms (two sharing a hall bath), only three are rented out if all the guests are not together, giving each room a private bathroom. The sunny Master Bedroom enjoys sweeping pastoral views; the Poppy Bedroom has a reading alcove; the Golden Bedroom is an inviting front corner room with a lovely sitting nook looking out to the ocean; and the handsome Northwest Bedroom offers wonderful views and the most lavish bathroom. Though the inn is elegant, with everything about it speaking of quality and impeccable attention to detail, its atmosphere is casual and relaxed, and guests are encouraged to settle in one of several public rooms or enjoy the extensive grounds. *Directions:* Drive south on Hwy 1 from the junction with the 128. Victorian Gardens is 8 miles past Elk on the left.

VICTORIAN GARDENS
Owners: Pauline & Luciano Zamboni
14409 South Hwy 1
Manchester, CA 95459, USA
Tel: (707) 882-3606, Fax: (707) 882-2718
4 rooms
Double: $190–$250
Open: all year, Credit cards: all major
karenbrown.com/california/victoriangardens.html

Rising from the sand dunes just 10 miles north of Monterey, Marina Dunes Resort offers you the opportunity to get closer to the Pacific Ocean than any other property in this guide. In fact, the bungalows are just a sand dune away from the pounding waves—so close that cars are not permitted and guests travel back and forth from their vehicles in battery-operated golf carts. Set in 20 one- and two-story buildings on 90 acres of dunes, the bungalows are the shorefont rooms of a 93-room complex. This arrangement affords lots of privacy for everyone and gives each of the resort units a spectacular view of Monterey Bay. Take in seascapes while sitting in front of your fireplace or soak up the salt air from your private balcony or patio. For dinner the restaurant serves western, beef, chicken, and seafood dishes as well as tapas at the bar. You can enjoy a swim in the pool, a soak in the Jacuzzi, or a pampering in the spa. There are plenty of opportunities for exploring Monterey with its famous Cannery Row and Aquarium but the absolute delight of staying here is that you can kick back in your bungalow, go beachcombing along the shore, or just contemplate life in front of the fire. *Directions:* Exit Hwy 1 at Reservation Road, Marina, turn west, and take the first right, Dunes Drive, where you find the hotel immediately on the left.

MARINA DUNES RESORT
Manager: Lisa Bindel
3295 Dunes Drive
Marina, CA 93933, USA
Tel: (831) 883-9478, (877) 944-3863
Fax: (831) 883-9477
60 rooms
Double: $199–$449
Open: all year, Credit cards: all major
karenbrown.com/california/marinadunes.html

The McCloud Guest House has a wonderful setting amidst spacious grounds of green lawns and huge shade trees, with Mount Shasta, northern California's 14,162-foot giant, in the distance. It is very private and quiet, yet is situated only two blocks from the attractive downtown. Built in 1907 as the estate of J. H. Queal, the president of the McCloud River Railroad Company, the inn is absolutely delightful in its Craftsman-style simplicity. Constructed entirely of wood, the square building is wrapped with a spacious verandah whose supporting columns reach up to a steeply pitched roof from which little dormer windows peek out into the trees. As you enter the foyer, the massive stone fireplace and wood-paneled walls create a country-lodge feeling. Guests have the use of a small games room and a library with books that they can borrow. They can also relax in the sauna and enjoy breakfast on the deck. Upstairs, the bedrooms surround a guest parlor where a pool table from the Hearst collection sits center stage. Each of the guestrooms has its own color scheme and personality, but all are decorated with period pieces such as antique dressers, white iron beds, and handmade quilts. *Directions:* From I-5 turn east on Hwy 89 for 12 miles to McCloud. Before the village turn left on Colombero Drive.

MCCLOUD GUEST HOUSE
Owner: Linda Baldwin
606 West Colombero Drive
P.O. Box 1510, McCloud, CA 96057, USA
Tel: (530) 964-3160
Fax: (530) 964-3202
5 rooms
Double: $125–$175
Open: all year, Credit cards: all major
karenbrown.com/california/mccloudguesthouse.html

With great determination, expenditure, and hard work, Lee and Marilyn Ogden renovated a long-abandoned historic building at the heart of the mountain town of McCloud and now the McCloud Hotel with its pretty yellow façade proudly dominates Main Street. Inside, the high, beamed ceiling and informal grouping of sofas and chairs set before a large fire give the feeling of a mountain lodge. Although the exterior of the hotel was in relatively good shape and required only cosmetic repairs, guestrooms benefit from the complete renovation and modernization of the interior. At the top of a wide, handsome staircase is an inviting parlor with access to the front expanse of porch. Rooms facing Main Street are a wonderful value, with a nice-size room, washbasin, toilet, and private bathroom. Rooms on the first and second floors at the back of the inn have four-poster beds and an additional but small sitting area. Four suites enjoy big Jacuzzi tubs, three of which are found in the room proper. The decor is similar in theme throughout, with the use of country patterns, old trunks, and washstands holding in-room washbasins. Breakfast and Saturday-afternoon tea are served at tables set in the lobby. *Directions:* From I-5 take the McCloud-Reno exit, driving east on Hwy 89 for 10 miles. Turn left on Colombero Drive, follow it into town, cross the tracks, and turn right on Main Street.

MCCLOUD HOTEL
Owners: Marilyn & Lee Ogden
408 Main Street
P.O. Box 730, McCloud, CA 96057, USA
Tel: (530) 964-2822, (800) 964-2823
Fax: (530) 964-2844
16 rooms
Double: $109–$198
Open: all year, Credit cards: all major
karenbrown.com/california/mccloudhotel.html

The Agate Cove Inn is a beautiful property situated on a bluff across the coastal road from the ocean. The heart of the inn is a charming 1860s blue-trimmed, white clapboard farmhouse where you find the reception area and an appealing lounge with comfy chairs facing a brick fireplace where a cozy fire crackles on chilly days. Windows stretch across the entire west wall of the lounge, giving guests a spectacular view of the coast as they enjoy a scrumptious hot breakfast. Two of the bedrooms are in the main farmhouse, while the others are scattered about the property in little cottages painted a pretty country-blue with white trim. Most of the rooms have a gas fireplace, a deck, and a view of the sea. Even the least expensive rooms, although smaller and simpler, are sweet and pretty. The inn was bought in 1999 by a charming young couple, Nancy and Dennis Freeze, who dreamed for years of opening their own inn. When they discovered the Agate Cove Inn they knew they had found the perfect spot. It is no wonder they fell in love with it—the little houses are so cute, and the setting superb. The view, looking out over brilliantly colored flowers to the sparkling blue sea framed by windswept cypress trees, is truly breathtaking. *Directions:* From Hwy 1 take Little Lake left (west), then Lansing right (north).

AGATE COVE INN
Owners: Nancy & Dennis Freeze
11201 North Lansing Street
P.O. Box 1150, Mendocino, CA 95460, USA
Tel: (707) 937-0551, (800) 527-3111
Fax: (707) 937-0550
10 rooms
Double: $129–$299
Open: all year, Credit cards: all major
karenbrown.com/california/agatecoveinn.html

The Blue Heron Inn is not the typical Mendocino Victorian, but a simple, New England-style house, painted white with blue trim, with a lovely red door. A white picket fence encloses the garden to each side, completing the adorable cottage look. On the ground floor is a delightful restaurant (The Moose Café) where daily specials (fresh fish and pasta dishes) are offered, complemented by a small wine list. Enjoy a Caesar salad for lunch and cioppino for dinner. In the morning a Continental breakfast with scones or muffins, fruit, and freshly squeezed orange juice is served here. Upstairs, you find three completely delightful bedrooms, each smartly furnished and containing a lovely queen-sized bed made with the most attractive linens. Sunset Room (in cool greens) captures ocean views across the rooftops and shares a modern bathroom with the adjacent Bay Room, which offers a tempting view of the ocean from its window. The Blue Heron Room has equally delightful decor, more space, and a pristine en-suite shower room. From this heart-of-town location it is just a half block to the ocean. *Directions:* Follow Hwy 1 north into Mendocino. Turn left at the Mendocino business district to Kasten Street then turn right.

BLUE HERON INN
Owner: Linda Friedman
390 Kasten Street
Mendocino, CA 95460, USA
Tel: (707) 937-4323, Fax: (707) 937-3611
3 rooms
Double: $95–$115
Open: all year, Credit cards: MC, VS
karenbrown.com/california/blueheroninn.html

Brewery Gulch Inn is the brainchild of Arky Ciancutti, a former physician and management consultant with a passion for the land. Redwood logs, originally harvested in the 1800s and preserved, buried deep in the silt of the neighboring Big River before being "rescued" by Arky, are a key ingredient in its construction. Set in 10 acres high on a bluff overlooking Smuggler's Cove, the architecturally distinctive, redwood-shake-covered inn contains ten guestrooms. The redwood is used throughout, blending with Craftsman-style furnishings and colors selected to harmonize with the inn's natural setting. Each room has an ocean view and fireplace, most have their own private deck, and all are luxuriously equipped with every modern convenience to make your stay complete. The inn's resident chef prepares gourmet breakfasts, afternoon hors d'oeuvres, and special-event dinners with Brewery Gulch-grown organic products. Guests can sample local vintners' produce at the wine bar, warmed by the heat thrown from logs burning in an enormous, custom-built fireplace made of stainless steel and glass, the focal point of the living/dining room. *Directions:* Heading north on Hwy 1 you will see the Brewery Gulch Inn signpost to your right just before you get to Mendocino.

BREWERY GULCH INN
Owner: Arky Ciancutti
Manager: Glenn Lutge
9401 North Hwy 1
Mendocino, CA 95460, USA
Tel: (707) 937-4752, (800) 578-4454
Fax: (707) 937-1279
10 rooms
Double: $150–$295
Open: all year, Credit cards: all major
karenbrown.com/california/brewerygulch.html

The John Dougherty House has an excellent location, just steps from Mendocino's quaint shops and cute restaurants, yet only a few short blocks from the splendid headlands where you can stroll the bluffs with only the pounding of the surf, the cry of the seagulls, and the barking of the sea lions to disturb the silence. The heart of the inn is a beguiling blue cottage with perky white trim, dating back to 1867. Some of the guestrooms are in the main house, one in the adjacent wood-shingled water tower, another in the old carriage house, and others in cottages nestled in the beautifully kept garden. For the finest view, splurge on the Captain's Room, which has a spacious verandah looking out over the village to the bay. If this isn't available, choose either Raven or Osprey with their view balconies, king-sized four-poster beds, fireplaces, cable TVs, and jet tubs. The cozy gathering room has a breakfast table at one end and comfortable chairs grouped before a brick fireplace where a fire blazes on chilly days. When the weather is warm, most guests choose to enjoy the hearty breakfast outside on the terrace overlooking the garden and the sea. Country-style antiques and Marion's hand-painted stencils set the tone of the decor. *Directions:* Coming north on 101, take the first street into Mendocino. Turn right on Kasten, then left on Ukiah.

JOHN DOUGHERTY HOUSE
Owners: Marion & David Wells
571 Ukiah Street
P.O. Box 817, Mendocino, CA 95460, USA
Tel: (707) 937-5266, (800) 486-2104
Fax: none
10 rooms, 4 cottages
Double: $110–$240
Open: all year, Credit cards: MC, VS
karenbrown.com/california/johndougherty.html

The Joshua Grindle Inn, located just a short walk from the center of Mendocino, is surrounded by a 2-acre plot of land. A white picket fence encloses the front yard of this most attractive white clapboard farmhouse, which, although architecturally simple, has hints of the Victorian era in the fancy woodwork on the verandah. In the 1879 farmhouse you find the guest lounge, a sedate room with old paintings and portraits on the walls, a fireplace, white lace curtains, a trunk as a coffee table, and an antique pump organ. The light, airy guestrooms have a New England-country ambiance enhanced by early-American antiques and some have their own fireplace. Of the five bedrooms in the main building two overlook the town of Mendocino and the distant ocean. All of the bathrooms here have been remodeled with marble counters and whirlpool and deep soaking tubs. A natural-wood cottage, Saltbox Cottage, has two cozy bedrooms, each with custom pine cabinets and luxurious cast-iron waterfall tubs and showers. The most romantic rooms are those tucked into the age-weathered water tower in the rear garden. Especially attractive is Watertower II, a sunny, cozy room on the second floor with a glimpse of the ocean. *Directions:* Follow Hwy 1 north into Mendocino. After crossing the bridge into town, take the second left at the stoplight onto Little Lake Road.

JOSHUA GRINDLE INN
Owners: Cindy & Charles Reinhart
Manager: Christine Wagner
44800 Little Lake Road
P.O. Box 647, Mendocino, CA 95460, USA
Tel: (707) 937-4143, (800) 474-6353
Fax: none
10 rooms, 2 cottages, Double: $130–$265
Open: all year, Credit cards: MC, VS
Select Registry
karenbrown.com/california/joshuagrindleinn.html

Most of our selections for Mendocino feature the coastal splendor, but although not next to the ocean, the Mendocino Farmhouse has some very special qualities. It is located 1½ miles inland at the end of a narrow lane that weaves through a beautiful redwood glen, crosses a small creek, and then opens into a lovely meadow. There, amidst beds of flowers, next to a pond, and surrounded by a white picket fence, you find an appealing farmhouse with white trim. Inside, the decor is country, with antique accents giving it an eclectic style. The breakfast tables capture the sunshine in a many-windowed niche overlooking the flower garden. Eating outside under redwoods is an option in good weather. There are four bedrooms in the farmhouse, each sparkling-clean and with its own bathroom; two enjoy fireplaces. Our favorite rooms are Cedar and Pine, two very private rooms found in the converted barn surrounded by its own little garden. Each is rustic in mood with either cedar or bleached-pine paneling, a sitting area, and a large wood-burning fireplace. *Directions:* From Hwy 1 take Comptche-Ukiah Road east of Mendocino. Go 1-7/10 miles to Olson Lane and turn left to the end of the road.

MENDOCINO FARMHOUSE
Owner: Margie Kamb
Olson Lane
P.O. Box 247, Mendocino, CA 95460, USA
Tel: (707) 937-0241, (800) 475-1536
Fax: none
6 rooms, 1 cottage
Double: $115–$145
Open: all year, Credit cards: MC, VS
karenbrown.com/california/mendocinofarmhouse.html

Maria and Daniel Levin moved from the San Francisco Bay Area to Mendocino in pursuit of their dream bed and breakfast. After a false start with the building next door, which has now become their home and still houses several of their guestrooms, they found it in this former boarding house. Applying their own personal skills (she as an interior designer and he as a contractor), their joint efforts have transformed Packard House into a magnificently restored example of a "carpenter's Gothic" Victorian. Exquisitely decorated throughout and furnished with an elegant mix of antique and modern furnishings and museum-quality art, four rooms in the main house are supplemented by one suite in the adjacent building. All have king- or queen-sized beds with luxurious linens, and private bathrooms with jet tubs or steam showers. Limestone floors, tile, and marble complete the picture. Packard House is centrally located, one of four landmark homes on "Executive Row"— and an easy walk from all the attractions of Mendocino with its restaurants, shops, and galleries, and the Mendocino Headlands State Park. *Directions:* Follow Hwy 1 north into Mendocino. After crossing the bridge into town, take the second left at the stop light onto Little Lake Road. Turn left on Lansing and immediately right onto Little Lake Street (not Road!) and the inn is on your right in two blocks.

PACKARD HOUSE
Owners: Maria & Daniel Levin
45170 Little Lake Street
Mendocino, CA 95460, USA
Tel: (707) 937-2677, (888) 453-2677
Fax: (707) 937-1323
4 rooms, 1 cottage
Double: $145–$265
Open: all year, Credit cards: MC, VS
karenbrown.com/california/packard.html

Joan and Jeff Stanford have created a sophisticated hotel within several attractive two-story, natural-wood buildings on 10 sheltered acres just to the south of Mendocino village. Check in with one of the personable staff who are happy to offer sightseeing advice or help you select a video from the inn's vast library. Pick up souvenirs in the adjacent gift shop and make yourself at home with the friendly resident cats in the expansive living room. Beyond the living room lies the Raven restaurant, which serves vegetarian fare featuring organic vegetables grown on the property. All the rooms and suites have private patios with distant ocean views across the gardens and pastures where llamas graze. The rustic paneled walls are hung with artwork and the fireplaces or stoves are supplied with plenty of wood to warm you on nippy nights. Everything is fresh and pretty and smart. A wonderful bonus is the glass-enclosed sauna and "greenhouse" pool where guests can enjoy a swim, take a sauna, or soak in the spa even on blustery days. For those who enjoy a workout, there is also an exercise room. You are very welcome to bring your well-behaved dogs and children. Borrow a mountain bike and take a spin around town or explore the adjacent Big River by kayak or canoe. *Directions:* A quarter of a mile south of Mendocino village at the intersection of Hwy 1 and Comptche-Ukiah Road.

STANFORD INN BY THE SEA
Owners: Joan & Jeff Stanford
Hwy 1 & Comptche-Ukiah Road
Mendocino, CA 95460, USA
Tel: (707) 937-5615, (800) 331-8884
Fax: (707) 937-0305
33 rooms
Double: $265–$465
Open: all year, Credit cards: all major
karenbrown.com/california/stanfordinn.html

If you are looking for a place to stay in the heart of Mendocino that absolutely oozes decadent Victorian charm, then the Whitegate Inn is definitely for you. This enviable white clapboard home, built in 1883, is set off from the sidewalk by a white picket fence and, of course, a white gate. Inside, you step into an elegant home of the 19th century brimming with decorative Victorian antiques. To the right of the entry hall there is a parlor whose decor perfectly captures the Victorian era, with an Oriental carpet, original crystal chandelier, elaborate furniture, gilt mirrors, ornate lamps, fancy drapes, bouquets of fresh flowers, and displays of the owners' collection of crystal and cranberry glassware. The parlor opens to a formal dining room where a gourmet breakfast is presented each morning on a beautifully set table using English bone china and sterling silver. The guestrooms capture the same elegant Victorian mood with antique beds piled high with pillows and made with luxurious linens. Of course, the 21st century has intruded with efficient fireplaces, snug en-suite shower rooms, cable TV, CD/clock radios, and queen- or king-sized beds. Enjoy the peace and quiet of this location just a block away from the heart of town. *Directions:* From the junction with Hwy 128 drive 9 miles north on Hwy 1 to Mendocino. Turn west at the stoplight (Little Lake Road) then left on Howard Street and proceed two blocks.

WHITEGATE INN
Owners: Susan & Richard Strom
499 Howard Street
Mendocino, CA 95460, USA
Tel: (707) 937-4892, (800) 531-7282
Fax: (707) 937-1131
6 rooms
Double: $170–$289
Open: all year, Credit cards: all major
karenbrown.com/california/whitegateinn.html

Ann and Gene Swett converted their family home into what continues to be one of the very nicest country inns in California. Their Tudor-style home is most attractive—shaded by giant oak trees in an acre of wooded gardens full of colorful camellias, fuchsias, rhododendrons, and lush ferns all set in a quiet Monterey suburb. The inside of the house is an oasis of gentility and tranquillity where everything is done with the comfort of the guest in mind. All of the bedrooms in the main house, cottage, and carriage house have fireplaces, many have whirlpool tubs for two, and all are beautifully decorated and thoughtfully appointed. In the main house one of our favorite rooms is The Library with its book-lined walls, cozy fireplace, and private balcony overlooking the garden. My overall favorite is the Garden Cottage, a totally private retreat with a separate sitting room, spa for two, and a skylight for gazing at the stars. Breakfast is posted the night before and can be served at the long mahogany table in the dining room or in the privacy of your bedroom. A refrigerator is kept stocked with complimentary beverages, and juices, hot beverages, and cookies are always available. *Directions:* Exit Hwy 1 at Soledad/Munras, cross Munras, go right on Pacific and Martin Street is on the left in a ½ mile.

OLD MONTEREY INN
Owners: Ann & Gene Swett
Innkeeper: Patti Kreider
500 Martin Street
Monterey, CA 93940, USA
Tel: (831) 375-8284, (800) 350-2344
Fax: (831) 375-6730
9 rooms, 1 cottage, Double: $240–$450
Open: all year, Credit cards: MC, VS
Select Registry
karenbrown.com/california/oldmontereyinn.html

As an alternative to a bed and breakfast we recommend the Spindrift Inn, a lovely hotel with a great location overlooking Monterey Bay. Just down the street from the fabulous Monterey Bay Aquarium, its rooms overlook either the bustle of Cannery Row or the serenity of the bay. We stayed in a front room overlooking Cannery Row and were happy to find that the deep-set windows and heavy drapes blocked out the noise of late-night revelers. Guestrooms on the bay side enjoy wonderful water views and corner rooms are spacious and have a lovely window seat. Bedrooms are handsomely decorated with rich European fabrics and all have wood-burning fireplaces, beds topped with down comforters and feather beds, and bathrooms finished in marble and brass. The feeling is European and the amenities are first-class. A Continental breakfast of fresh-baked breads and a selection of fruit is served on a silver tray in the room and in the evening a buffet of wine and cheese is set out in the front lobby. There is always someone at the front desk to assist with information or reservations. This is an efficient, attractive, and comfortable hotel with a premier location. *Directions:* Take the Pacific Grove/Del Monte exit off Hwy 1. Follow signs to Cannery Row and the Aquarium—the Spindrift is on the right-hand side on Cannery Row.

SPINDRIFT INN
Manager: Randy Venard
652 Cannery Row
Monterey, CA 93940, USA
Tel: (831) 646-8900, (800) 841-1879
Fax: (831) 646-5342
42 rooms
Double: $229–$479
Open: all year, Credit cards: all major
karenbrown.com/california/spindriftinn.html

Karen (Brown) Herbert and her husband, Rick, have built their own romantic English manor-style hideaway, Seal Cove Inn. Located just half an hour's drive south of San Francisco, the inn is bordered by towering, windswept cypress trees and looks out over fields of wildflowers and acres of parkland to the ocean. You enter through a spacious entrance hall into an elegantly comfortable living room with a large fireplace centered between French doors. Adjoining the living room is a dining room and next to that, a small conference room—all with park and ocean views. Antiques are used throughout: grandfather clocks, cradles filled with flowers, handsome tables, antique beds, armoires, trunks, etc. Each of the large bedrooms has a wood-burning fireplace, comfortable reading chairs, television, VCR, hot towel rack, and a refrigerator stocked with complimentary soft drinks and wine. Best yet, each of the bedrooms has a view of the distant ocean and doors opening either to a private balcony or onto the terrace. From the inn you can walk to a secluded stretch of beach or stroll through the forest along a path that traces the ocean bluffs. Karen has already had the pleasure of welcoming many guests to Seal Cove Inn who are also readers of her travel guides. *Directions:* From San Francisco take Hwy 1 south to Moss Beach (about 20 miles). Turn west on Cypress (at the Moss Beach Distillery sign). Seal Cove Inn is one block off the road on the right.

SEAL COVE INN
Owners: Karen & Rick Herbert
Manager: Dawn Grover
221 Cypress Avenue
Moss Beach, CA 94038, USA
Tel: (650) 728-4114, (800) 995-9987
Fax: (650) 728-4116
10 rooms, Double: $200–$300
Closed: Christmas, Credit cards: all major
Select Registry
karenbrown.com/california/sealcoveinn.html

The Pelican Inn, nestled among pine trees, jasmine, and honeysuckle, is a wonderful re-creation of a cozy English tavern with a few attractive guestrooms tucked upstairs. Wide-planked wood floors, an appealing small bar (with dart board), low, beamed ceilings, a giant fireplace with priest hole (secret hiding place), a cozy little guest lounge, and a dining room with trestle tables complete the first-floor scene. Besides the large indoor dining room, there is also a trellised patio where guests can have snacks or dine (in the evenings the candlelit tables are set with linens). (Note that the restaurant is closed on Mondays from November to April.) Upstairs there are seven cozy bedrooms where the English motif is carried out with heavily draped half-tester beds, Oriental carpets, a decanter of sherry, and fresh flowers. Rooms are small but cozy and reminiscent of a wonderful old English inn. The location of the Pelican Inn is fabulous: only a few minutes' drive from the giant redwood grove at Muir Woods and a short walk to the ocean. Note: Reservations are needed six months in advance for weekends. Also, the pub is very busy at weekends and noise from the revelers can persist until the 11 pm closing time. *Directions:* From Hwy 101 take the Stinson Beach/Hwy 1 turnoff. At the Arco station, go left for 5 miles on Hwy 1 to Muir Beach. Pelican Inn is on the left.

PELICAN INN
Owners: Ed & Susan Cunningham
Innkeeper: Katrinka McKay
10 Pacific Way
Muir Beach, CA 94965-9729, USA
Tel: (415) 383-6000, 866-383-6005
Fax: (415) 383-3424
7 rooms, Double: $200–$240
closed Mon, Nov to Apr
Open: all year, Credit cards: MC, VS
karenbrown.com/california/pelicaninn.html

As the gold boom passed, Murphys was left to sleep under its locust and elm trees until tourists discovered its beauty and slower pace of life. A few old stone buildings survive, one housing the Old Timers' Museum filled with pioneer and Gold Rush regalia. Dunbar House, 1880 is a handsome inn with a wraparound porch where guests can sit and sip Gold Country wine or enjoy a refreshing glass of lemonade. Bob and Barbara have lavished their time and attention on making their small inn extremely comfortable. Each cozy guestroom has a fireplace, a small refrigerator with ice and a bottle of wine, and a TV with VCR hidden away in an armoire. The Sequoia Room has a king-size bed and a two-person bath. The Cedar Room, just off the downstairs parlor, is a suite offering a luxurious Jacuzzi. Upstairs, the Ponderosa Room has a king bed, large claw-foot tub, and views of the garden, and the Sugar Pine Room is a two-room suite with a private balcony. Breakfast, served in the dining room by the fire, in the century-old garden, or in the privacy of your room, includes juice spritzer, fresh fruit, scones, a main entree, and a hot beverage. An appetizer selection is offered in the afternoon. *Directions:* From Angels Camp drive 9 miles east on Hwy 4. Turn left onto Main Street, go two blocks, and turn left into Dunbar House's driveway.

DUNBAR HOUSE, 1880
Owners: Barbara & Bob Costa
271 Jones Street
Murphys, CA 95247, USA
Tel: (209) 728-2897, (800) 692-6006
Fax: (209) 728-1451
5 rooms
Double: $190–$245
Open: all year, Credit cards: all major
Select Registry
karenbrown.com/california/dunbarhouse.html

Sitting quietly on its corner lot on First Street for close to a hundred years and previously used as a family home and commercial offices, this fine old shingle-sided structure has been carefully made over in readiness for its new life as the Blackbird Inn. Resplendently renovated with a new interior in the Greene and Greene style of Arts and Crafts architecture, it provides a haven of welcome and comfort just a few minutes' walk away from the delights of downtown Napa. The sitting room with its exquisite leaded stained-glass front door, large fieldstone fireplace, comfy sofas, stained-glass accents, soft-hued lighting, and gleaming mahogany woodwork sets the tone. The eight guestrooms, five up the imposing staircase, three on the main floor, are varied in size but similar in standard and amenities. Most have gas fireplaces, two have private, albeit small, decks, and half have Jacuzzi tubs. All are decorated in a pleasing Craftsman style—many pieces of furniture were handcrafted by the owner. Copia, the impressive food, wine, and garden exposition, is about a mile away on First Street. Spend your days exploring the Napa Valley and return to the inn to relax with a glass of wine and delicious hors d'oeuvres. *Directions:* Take the downtown Napa exit from Hwy 29 and turn left on Jefferson. Blackbird Inn is located at the corner of First and Jefferson.

BLACKBIRD INN
Innkeeper: Michael Harris
1755 First Street
Napa, CA 94559, USA
Tel: (707) 226-2450, (888) 567-9811
Fax: (707) 258-6391
8 rooms
Double: $135–$275
Open: all year, Credit cards: all major
karenbrown.com/california/blackbird.html

Conveniently situated just north of the town of Napa, Milliken Creek is nestled on 3 lushly wooded, secluded acres fronting onto a quiet stretch of the Napa River. Owners David Shapiro and Lisa Holt have overseen the renovation of the original coach house, constructed circa 1857 and reputedly the first stagecoach stop on the Silverado Trail. Bedrooms are accommodated in the Main and South Houses and the very private Cottage. All are similarly decorated in a modern yet casual style, and provide a mix of river views, fireplaces, private balconies, decks, and whirlpool tubs. A hot French country breakfast is served in your room each morning. In the afternoon a generous tasting of wine and cheese features some of the area's finest selections. David, a former professional musician, may even entertain you at his keyboard in front of the fireplace. Tall trees shade the gardens and fountains, and future plans call for a yoga gazebo and pool. Relax and soak up the ambiance of the inn and its slow-moving river, and sample the epicurean delights of nearby Napa Valley restaurants. *Directions:* Take the Trances exit from Hwy 29 in Napa, drive through the town, and, immediately after a left-hand turn for the Silverado Trail, bear right across the Milliken Creek Bridge (signposted Napa). Turn right at the stop sign (Silverado Trail southbound). Milliken Creek is on the right after a mile—its entrance is marked by a black sign with an "M."

MILLIKEN CREEK
Owners: Lisa Holt & David Shapiro
Manager: Nancy Nealon
1815 Silverado Trail
Napa, CA 94558, USA
Tel: (707) 255-1197, (888) 622 5775
Fax: (707) 255-3112
12 rooms, 1 cottage ($595–$1,295)
Double: $375–$650
Open: all year, Credit cards: MC, VS
karenbrown.com/california/milliken.html

Surrounded by 600 acres of vineyards, Oak Knoll Inn has an idyllic settings in the Napa Valley. You find the entry and prettily decorated front sitting room in the original stone farmhouse. Another building was added to each side to house guestrooms, each with a private entrance opening onto a wraparound deck overlooking the vineyards. Breakfast is a feast served on winter mornings in front of the stone fireplace and on warm mornings outside on the deck where you can often watch the graceful hot-air balloons as they drift silently over the vineyards. The guestrooms are luxurious in size, magnified further by the high vaulted ceilings. My favorite, number 6, has an arched window that towers to the height of the ceiling and offers a splendid view of the vineyards. Each bedroom enjoys a king-size bed, a sitting area before a fireplace, and thick stone walls, which provide efficient insulation. The bedrooms have been individually decorated with lovely, richly-hued fabrics in a traditional style. After sampling Napa Valley's many wineries, you can sit poolside with a glass of wine and enjoy the quiet and beauty of a backdrop of vineyards and the valley's gorgeous hills. *Directions:* Go north on Hwy 29 through Napa, then right on Oak Knoll Avenue, which has a left-right zigzag across Big Ranch Road. The inn is on the left.

OAK KNOLL INN
Owners: Barbara Passino & John Kuhlmann
2200 E. Oak Knoll Avenue
Napa, CA 94558, USA
Tel: (707) 255-2200, Fax: (707) 255-2296
4 rooms
Double: $250–$450
Open: all year, Credit cards: MC, VS
karenbrown.com/california/oakknollinn.html

La Residence is an inn that has grown around The Mansion—a beautiful Gothic-revival home built in the 1870s. In later years, additions more Victorian in style changed the appearance of the house. Nine rooms, housed in the original mansion, are dramatic in their decor, which blends well with the grand feeling of the home. Rooms vary from cozy, top-floor rooms tucked under slanted ceilings to spacious and elegant accommodations with fireplaces on the first floor. The 11 rooms in French barn, are well designed and commodious, each enjoying a private bath, fireplace, and French doors opening onto a patio or balcony. These bedrooms are handsomely decorated with pine antiques imported from France and England and Laura Ashley prints. Four beautiful, very private, suites decked out in lovely French decor are found on the edge of the vineyard. Breakfast is served in the French-country dining room with tables set before a blazing fire. Relax by the pool after a day of sightseeing. The splash of large fountains and a substantial planting of trees shield you from road noise from the nearby highway. *Directions:* Travel north on Hwy 29 through Napa. Take the first right turn after the Salvador intersection onto Howard Lane that winds back south to the inn.

LA RESIDENCE
Owners: David Jackson & Craig Claussen
4066 Howard Lane
Napa, CA 94558, USA
Tel: (707) 253-0337, (800) 253-9203
Fax: (707) 253-0382
24 rooms
Double: $225–$375
Open: all year, Credit cards: all major
karenbrown.com/california/laresidence.html

Chuck and Elaine Matroni are always ready to serve, spoil, and pamper guests in their three-story, soft-blue Queen Ann Victorian home, tiered on a hillside above gardens and lawn cascading down to the babbling Deer Creek. The parlors and dining room are typically Victorian with their formal furnishings and Oriental accents. The country kitchen is the heart of the home, where guests gather to chat to the innkeepers as they prepare a gourmet, multi-course breakfast, which is served either in the dining room or outside on the verandah. Deer Creek has five guestrooms, each named for the women who have owned the home since 1860. Sheryl's Room is a cheerful front corner room whose iron bed is set on an Oriental carpet. Lela's Room boasts a dramatic four-poster bed and a claw-foot tub framed in an alcove, romantically draped with lace curtains. Winifred's Room features a canopied bed, an in-room claw-foot tub, and a private deck. The antique oak furniture in Ida's Room is lovely against a floral backdrop and the trundle bed accompanying the white and brass day bed comfortably accommodates an additional person. Elaine's Room enjoys a lace-draped bed, a large Roman tub, and a private patio overlooking the grounds and the creek. *Directions:* Exit Hwy 20/49 at Broad Street, traveling south across the creek, and turn left on Nevada Street.

DEER CREEK INN
Owners: Elaine & Chuck Matroni
116 Nevada Street
Nevada City, CA 95959, USA
Tel: (530) 265-0363, (800) 655-0363
Fax: (530) 265-0980
5 rooms
Double: $125–$225
Open: all year, Credit cards: all major
karenbrown.com/california/deercreekinn.html

When gold was discovered, Nevada City became an affluent boomtown. It remains prosperous-looking today, its beautifully restored downtown area full of tempting restaurants and inviting shops. Just beyond Broad Street's historic shopping district, enclosed within a mature garden of long rolling lawns, tidy bushes, and flowers, sits Grandmere's Inn, a stately Colonial Revival home built in 1856 for Aaron Sargent, a U.S. Senator, and his suffragette wife, Ellen, whose friend, Susan B. Anthony, often stayed here. Sargent authored the bill that eventually gave women the right to vote. Now Grandmere's is a lovely country inn decorated with flair, and each of the rooms has a very different personality. The Senator's Chambers is a delightful ground-floor suite with a lovely bedroom and a separate parlor with sofa drawn before the fireplace. The Diplomat's Suite is a spacious upstairs bedroom with a sitting area. Ellen's Garden Room, a romantic downstairs hideaway, has a private garden entry, light, airy decor, and lots of room. In the morning the aroma of coffee fills the air and at 9 o'clock a full coarse breakfast is served in the spacious dining room. Enjoy the romance of Nevada City by taking a carriage ride round the town. *Directions:* From Hwy 49 exit at Broad Street, turn left, and the inn is at the top of the street, on the left.

GRANDMERE'S INN
Manager: Diane Barham
449 Broad Street
Nevada City, CA 95959, USA
Tel: (530) 265-4660, Fax: (530) 265-4561
3 rooms, 3 suites
Double: $156–$220
Open: all year, Credit cards: all major
karenbrown.com/california/grandmeres.html

Heavy iron gates swing open magically, allowing you to enter a world far removed from the everyday activity of Oakhurst, a town just to the south of Yosemite National Park. You enter through the château's heavy doors, cross a cool, flagged limestone foyer, and step down into a stunning living room opening onto a circular tower room where a grand piano sits beneath a whimsically frescoed ceiling. Doors open to reveal a sunny breakfast room and a tiny chapel. A spiraling stone staircase leads up to the individually decorated bedrooms named for herbs and flowers: Saffron has an enormous ebony bed and black-marble fireplace; Lavender is sunny in colors of periwinkle blue and lavender; and Elderberry is cool in blue and white. Each of the splendid bedrooms has a wood-burning fireplace, goose-down duvet, hidden CD player, luxurious bathroom with a deep soaking tub (many large enough for two), the finest toiletries, thick towels, and the softest of robes. In the evening, walk across the garden, by the swimming pool, to the Elderberry House Restaurant where the château's owner, Erna Kubin-Clanin, presents a spectacular fixed-price six-course dinner. A beautiful new villa offers two luxurious bedrooms. *Directions:* From the center of Oakhurst take Hwy 41 toward Fresno. As the road climbs the hill, turn right at Victoria Lane and drive in through the wrought-iron gates.

CHATEAU DU SUREAU
Owner: Erna Kubin-Clanin
48688 Victoria Lane
P.O. Box 577, Oakhurst, CA 93644, USA
Tel: (559) 683-6860, Fax: (559) 683-0800
10 rooms, 1 villa ($2,800)
Double: $410–$550*
*Service charge: 12%
Closed: first two weeks of Jan, Credit cards: all major
Relais & Chateaux
karenbrown.com/california/chateaudusureau.html

Occidental nestles between the rugged Sonoma coast and the vineyards of the Russian River valley. The Inn at Occidental, a block up from Main Street, dates from 1877. From the wraparound porch you enter the living room whose elegant furnishings are set in front of an inviting fireplace. The dining room where breakfast is served is located in the wine cellar. Breakfast offerings include freshly baked pastries, seasonal fruit, and such tempting delights as orange pancakes. Beautiful fir floors accented with lovely Oriental carpets are found throughout the public rooms. Each guestroom's decor echoes the colors in the original art displayed in the room and feather beds topped with down comforters assure a wonderful night's sleep. Recently remodeled and with an addition of an entire new suite of rooms, the inn now has 16 rooms with appealing amenities such as a romantic fireplace, a hot tub in a private garden oasis, or a luxurious spa tub. A neighboring cottage is perfect for a family or long-term stay. Conference facilities are available in a downstairs room with English oak furnishings and stone fireplace. Jerry, Tina and their staff make this inn very special. *Directions:* One hour north of San Francisco. Take Hwy 101 to Hwy 116 west to Sebastopol then take the Bodega Hwy west for 6 miles toward Bodega Bay to the Bohemian Hwy to Occidental.

INN AT OCCIDENTAL
Owners: Tina and Jerry Wolsborn
P.O. Box 857, Occidental, CA 95465, USA
Tel: (707) 874-1047, (800) 522-6324
Fax: (707) 874-1078
16 rooms, 1 cottage ($560–$650)
Double: $225–$320
No restaurant, but special wine-maker dinners
Open: all year, Credit cards: all major
Select Registry
karenbrown.com/california/innatoccidental.html

Sandwiched between the busier resorts of Monterey and Carmel, Pacific Grove has managed to avoid much of their more touristy ambiance and retains the air of being an inviting Victorian summer retreat. The Gosby House Inn is a perfect place to retreat to, with certainly a lot more fun and frolic than in days gone by when it was the summer home of a stern Methodist family. While the decor is decidedly Victorian in flavor, it has an air of whimsy and fun that banishes all formal stuffiness: teddy bears are posed rakishly on each bed. The bedrooms are scattered upstairs and down, some have garden entrances and two deluxe rooms occupy an adjacent clapboard house tucked behind the pretty garden. Over half the bedrooms have fireplaces and all have well designed and decorated bathrooms. Each room is appealingly decorated in soft colors and many benefit from the romantic touch of antique beds. Our particular favorites are 21 a garden cottage, and 22 and 23 in the Carriage House with spa tubs and huge decks. Before you step out for dinner, enjoy hors d'oeuvres and wine in the living room. A full breakfast is set out downstairs between 8 and 10 every morning. *Directions:* Take Hwy 1 to Hwy 68 west to Pacific Grove. Continue on Forest Avenue to Lighthouse Avenue, turn left, and go three blocks.

GOSBY HOUSE INN
Innkeeper: Kalena Mittelman
643 Lighthouse Avenue
Pacific Grove, CA 93950, USA
Tel: (831) 375-1287, (800) 527-8828
Fax: (831) 655-9621
22 rooms
Double: $100–$200
Open: all year, Credit cards: all major
karenbrown.com/california/gosbyhouse.html

The Green Gables Inn is sensationally positioned overlooking Monterey Bay. This romantic, half-timbered, Queen Anne-style mansion with many interesting dormers is as inviting inside as out. The living room and dining room have comfortable arrangements of sofas and chairs placed to maximize your enjoyment of the view. Many of the upstairs bedrooms, set under steeply slanting beamed ceilings with romantic diamond-paned casement windows, offer ocean views. While the Garret room does not have an ocean view, it is the coziest of hideaways. All but one of the upstairs bedrooms share bathrooms. The elegant ground-floor suite has a sitting room and fireplace, while the rooms in the adjacent carriage house all have fireplaces, sitting areas, and private bathrooms. As a guest at the Green Gables Inn you will certainly not perish from hunger or thirst—beverages are available all day, goodies are readily at hand in the cookie jar, and wine and hors d'oeuvres appear in the evening. Breakfast, too, is no disappointment: it's a hearty buffet of fruit, homemade breads, and a hot egg dish. *Directions:* From Hwy 1 take the Pacific Grove-Del Monte exit. As you go through the tunnel, Del Monte becomes Lighthouse Avenue, which you follow into Pacific Grove. Go right one block and you are on Ocean View Boulevard—the inn is on the corner at Fifth Street.

GREEN GABLES INN
Innkeeper: Lucia Root
301 Ocean View Avenue
Pacific Grove, CA 93950, USA
Tel: (831) 375-2095, (800) 722-1774
Fax: (831) 375-5437
11 rooms
Double: $120–$275
Open: all year, Credit cards: all major
karenbrown.com/california/greengablesinn.html

The Inn at 213 Seventeen Mile Drive sits on the tip of the Monterey Peninsula, an area renowned for its natural beauty and winter visitors, the Monarch butterflies. A classic example of a 1920s Craftsman-style house, it has been lovingly restored by its current owners, the Greening family, who spared no effort to maintain the integrity of the original building, renovating the extensive redwood paneling and wood floors, installing wonderful en-suite bathrooms, and purchasing complementary antique furniture. There are seven delightful rooms in the main house, three at the front (Blue Heron, Sanderling and Turnstone) having views (albeit distant) of the Pacific Ocean. My favorite, Blue Heron, has its own private sun porch and balcony. Tucked away in the gardens at the back of the house are four guest cottages. I particularly liked Guillemot with its high-pitched redwood ceiling and huge window seat. Breakfast is served in the dining room, the old billiard room, or, weather permitting, on the patio. Here you are minutes by car from Pebble Beach, Carmel, and the delights of Monterey with its Cannery Row and Aquarium. Make your choice or simply soak in the hot tub and curl up in front of the sitting-room fire. *Directions:* Take Hwy 1 to Hwy 68 west to Pacific Grove. Continue on Forest Avenue to Lighthouse Avenue, turn left, and go nine blocks to the inn.

INN AT 213 SEVENTEEN MILE DRIVE
Owners: Glynis & Tony Greening
Manager: Sally Goss
213 Seventeen Mile Drive
Pacific Grove, CA 93950, USA
Tel: (831) 642-9514, (800) 526-5666
Fax: (831) 642-9546
14 rooms
Double: $145–$240
Open: all year, Credit cards: all major
karenbrown.com/california/seventeen.html

Casa Cody, a moderately priced hotel in the heart of Palm Springs, although quite simple, stands out like a gem. There is a nostalgic, old-fashioned comfort to this one-story, pink-stuccoed building with turquoise trim, the oldest continuously functioning hotel in Palm Springs. It had fallen into a state of hopeless-looking disrepair until bought by Therese Hayes and Frank Tysen, who restored it with hard work, lots of imagination, and much love. The Casa Cody once again blossomed into an appealing small hotel with a nice choice of accommodations ranging from a standard double to a spacious two-bedroom, two-bath suite. Many of the rooms have the added bonuses of kitchenettes and fireplaces. The interior decor exudes a fresh, clean "Desert" look, with a southwest color scheme and handmade furniture. This friendly, comfortable inn is a remarkable value, especially the reasonably priced studio units such as 1, 2, 3, 4, 21, and 23, which have both fireplaces and well-equipped kitchens. We loved the 1920s doll-house-like, one-bedroom cottage tucked in under the trees in the corner of the property. Our favorite is the two-bedroom Old Adobe House, where Charlie Chaplin used to stay. *Directions:* Drive south through Palm Springs on Palm Canyon Drive. Turn right on Tahquitz-McCallum Road, then left on Cahuilla Road, and Casa Cody is half a block along on the right.

CASA CODY
Owners: Therese Hayes & Frank Tysen
Innkeeper: Elissa Goforth
175 South Cahuilla Road
Palm Springs, CA 92262, USA
Tel: (760) 320-9346, (800) 231-2639
Fax: (760) 325-8610
20 rooms, 3 cottages
Double: $89–$349
Open: all year, Credit cards: all major
karenbrown.com/california/casacody.html

Along with the scent of flowers, a gentle, friendly ambiance permeates the air of the Desert Hills Hotel, enhanced by the charming graciousness of your hostess, Joanne Petty, who built the hotel with her husband in 1956. The location is excellent—an easy walk to the heart of Old Palm Springs yet snuggled up against the rugged San Jacinto Mountains. The hotel does not have an antique ambiance, but rather a timeless theme of restful, pleasing, pastel desert colors. The tidy, attractive guestrooms (most with kitchenettes) are constantly upgraded and maintained in tip top condition. Excellent lighting, quality mattresses, and spotless bathrooms further attest to outstanding management. The rooms face a lush lawn and well-tended gardens surrounding a pretty pool. From the outside the one-story Desert Hills looks like most of the other hotels of similar vintage—you only realize its uniqueness when you see that every detail shows loving care. The Desert Hills is not a flashy, trendy hotel that would appeal to those looking for action, but rather the old-fashioned kind of tranquil oasis where you can settle in for an extended time, relaxing by the pool, hearing the wind whisper through the palm trees, and feeling like a friend of the family. Guests enjoy Continental breakfast, outdoor barbecues, a hot Jacuzzi, and bicycles. *Directions:* Turn west off Palm Canyon on Arenas and go six blocks—the hotel is on the northwest corner of Arenas.

DESERT HILLS HOTEL
Owners: Joanne & Alan Petty
601 West Arenas Road
Palm Springs, CA 92262, USA
Tel: (760) 325-2777, (800) 350-2527
Fax: (760) 325-6423
14 rooms
Double: $90–$250*
*Breakfast not included
Open: all year, Credit cards: all major
karenbrown.com/california/deserthillshotel.html

As you enter the large wrought-iron gates of the Ingleside Inn, you have the impression of being a guest on a private estate. This is not surprising, since the Ingleside Inn was once the home of the Humphrey Birge family, manufacturers of the Pierce Arrow automobile. Although the hotel is located in the heart of Palm Springs, it is an oasis of tranquillity. The parklike grounds are surrounded by a high adobe wall and the San Jacinto Mountains rise steeply behind the hotel, forming a dramatic backdrop. A pretty pool and gazebo highlight the front lawn. Some of the guestrooms open off an inner courtyard, while others are nestled in nearby cottages. Each room is individually decorated with antiques. All have whirlpool tubs, coffee makers, and refrigerators stocked with complimentary light snacks and juices. Many rooms have the added bonus of wood-burning fireplaces. Breakfast is served either on the verandah, poolside, or on your private patio. The owner of Ingleside Inn, Melvyn Haber, also owns the famous Melvyn's restaurant located next to the lobby. In the evening the restaurant traffic intrudes somewhat upon the solitude, but it is wonderfully convenient to have such an excellent restaurant so close at hand. *Directions:* From Los Angeles on Hwy 10 East exit to Hwy 111 and proceed for 12 miles. Turn right on Ramon Road.

❄ 🏧 ☎ 🧍 👫 🏇 ⛾ P ⑪ ≈ ⌨ ♿

INGLESIDE INN
Owner: Melvyn Haber
200 West Ramon Road
Palm Springs, CA 92264, USA
Tel: (760) 325-0046, (800) 772-6655
Fax: (760) 325-0710
30 rooms, 2 cottages
Double: $95–$395*
 *Breakfast not included
Open: all year, Credit cards: all major
karenbrown.com/california/inglesideinn.html

The magic of the desert can best be captured on balmy, starlit nights from the bougainvillea-shrouded patios of intimate hotels with the laid-back style and grace of yesterday. A rare example of such perfection is the Korakia Pensione, a 1920s Moorish-style villa just four blocks from the heart of Palm Springs, which was rescued from dilapidation by Doug Smith, an architect specializing in restoring historic buildings. With a backdrop of the San Jacinto Mountains, this delightful inn has the flavor of Morocco mingled with the romance of the Greek islands: simple whitewashed walls, Oriental carpets, handmade furniture, lovely natural fabrics, antiques, Moroccan fountains, fragrant fruit trees, torches blazing by the pools, and bougainvillea-draped archways create a stunning ambiance. Bedrooms mostly offer lots of privacy and are found around two swimming pools either in the original Moroccan-style pension or across the street in the Mediterranean-style villa. For a treat, request one of our favorite rooms, the Nash House or the Artist Studio. Private dinners are available Thursday through Sunday nights, served either in the room or poolside, and you can also enjoy old black-and-white movies outdoors on a Saturday night, a relaxing massage, Moroccan tea in the afternoon, and a full breakfast on the sun-drenched patio. *Directions:* Turn west off Palm Canyon on Arenas, go four blocks, and turn south on Patencio Road.

❄ ▥ 🖃 ☎ ⅋ ⅋⅋ ⅋ 🍸 P ≈ ⅋ ⅋

KORAKIA PENSIONE
Owner: Doug Smith
Manager: Flor Schectel
257 South Patencio Road
Palm Springs, CA 92262, USA
Tel: (760) 864-6411, Fax: (760) 864-4147
27 rooms, 15 cottages, 2 houses
Double: $139–$595
Dinner available Thur-Sun
Open: all year, Credit cards: MC, VS
karenbrown.com/california/korakia.html

Once a sleepy desert town, Palm Springs was discovered in the 1920s by glamorous movie stars who made it their secret hideaway. This balmy paradise also captivated the heart of Samuel Untermyer, a New Yorker and famous anti-trust lawyer of the time, who bought a beautiful estate, The Willows, snuggled next to the mountains just a few blocks from the center of town, where in winter he entertained many distinguished friends. The home remained a private residence until opening in 1996 as a deluxe small hotel after a total renovation that returned it to its former elegance and successfully captured the ambiance of the 1930s. The clay-colored building with wrought-iron trim and red-tiled roof is softened by a profusion of greenery and brightened by a cheerful array of colorful flowers. A pool nestles on the lower garden area—but an equally inviting nook for a refreshing drink is a beautiful flagstone terrace enclosed on one side by a wall of natural rock with a cascading waterfall. Every lovely guestroom has its own personality, with the price basically reflecting its size. The rates are expensive, but you will feel like guests in a private home displaying the opulence of a bygone era. *Directions:* Located in the heart of Palm Springs. From either Palm Canyon Drive or Indian Canyon Drive, take Tahquitz Canyon Way west. In a few blocks the street dead-ends. The Willows is at the end of the road on your right.

THE WILLOWS
Owners: Tracy Conrad & Paul Marut
412 West Tahquitz Canyon Way
Palm Springs, CA 92262, USA
Tel: (760) 320-0771, (800) 966-9597
Fax: (760) 320-0780
8 rooms
Double: $295–$575
Open: all year, Credit cards: all major
karenbrown.com/california/thewillows.html

Lake La Quinta Inn is a stunning, boutique-style inn: a two-story, creamy-beige stucco building that hints of the romance of a French château with its steeply pitched slate roof, whimsical chimneys, and jaunty dormer windows. The inn is not in the heart of Palm Springs, but in La Quinta, one of the most opulent of the wealthy towns catering to ardent golfers who come to play on some of the most outstanding courses in the world. As you step inside the inn, the tasteful, refined elegance and the outstanding warmth of welcome give the feeling that you are a guest in a friend's home. The living room, with French doors opening onto the terrace, which overlooks the small lake, has comfortable chairs and sofas cozily grouped around a fireplace. The splendid dining room also looks out to the lake. There are only 13 guestrooms, varying in size from a standard room to a super-deluxe suite. Although each of the luxuriously appointed bedrooms has its own personality, they all are similar in mood with fireplaces, balconies or terraces facing the lake, splendid large bathrooms with double sinks, and top-quality linens. You might never want to leave the beautiful pool tucked in the garden, but if you are a golfer, Tim can arrange preferred tee times for you—there are over 100 golf courses to choose from. *Directions:* Take Interstate 10 to Washington and turn right. Drive 6 miles and turn left on Lake La Quinta drive after 47th Avenue.

LAKE LA QUINTA INN   New
Innkeeper: Tim Ellis
78-120 Caleo Bay
Palm Springs-La Quinta, CA 92253, USA
Tel: (760) 564-7332, (888) 226-4546
Fax: (760) 564-6356
13 rooms
Double: $189–$499
Open: all year, Credit cards: all major
karenbrown.com/california/lakelaquinta.html

When the last of Janet Marangi's four children left the nest, she fulfilled her dream of opening a bed and breakfast. Just two blocks from the colorful center of South Pasadena, she found an 1895 Victorian-style farmhouse, now painted a pretty buttercup yellow, accented by white trim. A white picket fence and encloses a perfectly groomed front lawn. Rose bushes line the fence and border the path leading to the spacious front porch. Janet's goal was to instill a totally comfortable, homey ambiance, and she has succeeded admirably. The furnishings are mostly pieces lovingly collected over the years by Janet while browsing for antiques. The living room is painted a rich green, which sets off the traditional furniture and rich floral fabrics. The bedrooms are appealingly decorated, each representing an artistic period. Niceties such as fresh roses, water, port, European candy, and English towels are found in all rooms. The Eighteenth-Century English is a cheerful room with king-sized canopy bed, old-fashioned rose-patterned wallpaper, antique desk, and white lace curtains. Of the ten rooms, five are in the adjacent cottage: three are two-room suites with fireplaces, Jacuzzi tubs, and canopy beds. You can easily travel into into Los Angeles on the light rail. *Directions:* Fifteen minutes from downtown Los Angeles. Take Hwy 110 (Pasadena Freeway), exiting at the Orange Grove off-ramp. Turn right on Orange Grove, go two blocks, and turn left on Magnolia.

❄ ⚓ 🍺 ✎ ☎ 🚶 👫 🐎 🍸 P 🐕

ARTISTS' INN
Owner: Janet Marangi
1038 Magnolia Street
Pasadena (South), CA 91030, USA
Tel: (626) 799-5668, (888) 799-5668
Fax: (626) 799-3678
10 rooms
Double: $120–$205
Open: all year, Credit cards: all major
karenbrown.com/california/theartistsinn.html

Built in the 1880s, this lovely three-story home with dormer windows and wraparound porch set on a lush lawn shaded by mature trees is just 12 minutes from downtown Los Angeles. On one side of the entry you find the cozy library decorated in dark greens and plaids looking out onto the swimming pool and on the other side, through French doors, is the formal living room with its piano and sofas set in front of the fireplace. Central to the living room, the hand-carved wood fireplace opens up at the back so that it also warms the adjacent breakfast room. It is fun to peek into the butler's pantry just beyond the dining room: its tin roof is original to the home and its shelves display a lovely collection of Christmas Spode. The Prince Albert and English Holiday rooms are on the second floor and each has lovely old wooden floors, queen beds, and a private bathroom. The third floor boasts three romantic bedrooms tucked under the eaves. Thoughtful amenities like a refrigerator stocked with complimentary refreshments, cookies, and brownies as well as in-room touches such as large fluffy towels, robes, fresh flowers, and a basket of fruit make you feel very welcome and cared for. *Directions:* From either the 134, 210, or 110 freeways, take the Orange Grove Avenue exit. The Bissell House is located on Pasadena's historical Millionaires' Row on the southwest corner of Orange Grove and Columbia. The entrance is on Columbia.

BISSELL HOUSE
Owners: Russ, Leonore & Ivis Butcher
201 Orange Grove Avenue
Pasadena (South), CA 91030, USA
Tel: (626) 441-3535, (800) 441-3530
Fax: (626) 441-3671
5 rooms
Double: $140–$185
Open: all year, Credit cards: all major
karenbrown.com/california/bissellhouse.html

Justin Winery has a glorious setting, tucked in gently rolling hills 17 miles west of Paso Robles. The winery complex (consisting of the tasting room, the Baldwins' home, reception, boutique, restaurant, and guestrooms) is beautiful and the setting is serene. The attractive wooden buildings are painted a dove gray, accented by white trim, and set off to perfection by lush lawn and well-tended gardens. The three suites (the Tuscany, the Provence, and the Sussex) combine the luxury and amenities of a five-star hotel with the friendliness of a family-run inn. The suites feature European antiques, fine fabrics, feather beds, imported linens, down comforters, frescoed ceilings, flower-filled windowboxes, marble bathrooms with hydro spas, and wood-burning fireplaces. The Sussex suite (the largest of the three) opens onto the garden while the Provence and Tuscany suites have balconies where you can sip a glass of wine while looking over the vineyards. Guests also have the use of a pretty swimming pool tucked in the garden. Amazingly for such a small inn, there is a restaurant, Deborah's Dining Room, which is open every night. In this cozy, elegantly decorated dining room a gourmet set dinner is served nightly. *Directions:* From Hwy 101, at Paso Robles, exit at 24th Street. Go west (24 becomes Naciemiento Lake Road) for 7 miles and bear left onto Chimney Rock Road.

JUST INN
Owners: Deborah & Justin Baldwin
11680 Chimney Rock Road
Paso Robles, CA 93446, USA
Tel: (805) 238-6932, (800) 726-0049
Fax: (805) 238-7382
3 rooms
Double: $245–$295
Open: all year, Credit cards: all major
karenbrown.com/california/justinn.html

As in the best bed and breakfasts, Deborah and Douglas Thomsen welcome guests with genuine hospitality. Instead of sharing the house with their hosts, guests have their own "home", a carriage house from which they can come and go at leisure. The two bedrooms are found off the western-motif living room—a perfect setup for two couples traveling together. One of the bedrooms has the same western motif while the other sports a Ralph Lauren look with bold-patterned floral fabrics and dark wicker furniture. Each room enjoys its own sitting area in addition to sharing the central living room. Everything looks decorator-perfect, which is not surprising as Deborah was an interior designer before she and Douglas left the hectic Orange County lifestyle to build their dream home. You wind uphill to the main house and as you approach, a gate slowly swings open and you continue on up to the large, elegant, two-story, gabled manor constructed of wood, stucco, and stone. Just steps away is the guest house. Deborah not only prepares a full breakfast each morning, but also delights in assisting her guests plan their sightseeing—she helped us with our wine itinerary of the Paso Robles area and has lots of great information on the nearby coastal region. *Directions:* From Hwy 101, at Paso Robles take Hwy 46 west for 8 miles. Turn right on Vineyard Drive for 2½ miles. The entrance is on your left.

ORCHARD HILL FARM
Owners: Deborah & Douglas Thomsen
5415 Vineyard Drive
Paso Robles, CA 93446, USA
Tel: (805) 239-9680, Fax: (805) 239-9684
2 rooms
Double: $145–$185
Open: all year, Credit cards: all major
karenbrown.com/california/orchardhillfarm.html

The newly built Summerwood Inn, with its nostalgic charm of a lovely country English-style home, makes an ideal choice if you want to stop en route between San Francisco and Southern California. Its setting is superb—nestled in a spectacularly beautiful area of gently rolling hills, either covered with vineyards or dotted with oak trees. You enter the long, low, white frame home with its old-fashioned wraparound porch and overhanging roof through large double doors into a spacious entry hall. To the left is a formal dining room, to the right is a sun-filled living room—bright and cheerful with sofas and chairs covered in colorful English-style fabrics. In the morning guests can choose from five items on the breakfast menu. Wine and cheese are served in the afternoon, and coffee or tea and a dessert at night. The guestrooms, all large and individually decorated, have a mood of comfortable elegance. Each bedroom has either a private terrace or balcony that looks out over the Summerwood vineyards (my personal favorites are the rooms in the rear that have the most expansive views) and a beautifully appointed bathroom. All of the rooms have their own gas log fireplaces. The adjacent Summerwood Winery has a gift shop and offers wine tasting. The inn makes a good base for visiting Hearst Castle, which is just a short drive away by a scenic road. *Directions:* From Hwy 101, at Paso Robles take Hwy 46 west for 1¼ miles. Summerwood Inn is on your right.

SUMMERWOOD INN
Innkeeper: Andrea Boatman
2130 Arbor Road
Paso Robles, CA 93447, USA
Tel: (805) 227-1111, Fax: (805) 227-1112
9 rooms
Double: $195–$345
Open: all year, Credit cards: all major
karenbrown.com/california/summerwoodinn.html

People simply driving by the Inn at Playa del Rey would probably not be drawn inside by the inn's exterior and location on a busy road. However, this newly constructed Cape Cod-style inn, just three blocks from the beach, backs onto the Ballona Wetlands, a 350-acre bird sanctuary, and was beautifully designed to complement rather than compete with the setting and natural surroundings. Large picture windows frame a panorama of a grassy expanse of wetlands and distant marina. A narrow channel banded by an inviting bike path weaves through the wetlands, often navigated by tall-masted boats charting a course to the ocean. The decor is light and airy, with pine furnishings matched with lovely fabrics and attractive wallpapers. The spacious guestrooms are each individual in style and floor plan, and maximize any opportunity to incorporate views. The choice rooms are, of course, those at the back of the inn with unobstructed views of the wetlands. Rooms at the front are less expensive and enjoy the morning light while dual-glazed and shuttered windows minimize the noise of traffic. Public areas include an outdoor courtyard and a lovely breakfast room and living room running the length of the back of the building, banked by French doors. *Directions:* Exit the San Diego Freeway (405) onto the Marina Freeway (90) and travel west toward Marina del Rey. The freeway ends at a stoplight at Culver Blvd. Turn left and drive west for 2 miles to the inn.

INN AT PLAYA DEL REY
Owner: Susan Zolla
Innkeeper: Heather Suskin
435 Culver Boulevard
Playa del Rey, CA 90293, USA
Tel: (310) 574-1920, Fax: (310) 574-9920
21 rooms
Double: $150–$350
Open: all year, Credit cards: all major
karenbrown.com/california/innatplayadelrey.html

The East Brother Light Station, sitting snugly on its own tiny island, dates back to 1873 when it was built to guide ships through a 2-mile-wide strait connecting San Francisco and San Pablo Bays. Adjoining the tower beacon, a small house with gingerbread trim was built for the lightkeepers and their families. This nostalgic lighthouse was doomed for destruction until a group of concerned citizens banded together in 1979, raised the funds, and rescued it. As a boy, one of the saviors, Walter Fanning, spent many happy hours at the light station, where his grandfather was the lightkeeper. Today guests enjoy the island in far more comfortable circumstances than the keepers of old. Guests are brought by boat in the afternoon, treated to a champagne tour and delicious four-course dinner with wines, popovers and coffee in a morning and a full breakfast. There are five pleasantly decorated guestrooms, all with a view of the bay. The innkeepers, Carolyn and Curt, live on the island, prepare the meals, and graciously tend to the needs of their guests. Because all the water is caught from rainfall and is limited, only guests staying more than one night may use the showers. *Directions:* The East Brother Light Station, located in San Pablo Bay, is reached by boat. When you call for reservations, ask for further information.

EAST BROTHER LIGHT STATION
Innkeepers: Captain Curt & First Mate Carolyn
117 Park Place
Point Richmond (San Francisco Bay), CA 94801, USA
Tel: (510) 233-2385, Fax: none
5 rooms
Double: $290–$410*
 *Includes breakfast & dinner with wine
Restaurant: for guests only
Open: all year, Thur to Sun, Credit cards: all major
karenbrown.com/california/eastbrother.html

The known history of the Rancho Santa Fe property dates back to 1845 when an 8,842-acre land grant was given to Juan Maria Osuna. In 1906 the Santa Fe Railroad purchased the land grant, changed the name to Rancho Santa Fe, and planted millions of eucalyptus seedlings with the idea of growing wood for railroad ties. The project failed, so the railroad decided instead to develop a planned community and built a lovely Spanish-style guesthouse for prospective homebuyers. This became the nucleus for what is now the Inn at Rancho Santa Fe and houses the lounge, dining rooms, offices, and a few guestrooms. The lounge is extremely appealing, like a beautiful living room in a private home, with a large fireplace, comfortable seating, impressive floral arrangements, and a roaring fire. The dining rooms have a cozy atmosphere. The grounds are lovely, filled with flowers and shaded by fragrant eucalyptus trees. Here you find our favorite rooms tucked away in cottages, ranging in size from a snug queen-bedded room with private patio (a standard room) to a luxurious three-bedroom house. We especially loved the rooms with a private patio and fireplace, though have to admit we were smitten by room 133, a tiny little cottage. Slip away to the inn's beach house in nearby Del Mar or enjoy the pool and tennis courts on the property. *Directions:* From San Diego go north for 25 miles on I-5, take the Lomas Santa Fe Drive turnoff east, and travel 4-2/10 miles to the inn.

INN AT RANCHO SANTA FE
Owner: Duncan Royce Hadden
5951 Linea del Cielo at Paseo Delicia
P.O. Box 869, Rancho Santa Fe, CA 92067, USA
Tel: (858) 756-1131, (800) 843-4661
Fax: (858) 759-1604
77 rooms
Double: $185–$695*
*Breakfast not included: $10–$15
Open: all year, Credit cards: all major
karenbrown.com/california/innatranchosantafe.html

Rancho Valencia Resort is a luxurious Relais & Châteaux hotel tucked away in the hills above Rancho Santa Fe minutes from the picturesque seaside town of Del Mar. This tranquil, secluded hideaway offers privacy, relaxation, and recreation on a very intimate scale. Sports enthusiasts love it here, for the resort has 18 tennis courts and privileges at exclusive private golf clubs. Garden paths bordered by an abundance of flowers wind through the grounds to the 26 casitas scattered throughout the property. One is a luxurious three-bedroom home while the rest are either spacious studios or suites. All have cathedral ceilings with exposed beams, lovely fireplaces, plantation-shuttered windows, and French doors leading to private garden patios. The heart of the property is the clubhouse with its central courtyard patios set with tables amidst terra-cotta pots overflowing with flowering plants. Rancho Valencia's signature restaurant offers casual, elegant dining inside and alfresco dining on the tiered terrace overlooking the tennis courts and the valley. *Directions:* From I-5 in Del Mar, take the Via de la Valle Road east to El Camino Real to San Dieguito Road east and follow signs to the resort.

RANCHO VALENCIA RESORT
Director: Michael Ullman
5921 Valencia Circle
P.O. Box 9126, Rancho Santa Fe, CA 92067, USA
Tel: (858) 756-1123, (800) 548-3664
Fax: (858) 756-0165
49 rooms, Double: $470–$1,420*
* *Breakfast not included: $18*
Relais & Chateaux
Open: all year, Credit cards: all major
karenbrown.com/california/ranchovalencia.html

Tiffany House is a pretty, dove-gray Victorian set back behind a white picket fence. From the formal parlor decorated in 1850s furniture and rich hues of dark blue, a staircase leads to three guestrooms in the main house. The Victorian Rose Room is dressed in colors of greens, mauves, and blacks, reminiscent of the Victorian period, and a claw-foot tub is staged dramatically in the alcove of the turret with distant but unobstructed views of Mount Lassen. Off the landing to the right is the attractive, light, and airy Oak Room whose colors of red, white, and blue complement the nostalgic Americana theme. This room has an inviting sitting area tucked under the eaves and overlooks the peaceful back garden. The Tierra Room is a pretty, restful room with its white iron bed and delicate blue-and-white prints all set under the delightful angles and eaves of the roofline. Accessed off the back garden patio with its own private entrance is Lavinia's Cottage, a light, airy, and spacious room with pine walls, a romantic, high iron bed, and an in-room Jacuzzi. From the corner sitting area an expanse of paned windows gives a lovely view of Mount Lassen. There is a charming garden with a romantic gazebo, and on a lower terrace, a splendid large swimming pool. *Directions:* From I-5, travel west on Lake Boulevard for 8/10 mile to Market Street. Go south on Market. Turn right at the first street, Benton Drive, then right again at the next street, Barbara Road.

❄ ☕ 🚼 💳 ⫟ 🚶 P ≈ 🚣

TIFFANY HOUSE
Owners: Susan & Brady Stewart
1510 Barbara Road
Redding, CA 96003, USA
Tel: (530) 244-3225, Fax: none
3 rooms, 1 cottage
Double: $100–$150
Open: all year, Credit cards: all major
karenbrown.com/california/tiffanyhouse.html

High on a hillside above the Silverado Trail, with magnificent views south along the Napa Valley, Auberge du Soleil sets the standard for luxurious self-indulgence. The bedrooms are housed in cottages nestled amidst manicured slopes of olive trees and are decorated in Mediterranean style—terra-cotta tiles and cool earth tones are the backdrop for splashes of color from large modern artwork and brilliant yellow and vermilion soft furnishings. Beautifully appointed, oversized bathrooms are equipped with large tubs, walk-in showers, and an abundant supply of fluffy white towels and robes. After a hard day of shopping, lunching, or touring the nearby vineyards, settle down to savor the sunset on your private trellis-covered patio. Stroll the trail of modern sculptures, swim in the pool, or let the specialists at the spa soothe and pamper you. Sample the gastronomic delights of the restaurant with its sensational view matched only by the cuisine. Featuring a full range of regional delicacies, a most impressive wine list, and attentive staff, dinner is an integral part of the Auberge du Soleil experience. For those with smaller appetites the bar offers lighter fare in a cozy atmosphere or outside on the wraparound deck. *Directions:* From Napa go north on Hwy 29 towards Calistoga. At Rutherford turn right on Rutherford Crossroad, cross the Silverado Trail on a left-right jog, and take Rutherford Hill Road up the hill to Auberge du Soleil.

AUBERGE DU SOLEIL
Manager: Phillipa Perry
180 Rutherford Hill Road
Rutherford, CA 94573, USA
Tel: (707) 963-1211, (800) 348-5406
Fax: (707) 963-8764
50 rooms, Double: $550–$3,500*
*Breakfast not included: $18
Open: all year, Credit cards: all major
Relais & Chateaux
karenbrown.com/california/soleil.html

Situated in a private 250-acre valley, Meadowood, an appealing complex of sand-gray gabled wooden buildings with crisp white trim, is a resort community in a secluded setting sheltered by towering Ponderosa pines and Douglas firs. Wooded areas open up to a nine-hole golf course, croquet lawns, tennis courts, and swimming pools. With accommodation spread out across the property (lots of privacy here), guests are often driven in golf carts to the centrally located clubhouse, a three-story structure overlooking the golf course. Here you find The Restaurant, featuring wine-country cuisine in an elegant setting, The Grill, offering meals in a less formal setting, a golf shop, and conference facilities. There are 13 guestrooms in the Croquet Lodge, which overlooks the perfectly manicured croquet lawn. Other bedrooms are found in clusters of lodges scattered about the property. The atmosphere, relaxed, informal, and unpretentious, is accurately described as "California casual." The accommodations are expensive but lavishly appointed and attractively furnished, reflecting an incredible attention to every luxurious detail. Guests keep busy with a state-of-the-art health spa, hiking trails, bicycles, and a resident wine tutor. *Directions:* From Napa go north on Hwy 29 towards Calistoga. At Saint Helena turn right on Pope Street. Go left on the Silverado Trail, first right on Howell Mt. Road, and first left on Meadowood Lane.

MEADOWOOD NAPA VALLEY
Manager: Philip Kendall
900 Meadowood Lane
Saint Helena, CA 94574, USA
Tel: (707) 963-3646, (800) 458-8080
Fax: (707) 963-3532
85 rooms, Double: $515–$850*
 *Breakfast not included
Open: all year, Credit cards: all major
Relais & Chateaux
karenbrown.com/california/meadowood.html

Just off Hwy 29 at the corner of El Bonita, on the outskirts of Saint Helena, the Vineyard Country Inn backs onto an expanse of vineyards. Constructed to resemble a French country manor, the inn's attention to detail and the quality of appointments are impressive. Handsome slate roofs dotted by whimsical brick chimneys top the complex of buildings. A path winds from the main building, which houses the lobby and attractive breakfast room, past the enclosed pool and Jacuzzi, through patches of flowering garden to the guestrooms. Accommodations are all suites enjoying a sitting area in front of a wood-burning fireplace, and a bedroom furnished with either a king bed or two queen sleigh beds. The decor is clean and elegant in its simplicity. Bathrooms have lovely tile and wallpaper and are beautifully fresh and modern. Under beamed ceilings, the downstairs bedrooms (except for two) open onto patios; all the upstairs rooms open onto private decks. The Vineyard Country Inn's guestrooms are spacious and offer excellent value for money in comparison to other luxury accommodation in the valley. A bountiful breakfast buffet is served and trays are available so that you can take your repast back to the privacy of your room. *Directions:* From San Francisco take Hwy 101 north to Hwy 37 east, then Hwy 37 to Hwy 121/129. Located on Hwy 29 at El Bonita.

VINEYARD COUNTRY INN
Owners: Michael & Mary Ann Pietro
Innkeepers: Ortwin & Patricia Krueger
201 Main Street
Saint Helena, CA 94574, USA
Tel: (707) 963-1000, Fax: (707) 963-1794
21 rooms
Double: $170–$295
Open: all year, Credit cards: all major
karenbrown.com/california/vineyardcountry.html

The Wine Country Inn is one of those delightful places that thumbs its nose at being minimalist, chic, and cozy—it delights in being spacious, comfortable, and courteous. Occupying a collection of wood and stone buildings set on a low hillside, surrounded by expansive vineyards, 3 acres of ground give a spacious feel to this quiet spot, which is central to everything in the Napa Valley. The spaciousness is echoed in the room sizes—there's not a snug room in the place. Relax, spread out, and enjoy the tranquil setting. Fourteen rooms are housed in the main building, six in the Brandy Barn, and four in the Hastings House. Many of the rooms have private outdoor hot tubs, patios, balconies, and fireplaces. The latest additions are individual cottages set on the hillside and down overlooking the vineyards. Decor ranges from rustic barnwood to contemporary. Do not be concerned about staying in one of the older rooms for everything is pleasingly maintained. Relax by the lovely pool and take your wine and hors d'oeuvres (delicious homemade appetizers) onto the deck to soak up the view across the vineyards to distant hills. An excellent breakfast is served. *Directions:* Two miles north of Saint Helena on Hwy 29 turn right onto Lodi Lane. The Wine Country Inn is in a quarter of a mile down on the left.

WINE COUNTRY INN
Owner: Jim Smith
Manager: Deniese Steelman
1152 Lodi Lane
Saint Helena, CA 94574, USA
Tel: (707) 963-7077, (888) 465-4608
Fax: (707) 963-9018
24 rooms, 5 cottages, Double: $195–$610
Open: all year, Credit cards: MC, VS
Select Registry
karenbrown.com/california/winecountryinn.html

This guide features small hotels with charm, so how could we consider including a resort hotel with 688 rooms! The reason is quite simple: there is just nothing else in California to compare with the marvelously whimsical Hotel del Coronado. It's an elegant hideaway with lots of action, plenty of pizzazz, fabulous architecture, and an incredible sandy beach. Whether you want to enjoy an action-packed family vacation or relax on a secluded portion of the beach, the Hotel del Coronado can accommodate you. Its history dates back to 1887 when Elisha Babcock and H. L. Story purchased Coronado Island and reserved the prime 31 acres of real estate for building of one of the world's largest wooden structures. Within a year, their dream came true. The Hotel del Coronado, a white Victorian, gingerbread hotel—a fantasy of turrets, wraparound porches, funny little towers, and perky gables—was ready to open. Over the years, more buildings have been added and while the original structure remains on the outside much as it was over a hundred years ago, the interior has been restored to include classic design and air conditioning. If you want a contemporary beachfront room, opt for the Ocean Towers, but if you value nostalgia, ask to be in the Victorian building. *Directions:* Take I-5 to the Coronado Bridge then turn left on Orange Avenue.

HOTEL DEL CORONADO
Manager: Michael Hardisty
1500 Orange Avenue
San Diego–Coronado, CA 92118, USA
Tel: (619) 435-6611, (800) 468-3533
Fax: (619) 522-8262
688 rooms
Double: $260–$2,300*
 *Breakfast not included
Open: all year, Credit cards: all major
karenbrown.com/california/hoteldelcoronado.html

The slogan of the Crystal Pier Hotel & Cottages—"Sleep over the Ocean"—aptly expresses what is unique and special about this property. Charming white clapboard cottages trimmed in blue and dressed with windowboxes cover the length of both sides of this private/public pier in colorful Pacific Beach. When the tide is in, the surf washes beneath the cottages and wooden slats of the pier. Cottages all enjoy an expanse of deck and unobstructed views of ocean, surfers, and beachcombers. It is easy to get to know your neighbors while watching the sunset over the ocean as only low white picket fences divide each patio. The most private units are those towards the end of the pier for they are set at an angle and have private patios and the most spectacular ocean views. All the cottages enjoy a little kitchen and living room and are priced according to whether they are a spacious studio, one bedroom with bath, or two bedrooms with two baths. Although it is locked in the evening and has 24-hour security, the pier is open to the public by day. Be advised that the morning starts early on the pier with fishing at its end, the rumble of guests' cars on the wooden slats, and the arrival of beachcombers, lifeguards, and surfers on the beach below. *Directions:* Leave I-5 at Balboa/Garnet Ave. The pier is at the end of Garnet Avenue on Ocean Front Walk.

CRYSTAL PIER HOTEL & COTTAGES
Manager: Jim Bostian
4500 Ocean Boulevard in Pacific Beach
San Diego–Pacific Beach, CA 92109, USA
Tel: (858) 483-6983, (800) 748-5894
Fax: (858) 483-6811
29 cottages
Double: $195–$320*
*Breakfast not included
Open: all year, Credit cards: MC, VS
karenbrown.com/california/crystalpier.html

The Inn at Union Square has a convenient and strategic location, right in the heart of San Francisco—just steps from Union Square, theaters, and shopping. Owned by Nan and Norm Rosenblatt, this is a professionally managed, boutique hotel. The small lobby is entered from the street and appears to be the entryway of a country home. An elevator takes guests to the upper floors. As you step off the elevator, each floor has its own little sitting area with chairs grouped comfortably around a fireplace where complimentary wine and hors d'oeuvres are served in the evening from 5:30 to 8 pm. Newspapers are left outside each door in the morning. Guests can either go to the lounge for an expanded Continental breakfast or take a tray to their room. The decor in each of the rooms is most attractive, with a traditional mood created by the use of beautiful fabrics and fine furniture. Some of the rooms have their own fireplaces and the penthouse suite has a sauna and whirlpool tub. Every room, from the least expensive small rooms to the deluxe suites, is spotlessly maintained and appealing. All rooms are equipped with voice mail, dual-line phones, and modems. Room service is available. The inn has membership to a full-service gym. *Directions:* Located one block off Union Square on Post Street, between Stockton and Powell.

INN AT UNION SQUARE
Owners: Norm & Nan Rosenblatt
440 Post Street
San Francisco, CA 94102, USA
Tel: (415) 397-3510, (800) 288-4346
Fax: (415) 989-0529
30 rooms
Double: $155–$375
Open: all year, Credit cards: all major
karenbrown.com/california/innatunionsquare.html

The Hotel Majestic was built in 1902 as a private home but was converted to a hotel just two years later, making it San Francisco's longest-operating hotel. Located west of Van Ness, the Majestic offers a quiet refuge away from the bustle of the city (though there is a free morning shuttle to the financial district). The hotel is aptly described by the innkeeper as "romantic with a touch of elegance." Rich, muted colors, subtle, contrasting trims, crown moldings, high ceilings, soft lighting, tapestry carpets, lovely artwork, and traditional furnishings all contribute to that elegance. The guestrooms are all similar in handsome appointments but vary dramatically in size. Standard rooms are cozy and comfortable for a single traveler or short stay, while at the other extreme there are nine luxury suites with canopied king beds, sitting rooms with fireplace, and commodious bathrooms. The Avalon Bar is a very appealing evening rendezvous spot and Perlot, one of the city's most romantic dining rooms, offers fine cuisine in an intimate setting. *Directions:* Take the Lombard Street exit off of the Golden Gate Bridge and go 13 blocks, turning right on Van Ness Avenue. After 15 blocks turn right on Sutter Street, driving 2 blocks to Gough. Cross the street and park on the right. The hotel is at the corner of Sutter and Gough.

HOTEL MAJESTIC
Innkeeper: Brooks Bayly
1500 Sutter Street
San Francisco, CA 94109, USA
Tel: (415) 441-1100, (800) 869-8966
Fax: (415) 673-7331
58 rooms, Double: $170–$375*
*Breakfast not included
Open: all year, Credit cards: all major
Select Registry
karenbrown.com/california/hotelmajestic.html

The Petite Auberge is a lovely little hotel on Bush Street sitting next to its sister "Four Sisters" hotel, the White Swan. Whereas the White Swan has an English flavor, the Petite Auberge is like a romantic French country inn snuggled at the heart of the city, just steps from the famous theater district and exclusive shopping and fine dining. The façade is most appealing—a slim, four-story building with a column of bay windows bordered by narrow windows decorated with flowerboxes. A collection of French dinner plates, art posters and teddy bears give a warm welcome to the cozy entry. Each guestroom is attractively decorated with delicate colors, all have private baths, and many have fireplaces. Downstairs there is a most inviting suite with a fireplace, spa tub, and private outside entrance and deck. Wine, sherry, and hors d'oeuvres are available at 4:30 pm for those guests who want a quiet moment after a busy day. A delicious breakfast is served buffet style in the delightful breakfast room with its French marketplace mural and French doors giving onto a pretty patio where you can sit in pleasant weather. Breakfast includes a selection of teas and coffee, homemade breads, fruit, a hot dish, cereals, and pastries. *Directions:* Take Van Ness Avenue north to Bush Street. Turn right on Bush and go about 1 mile. The inn is between Taylor and Mason.

 P

PETITE AUBERGE
Innkeeper: Lou Rosenberger
863 Bush Street
San Francisco, CA 94108, USA
Tel: (415) 928-6000, (800) 365-3004
Fax: (415) 673-7214
26 rooms
Double: $139–$229
Open: all year, Credit cards: all major
karenbrown.com/california/petiteauberge.html

Union Street is always a favorite place to dine, shop, and play and the several blocks stretching out at the foot of exclusive Pacific Heights offer charming restaurants and pretty boutiques in quaint Victorian houses. Right in the heart of this attractive area, snuggled into a pretty, light-yellow Victorian house with green trim, is the Union Street Inn. Steps on the left side of the building lead up to the front door, which opens into a small reception foyer. To the left is an old-fashioned parlor, comfortably furnished with antiques. Doors from the parlor lead out to the most special feature of the inn—an exceptionally attractive, English-style garden where a brick path meanders through a medley of shrubs, flowers, and shade trees. At the end of the garden, behind a white picket fence, is a cute cottage converted into a guest suite. In the house itself are five more guestrooms, each individually decorated in a traditional style. My favorite is the English Garden Room, which has its own small deck overlooking the garden. All of the rooms have a welcome basket of fresh fruit. Continuing the mood of hospitality, refreshments are set out for guests each afternoon, and in the morning a full breakfast is served. Your hosts, Jane Bertorelli and David Coyle, oversee every detail of the inn and personally welcome guests. *Directions:* From Hwy 101 north, take Lombard Street, turn right on Steiner, then left on Union. The inn is between Fillmore and Steiner.

UNION STREET INN
Owners: Jane Bertorelli & David Coyle
Manager: Katie Edison
2229 Union Street
San Francisco, CA 94123, USA
Tel: (415) 346-0424, Fax: (415) 922-8046
6 rooms
Double: $169–$279
Open: all year, Credit cards: all major
karenbrown.com/california/unionstreetinn.html

The Washington Square Inn has a great location in the North Beach area, facing historic Washington Square. Within easy strolling distance you find a wealth of wonderful little places to eat and a bit farther, but an interesting walk through Chinatown, are the theaters and shops of the Union Square area. From the moment you enter, the ambiance of the French countryside surrounds you—an antique dining table, mellowed with age and surrounded by country chairs, stretches in front of large windows framed with tie-back drapes. Large gilt mirrors, pots of orchids, and a fireplace with an antique wooden mantel add to the country appeal. In the afternoon guests have tea or wine and hors d'oeuvres in front of the fire and in the morning an expanded Continental breakfast of juice, fruit, muffins, breads, croissants, and hot and cold cereals is served here (if guests prefer, breakfast will be brought to their room). Two staircases lead to the guestrooms, each individually decorated. From the simplest room to the most luxurious suite, each of the rooms, dressed with beautiful coordinating fabrics, exudes a lovely country charm. A couple of rooms have cozy bay windows accented with inviting sitting nooks. The restaurant next door, Moose's, serves fine cuisine. *Directions:* In North Beach, on Washington Square, between Union and Filbert.

WASHINGTON SQUARE INN
Innkeeper: David A. Norwitt
1660 Stockton Street
San Francisco, CA 94133, USA
Tel: (415) 981-4220, (800) 388-0220
Fax: (415) 397-7242
15 rooms
Double: $145–$245
Open: all year, Credit cards: all major
karenbrown.com/california/washingtonsquareinn.html

The White Swan Inn, a small, London-style hotel with English-country decor, has a splendid location just steps from a wide selection of quaint restaurants and a five-minute walk from San Francisco's fabulous Union Square shopping and theater district. But the appeal of the White Swan is far greater than its setting: from the moment you enter, you will know immediately that this is not a standard commercial hotel. Off the entry a small sitting area and a reception desk greet you, but the heart of the inn is down a flight of stairs where a spacious lounge awaits, with one section set up with tables and chairs for a full buffet breakfast. Wine, sherry and hors d'oeuvres are set out at 4:30 pm. Beyond the eating area is a pretty living room with a fireplace and comfortable lounge chairs. Next door is the library, with a cricket bat mounted on the wall—another cozy area for relaxing—and a small exercise room. Although the inn is in the center of the city, French doors open out from a conference room at the back onto a deck and small English-style garden. The bedrooms are beautifully decorated with pretty coordinating fabrics. Each room has a separate sitting area, fireplace (which can be turned on by a bedside switch), small refrigerator, wet bar, direct-dial telephone, and color television. This hotel is an absolute delight. *Directions:* Take Van Ness Avenue north, turn right on Bush and go about 1 mile. The inn is between Taylor and Mason.

WHITE SWAN INN
Innkeeper: Lou Rosenberger
845 Bush Street
San Francisco, CA 94108, USA
Tel: (415) 775-1755, (800) 999-9570
Fax: (415) 775-5717
26 rooms
Double: $179–$269
Open: all year, Credit cards: all major
karenbrown.com/california/whiteswaninn.html

The Gerstle Park Inn, a rambling, wood-shingled home on 1½ acres, is a beautiful inn set in a residential district of San Rafael, catering mostly to business travelers and local families, as well as tourists. The inn carries an air of sophistication wonderfully complemented by a homey and welcoming ambiance. Just off the entry are the formal living room with its Asian-inspired decor and the enclosed wraparound porch, which serves as an intimate and elegant breakfast room where a full, cooked-to-order breakfast is served each morning. Upstairs, rooms range from the Redwood Suite, cozy and romantic with a pine-planked, low-angled ceiling and wooded views afforded by a row of windows at ceiling height, to the San Rafael Suite, spanning the length of one end of the building, with its king bed and large deck facing the surrounding hills. The separate carriage house has two suites complete with well-stocked kitchens, breakfast nooks, living rooms, and private patios. Two stand-alone cottages also have kitchens and provide wonderful privacy. All the rooms enjoy amenities and conveniences such as two-line telephones with voice mail, televisions, VCRs, CD players, hairdryers, and robes. For Judy and Jim Dowling, your gracious and talented hosts, running Gerstle Park Inn is a dream fulfilled. *Directions:* Exit Hwy 101 at San Rafael Central exit. Go west on 3rd Street, then left on D Street, right on San Rafael Avenue, and left on Grove Street.

GERSTLE PARK INN
Owners: Judy & Jim Dowling
Manager: Barbara Searles
34 Grove Street
San Rafael, CA 94901, USA
Tel: (415) 721-7611, (800) 726-7611
Fax: (415) 721-7600
12 rooms, Double: $179–$245
Open: all year, Credit cards: all major
Select Registry
karenbrown.com/california/gerstleparkinn.html

The Cheshire Cat is comprised of two lovely beige-and-white Victorians sitting side by side and connected by a tranquil bricked patio (where breakfast is served on chilly days), and a third building, the James House, across the street. In the foyer of the main house a grouping of Alice in Wonderland figurines sets the whimsical theme of the inn. Each guestroom is unique in appeal although consistent in the Laura Ashley coordinated prints and wallpapers used in the decor, from plums and creams in the Mad Hatter Room to smoke-blue and cream in the Dormouse's Room. Two spacious suites, Tweedle Dum and Tweedle Dee, enjoy a fireplace, Jacuzzi, and their own entrance off the back garden. Three two-bedroom cottages, Woodford, Prestbury, and Mobberly, have a fully stocked kitchen, living room, fireplaces, and a private redwood deck with a hot tub. James House houses four beautiful guest accommodations: The Lion, on the ground floor, and White King, White Queen, and Unicorn on the first floor. White King is an especially appealing room with a large king bed set on pine flooring and seating in a pretty bay-window alcove. Its bathroom is large and luxurious with a Jacuzzi tub. *Directions:* Exit Hwy 101 at Mission Street, go east on Mission for five blocks, right on State Street for three blocks, and right on Valerio.

CHESHIRE CAT
Owner: Christine Dunstan
36 West Valerio Street
Santa Barbara, CA 93101, USA
Tel: (805) 569-1610, Fax: (805) 682-1876
21 rooms
Double: $169–$400
Open: all year, Credit cards: all major
karenbrown.com/california/thecheshirecat.html

Having always admired State Street for its whitewashed Spanish-style buildings, we were delighted to discover the Hotel Santa Barbara, situated in the heart of the plaza just one block from the town's open-air malls and quaint boutiques. There has been a hotel on this site since 1876, with the present structure being built in 1925 and recently restored and updated at a cost of $4 million. This family-managed hotel reminds you of the 1920s Hollywood movie era—in fact, it used to be a getaway for stars such as Clark Gable and Carol Lombard. With cool, tiled floors in the foyer and colors of sand and rust, the atmosphere is that of a Moroccan arched marketplace. There are comfy pillow-filled sofas and café-style seating in the area where your Continental breakfast is served. This is a four-storied, mission-style building with the guestrooms, some with Juliet balconies, facing onto a U-shaped courtyard. Rooms, all air-conditioned, are furnished in bold colors of blues and yellows and have elegant, stark-white bathrooms. The large, well-appointed suites are extremely comfortable. There is some street noise, so request a room away from the activity. Valet parking is available. Children under 16 stay free with a parent. *Directions:* From Hwy 101 exit at Carrillo, drive for several blocks, then turn right on Chapala. Turn left on Cota—the hotel is on the right, half a block down at the corner of Cota and State Streets.

HOTEL SANTA BARBARA
Manager: Tamara Erickson
533 State Street
Santa Barbara, CA 93101, USA
Tel: (805) 957-9300, (888) 259-7700
Fax: (805) 962-2412
75 rooms
Double: $209–$239
Open: all year, Credit cards: all major
karenbrown.com/california/hotelsantabarbara.html

The Secret Garden Inn is a charming complex of cottages shaded by trees and banded by a beautiful garden. Dominique Hannaux, the owner, hails from France and the Secret Garden Inn looks absolutely beautiful as a result of her focused attention and charming decor. Since she bought the inn a few years ago, Dominique has not made dramatic changes, but rather subtle ones to the decor that surprisingly make a huge difference to the appeal and ambiance of the inn. The main building houses an inviting living room, a lovely country dining room, and two of the guest accommodations. The other guestrooms are extremely private, located in individual cottages with their own entrance — very romantic, peaceful, and restful. Each room has its own decor and special appeal, such as Hummingbird with a private deck and hot tub and Nightingale with a spacious living room, fireplace, and private deck with hot tub. Central to the cottages at the back of the main house is a lovely, lush garden, which surrounds a patio shaded by persimmon, avocado, and mock orange trees. On mornings blessed with sunshine, tables are set here for breakfast. *Directions:* Take Hwy 101 to the Mission Street exit then go east on Mission for one block to Castillo Street. Turn right on Castillo, then left on Pedegossa, and left again on Bath Street. The Secret Garden Inn is on the right.

SECRET GARDEN INN
Owner: Dominique Hannaux
1908 Bath Street
Santa Barbara, CA 93101, USA
Tel: (805) 687-2300, (800) 676-1622
Fax: (805) 687-4576
11 rooms
Double: $121–$231
Open: all year, Credit cards: all major
karenbrown.com/california/secretgardeninn.html

The Simpson House Inn, a handsome, rosy-beige Victorian landmark with white and smoke-blue trim, is located on a quiet residential street only a five-minute walk from the historic downtown shopping attractions of State Street. The lush surrounding gardens of the inn include an acre of lawn banded by beautiful flowerbeds and mature shade trees. An irresistible feature of the inn is a cheerful back porch under an arbor of draping wisteria with white wicker chairs and comfy pillows: a perfect niche to enjoy the garden. In the main house the sitting room and dining room are quite formal. However, the formality disappears upstairs in the charming guest chambers, each individually decorated with hand-printed Victorian wallpapers to suit different tastes—from feminine to a more tailored look. Three cottages in the back garden are beautifully decorated in rich fabrics and intimate with a Jacuzzi tub nestled right into a bay window. The barn also offers spacious accommodations, light and airy, whose pine furnishings are perfect against the exposed beams of the original barn. Each room enjoys niceties such as robes, fresh flowers, and bottled water. In the evenings sherry and local wine are offered with an extensive Mediterranean hors d'oeuvres buffet. An efficient and friendly staff assists Dixie Budke with the duties of the inn. *Directions:* From downtown take Santa Barbara Street northeast toward Mission, then turn left onto Arrellaga.

SIMPSON HOUSE INN
Owners: Linda Sue & Glyn Davies
Manager: Dixie Adair Budke
121 East Arrellaga Street
Santa Barbara, CA 93101, USA
Tel: (805) 963-7067, (800) 676-1280
Fax: (805) 564-4811
11 rooms, 4 cottages, Double: $225–$600
Open: all year, Credit cards: all major
Select Registry
karenbrown.com/california/simpsonhouseinn.html

The foundations of The Babbling Brook Inn date back to the 1790s when padres from the Santa Cruz Mission built a grist mill on the property, taking advantage of the small stream to grind corn. In the late 19th century a tannery powered by a huge water wheel was constructed. Beside the historic wheel a rustic log cabin stands as the "heart" of the inn with a homey living room where guests congregate around a roaring fire with tea and coffee and homemade cookies and enjoy a tempting breakfast buffet (trays are provided so that you can take your morning repast back to your room). Here you find my favorite room, Artists, with its outdoor tub recessed into its private deck, which looks out over the entire property. Most of the other bedrooms are found in shingled houses nestled in the garden surrounded by pines and redwoods and overlooking the idyllic little meandering brook. Each house has one room on the ground floor and one above and is decorated in French-country style with pretty fabrics and colors, and enjoys lots of amenities including a fireplace. Most rooms have a private deck and some even have soaking jet bathtubs for two. *Directions:* From San Jose or San Francisco take Hwy 17 to Santa Cruz. Turn north on Hwy 1, which becomes Mission Street, then left on Laurel for one and a half blocks to the inn, which is on the right-hand side.

BABBLING BROOK INN
Innkeeper: Aurorah Cheney
1025 Laurel Street
Santa Cruz, CA 95060, USA
Tel: (831) 427-2437, (800) 866-1131
Fax: (831) 427-2457
13 rooms
Double: $139–$239
Open: all year, Credit cards: all major
Select Registry
karenbrown.com/california/babblingbrook.html

The Channel Road Inn dates back to 1910 when Thomas McCall built an elaborate wood-shingled home for his large family. A third story was later added, giving plenty of space for the 14 guestrooms it now offers. The house has an interesting location: just on the fringe of Pacific Palisades yet on a busy street that leads through a somewhat honky-tonk neighborhood to the wonderful playground of a beach. The downstairs lounge and dining areas of the inn are sedately decorated, beautifully in keeping with the style of the home. The guestrooms, tucked throughout the house, are all individually decorated and each has its own delightful personality. My favorite room was number 1, one of the less expensive rooms but delightful with a fresh white-and-blue color scheme and sharing a large, quiet rooftop terrace with the adjacent room 5. When making reservations, keep in mind that the rooms vary in size and decide whether you want a patio, soaking tub, or the relative quiet of an inside-facing room. A ground-floor handicap room has ramp access direct from its parking space. Bikes are available for excursions along the strand. Recover from your exertions with a soak in the hot tub. *Directions:* From Hwy 405 take 10 west, then Pacific Coast Hwy (Route 1) north for 2 miles. Make a hard right on West Channel Road, continue 1 block, and the inn is on the left.

CHANNEL ROAD INN
Owner: Susan Zolla
Manager: Christine Marwell
219 West Channel Road
Santa Monica, CA 90402, USA
Tel: (310) 459-1920, Fax: (310) 454-9920
14 rooms
Double: $165–$365
Open: all year, Credit cards: all major
Select Registry
karenbrown.com/california/channelroadinn.html

Shutters on the Beach is a stunning, deluxe, luxury hotel fronting directly onto the superb Santa Monica beach and although it is of new construction, the hotel has a delightfully nostalgic mood. The elegant, Cape Cod-like, whisper-gray, wood-shingled building is enhanced by white gingerbread trim. I am not sure how it is accomplished, but there is an engaging, homelike ambiance throughout—perhaps it is the wood-beam ceiling or the cozy groupings of plump, comfy sofas, or the fireplaces. The designer's goal was to create a hotel where guests would feel that they were staying at a friend's beach house rather than a commercial hotel: that goal has certainly been achieved. A garden terrace (where white lounge chairs are grouped around an attractive swimming pool) spans a small street to connect the beach house with a more traditional-looking hotel section. All of the guestrooms are attractive: nautical blues and aquas accent a predominantly white color scheme. An uncluttered, simple, yet elegant mood prevails, enhanced by Italian linens and furniture of excellent quality. Every room has heavy, wooden, white louvered shutters, which give the hotel its name. *Directions:* Go west on Hwy 10 (Santa Monica Expressway) to Santa Monica. Take the 4th Street exit south (right) onto Pico Boulevard. Shutters on the Beach sits where Pico Boulevard meets the beach.

SHUTTERS ON THE BEACH
Manager: Armella Stepan
One Pico Boulevard
Santa Monica, CA 90405, USA
Tel: (310) 458-0030, (800) 334-9000
Fax: (310) 458-4589
198 rooms
Double: $395–$2,500*
 *Breakfast not included
Open: all year, Credit cards: all major
karenbrown.com/california/shutters.html

Judy and Mike selected the Gables Wine Country Inn, an aristocratic Victorian home on the outskirts of Santa Rosa, with a dream of opening a bed and breakfast. Although the Gables enjoys an expanse of 3 acres at the back, with a wonderful old barn (home to a colony of owls), the house sits just off the very busy Petaluma Hill Road. A little traffic noise can be heard from the front guestrooms, but the back rooms overlooking the garden enjoy the quiet of the country setting. The decor throughout the inn is in keeping with the grandeur of the home. Guestrooms are spacious and pretty with a country-Victorian theme. Accommodation is also offered in country cottage behind the main house. There's a sitting area, fireplace, wet bar, Jacuzzi tub, TV, VCR, and video library, and a cozy upstairs sleeping loft. Judy is an accomplished cook and her casual afternoon tea features homemade cookies and brownies. Breakfasts are quite a repast with freshly squeezed juice, fruit, and a main course—a bounty that will take you right through to dinner. Mike is a talented craftsman and he is responsible for many of the fine finishes throughout the inn and all the hand-crafted furniture in the cottage. *Directions:* From San Francisco take Hwy 101 north, exiting at Rohnert Park Expressway. Turn right off the exit ramp and go 2½ miles, turning left on Petaluma Hill Road.

GABLES WINE COUNTRY INN
Owners: Judy & Mike Ogne
4257 Petaluma Hill Road
Santa Rosa, CA 95404, USA
Tel: (707) 585-7777, (800) 422-5376
Fax: (707) 584-5634
8 rooms, 1 cottage
Double: $175–$300
Open: all year, Credit cards: all major
karenbrown.com/california/thegables.html

The Vintners Inn is a natural choice for those who want to stay in a secluded hotel that has a close-to-everything location, perfect for visiting the Napa, Sonoma, or Russian River areas. Just off the 101 freeway, the Mediterranean-style building is set amid 90 acres of vineyards (be sure to request a room that faces these) and I was astonished to find that I could not hear any freeway noise. The spacious guestrooms are housed in three buildings that encircle a fountain in the bricked courtyard. The rooms are decked out in restful tones of beige in a French-country decor, and all offer oversized tubs, small refrigerators, robes, televisions, data ports, and patios or balconies. Rooms are priced according to size, with spacious patio and balcony rooms being the least expensive and extra-large junior suites with sitting areas, fireplaces, and luxurious bathrooms (Jacuzzi tub and shower) being the most expensive. In the morning a lavish full breakfast is set in the Provence Room: you can enjoy it here or on the patio, or take a tray to your room. On the edge of the vineyards is a Jacuzzi tub and those who must can work out in the gym. For dinner walk the few yards to the restaurant John Ash & Co. *Directions:* From San Francisco travel Hwy 101 north to Santa Rosa. Exit at River Road, turn left over the freeway, and take the first left onto Barnes Road. Turn left into the first driveway.

VINTNERS INN
Owners: Don & Rhonda Carano
Innkeeper: Percy Brandon
4350 Barnes Road
Santa Rosa, CA 95403, USA
Tel: (707) 575-7350, (800) 421-2584
Fax: (707) 575-1426
44 rooms
Double: $210–$395
Open: all year, Credit cards: all major
karenbrown.com/california/vintners.html

Just beyond Sausalito's yacht club and only steps away from the ferry dock, right on the water's edge, sits the Inn Above Tide, very cleverly converted to an inn from what was originally an apartment complex and then most recently an office building. All of its 30 rooms enjoy million-dollar views of the San Francisco Bay and skyline and are appropriately stocked with binoculars. Twenty-four of the rooms have wonderful little decks whose partitioning wall is of glass, creating the illusion of being right on the water. The remaining six rooms, although without a deck, are a little more spacious. The rooms, many of which have fireplaces, are attractive—light and airy so as not to compete with the view. The decor plays on a nautical theme with porthole windows and soft green-and-white prints with little fish. The two suites are both spectacular, spacious rooms with private decks and magnificent views of the city. The buffet in the drawing room is set in the evenings with a selection of wine and cheese, and in the mornings with a Continental breakfast (trays are available if you prefer to enjoy breakfast in your guestroom). If you want to use Sausalito as a base for exploring San Francisco, you can easily journey back and forth by ferry, avoiding the hassle and cost of a car. *Directions:* From San Francisco cross the Golden Gate Bridge and exit on Alexander Avenue. Alexander becomes Bridgeway. Turn right towards the water on El Portal.

❄ ⚓ ☕ 🏄 CREDIT ☎ ⛨ 🚶 👫 🏇 🍸 P 🚭 🛥 ♿ 🍇

INN ABOVE TIDE
Owner: William McDevitt
Manager: Mark Flaherty
30 El Portal
Sausalito, CA 94965, USA
Tel: (415) 332-9535, (800) 893-8433
Fax: (415) 332-6714
30 rooms
Double: $245–$750
Open: all year, Credit cards: all major
karenbrown.com/california/innabovetide.html

The Hotel Sausalito boasts a colorful past. Its early days saw activity as a bordello and as a speakeasy during Prohibition—with its location next to the docks, liquor from the trucks that rumbled past its doors conveniently ended up in its parlor. It is now home to the Purdies, a delightful Scottish family whose brogue will charm you, but who will impress you most with their warm, professional approach to innkeeping. A steep flight of stairs (there is an elevator) leads up to guestrooms from the small street-side entry. With a backdrop of walls washed in warm pastel tones, the furnishings are handsome—custom-designed and hand-crafted by local artisans—and have been selected to enhance the individuality of each guestroom. The size, outlook, and bathroom appointments determine the room tariff. Some of the rooms are snug, yet greatly appreciated by the traveler looking for value. Regardless of the guestroom's location or size, its appointments, such as furnishings, art, the finest linens, desktop phones with data port, voice mail, and cable television, are luxurious. We enjoyed one of the larger rooms overlooking Sausalito's main street, buffered from the noise by well-insulated windows. A lovely second-floor roof garden is a tranquil place to relax. Although breakfast is not served in the hotel, coupons are provided for coffee and pastries next door at Café Tutti. *Directions:* Refer to directions for the Inn Above Tide—they are neighboring hotels.

HOTEL SAUSALITO
Owners: Josephine & Billy Purdie
16 El Portal (at Bridgeway)
Sausalito, CA 94965, USA
Tel: (415) 332-0700, (888) 442-0700
Fax: (415) 332-8788
16 rooms
Double: $145–$270
Open: all year, Credit cards: all major
karenbrown.com/california/hotelsausalito.html

More New Orleans French Quarter than Southern California beach, the Seal Beach Inn dates back to the 1920s when the little town of Seal Beach was a wild party town of dance halls, offshore gambling ships, and bath houses. Today the only hint of the inn's glitzy past is its vintage neon sign, which blends in very nicely with owner Marjorie Bettenhausen-Schmaehl's collection of bygones, from old street lamps and ornate, wrought-iron railings to an 8-foot-tall Parisian frescoed fountain bubbling on the patio beside the pool. Every nook and cranny is filled with a profusion of colorful flowers, vines, shrubs, and trees. Not only are the guestrooms named after flowers, but the gardens contain all the namesake species—wisteria, honeysuckle, bougainvillea, zinnia. Several rooms have fireplaces, kitchens, Jacuzzi baths, and Roman soaking tubs. All have thick towels, fine linens, and grand furnishings that range from an old Persian mural and carved pre-Civil-War headboards to sumptuous Victorian pieces. A lavish breakfast buffet is laid out in the dining room each morning and coffee and teas are available all day in the adjacent library. You can walk to over 20 restaurants and the beach. Just down the road is Long Beach with its famous aquarium and the Queen Mary. *Directions:* Going south on the 405, exit at Seal Beach Boulevard. Go left to Pacific Coast Hwy, turn right then left on 5th street. The inn is two blocks down on the left.

SEAL BEACH INN
Owner: Marjorie Bettenhausen-Schmaehl
212 5th Street
Seal Beach, CA 90740, USA
Tel: (562) 493-2416, (800) 443-3292
Fax: (562) 799-0483
23 rooms
Double: $140–$399
Open: all year, Credit cards: all major
Select Registry
karenbrown.com/california/sealbeachinn.html

The Alisal Guest Ranch, a quintessential family resort located in the bucolic Santa Ynez Valley in the town of Solvang, appeals to the child of any age with its horseback riding, golf, tennis, country dancing, and western barbecues. Originally a land grant in the 1700s to a Spanish conquistador, Alisal has been a working cattle ranch and secluded hideaway since 1946. Its 73 cottages, ranging from studios to large suites, are all extremely comfortable and tastefully decorated and have wood-burning fireplaces. The "California ranch" decor is very inviting, with high beamed ceilings, Spanish tile, and fine western art. Each cottage is its own private retreat with garden views and covered porches—a home away from home. If quiet and privacy are your desires, visit the ranch during the week off season and stay in the cottages nearest the golf course—these are farthest from the main activities. Breakfast and dinner, which are included in the price, are taken in the large Ranch Room where you are assigned a table for the duration of your stay. We have heard about Alisal for years from friends who enjoy it as a family retreat to which they return again and again, generation after generation. *Directions:* Take Hwy 101 to Buellton and exit at Hwy 246 (Solvang/Lompoc). Coming from the north, turn left from the off ramp; from the south, turn right. Follow signs to Solvang and turn right on Alisal Road, past the golf courses, to the main entrance.

ALISAL GUEST RANCH & RESORT
Manager: David Lautensack
1054 Alisal Road
Solvang, CA 93463, USA
Tel: (805) 688-6411, (800) 425-4725
Fax: (805) 688-2510
73 cottages
Double: $410–$495*
*Includes breakfast & dinner
Open: all year, Credit cards: all major
karenbrown.com/california/alisalguestranch.html

The name of the inn, "Storybook", represents the theme that runs from its whimsical architecture to the decor of the guestrooms. It's a delightful inn that fits in perfectly with the mock early-20th-century Danish architecture of Solvang. Carol and Chip Orton descend from a long line of Santa Ynez Valley residents and like to share their Danish history and advise guests on which wineries to visit. Every afternoon around four o'clock Chip opens up an impressive array of local wines for the hors d'oeuvre hours. A full breakfast is cooked to order. Each bedroom is named for one of Hans Christian Anderson's magical stories such as The Ugly Duckling, The Little Mermaid, The Princess and the Pea, Thumbelina, and The Emperor's New Clothes. Subtle murals from the fairytale deck the walls of the room—Thumbelina floating amongst the lily pads, the little tin soldier standing guard—and books allow you to reread your tale. All the individually decorated rooms have gas fireplaces, some nice antiques, attractive canopy, sleigh, or four-poster beds, and fresh, pretty fabrics. Several have Jacuzzi tubs. It's a perfect location on a quiet side street just steps from Solvang's interesting shops and restaurants. *Directions:* Hwy 246 off Hwy 101 becomes Mission Drive, the main street of Solvang. Turn east off Mission onto First Street.

STORYBOOK INN
Owners: Carol & Chip Orton
409 First Street
Solvang, CA 93463, USA
Tel: (805) 688-1703, (800)786-7925
Fax: (805) 688-0953
9 rooms
Double: $129–$224
Open: all year, Credit cards: MC, VS
karenbrown.com/california/thestorybookinn.html

We have quickly fallen in love with the quiet pace, beautiful vistas, and fabulous food wine of the Sonoma Valley. Conveniently located just two blocks from the historic Sonoma Plaza, The Inn at Sonoma's casual décor extends to 19 well-appointed rooms, connected to the underground parking by elevator. Common features include fireplaces, 10-foot-high ceilings, private (albeit small) patios or balconies (for all but three rooms), and nicely appointed bathrooms. Our favorite rooms are those facing Broadway. We especially liked rooms 11 and 10 with their larger decks. An ample outdoor sundeck complete with huge hot tub and limited views of the surrounding hills completes the picture. Before you step out for dinner, enjoy hors d'oeuvres and wine before the huge fireplace in the living room or outside on the deck. After breakfast borrow one of the inn's bicycles to tour the town or walk to the shops and restaurants. The more adventurous can try a hot-air balloon or glider ride. A year-round temperate climate makes this a wonderful destination. *Directions:* Hwy 12 becomes Broadway as it heads north into Sonoma. The Inn at Sonoma is on your right two blocks before you arrive at the square.

INN AT SONOMA
Innkeeper: Chapman Retterer
630 Broadway
Sonoma, CA 95476, USA
Tel: 707-939-1340, (888) 568-9818
Fax: 707-939-8834
19 rooms
Double: $145–$250
Open: all year, Credit cards: all major
karenbrown.com/california/innsonoma.html

Just a four-block walk from Sonoma's historic plaza, MacArthur Place offers luxurious accommodation in a complex of Victorian buildings in 7 acres of manicured grounds with lawns trimmed by box hedges, flourishing rose gardens, majestic trees, ponds, fountains, and gardens decorated with modern sculpture. The original manor house has lots of appeal but our favorite rooms are those in the cottages in the grounds. The Caretaker's Cottage, a spacious suite, enjoys a Jacuzzi tub and a lovely private porch. New suites feature a wood-burning fireplace, jet hydrotherapy tub, wet bar, original art, and verandah or balcony overlooking the gardens. All rooms have splendid garden views, modern bathrooms with oversized showers, walk-in closets, down comforters, monogrammed robes, DVD and CD players, and dual-line telephones with data port and voice mail. The Garden Spa at MacArthur Place offers body treatments, massages, and facials based on elements found in the garden. An outdoor swimming pool and whirlpool are located next to the spa. A continental breakfast is served on the verandah in the gardens. Guests often dine at Saddles Restaurant, a delightfully casual steakhouse in the restored barn. *Directions:* Hwy 12 becomes Broadway as it heads north into Sonoma. MacArthur Place is on your right four blocks before you arrive at the square, on the corner of Broadway and MacArthur.

❄ ☕ ✂ 🖼 ☎ 👨‍🍳 🧍 👫 🍷 P 🍴 🚭 ≋ 🖼 🐾 ⛷ 🍇

MACARTHUR PLACE
Owner: Suzanne Brangham
Manager: Bill Blum
29 E. MacArthur Street
Sonoma, CA 95476, USA
Tel: (707) 938-2929, (800) 722-1866
Fax: (707) 933-9833
64 rooms
Double: $199–$475
Open: all year, Credit cards: all major
karenbrown.com/california/macarthurplace.html

On a full hilltop acre above the town of Sonora, the attractive Barretta Gardens Inn, built around 1903, sits off the road in the shade of its own mature and lush landscaped garden. Barretta Gardens benefits from the enthusiasm, dedication, and graciousness of its proprietors, Sally and Bruno Trial. Bruno's freshly baked pastries are a part of the morning breakfast. On one side of the living room is the dining room whose chandelier is original to the home. Two guestrooms are found on the entry level. The Odette, off the living room with a private entrance, is set under 10-foot-high ceilings and a crystal chandelier, and enjoys an appealing plant-filled sitting room furnished with white wicker furniture. Italian beds have been converted to accommodate a queen mattress. The attached bathroom with whirlpool spa for two has lace-covered windows overlooking the rose garden and foothills. The Isabelle room, with its wall of windows looking out to the Sonora hills, is dressed in greens and maroons and enjoys a large Jacuzzi tub for two. Upstairs, the Chantal room is pretty in a wash of rose, while the Liliane room has a brass king-size bed. A small parlor sits between the Liliane room and the pretty Janine room, which together can be rented as a two-room suite or as a one-room suite with just the Janine. *Directions:* Take Hwy 108 to Washington. Make a right on Restano Way, a right at Mono Way, and a left on Barretta.

BARRETTA GARDENS INN
Owners: Sally & Bruno Trial
700 South Barretta Street
Sonora, CA 95370, USA
Tel: (209) 532-6039, (800) 206-3333
Fax: (209) 532-8257
5 rooms
Double: $100–$250
Open: all year, Credit cards: all major
karenbrown.com/california/barrettagardens.html

Sutter Creek is a charming Gold Country town whose main street is bordered at either end by New England-style residences with their green lawns and neatly clipped hedges. One of these attractive homes is the Foxes, an idyllic hideaway created and run for many years by Min and Pete Fox. We welcome new owners Bob Van Alstine and Jim Travnikar. who are adding their personal touches to this sophisticated bed and breakfast where every spacious guestroom is decorated with exquisite flair. Four rooms are found in the main house and three in the carriage house to the rear. We especially love the Victorian and Anniversary rooms, found upstairs in the main house, with their luxurious tiled bathrooms, walk-in showers, and antique claw-foot tubs. Most of the rooms have fireplaces and all have TVs, VCRs, and refrigerators placed in antique armoires. Each room has a sitting area with a table for breakfast, which is cooked to order and brought to your room with silver service accompanied by a large pot of coffee or tea. Bob Van Alstine and Jim Travnikar.definitely pamper their guests. *Directions:* From Sacramento take Hwy 50 toward Placerville and Lake Tahoe. At the Watt Avenue exit, drive south to Hwy 16. Drive east on Hwy 16 and continue to the junction with Hwy 49 then turn south to Sutter Creek. The Foxes is located on the north end of Main Street on the west side.

FOXES
Owners: Bob Van Alstine & Jim Travnikar.
77 Main Street
P.O. Box 159, Sutter Creek, CA 95685, USA
Tel: (209) 267-5882, (800) 987-3344
Fax: (209) 267-0712
7 rooms
Double: $155–$215
Open: all year, Credit cards: all major
karenbrown.com/california/thefoxes.html

Grey Gables Inn is a pretty, soft-gray-blue house detailed with white trim sitting appealingly behind an English boxwood hedge within easy walking distance of the wonderful array of shops and restaurants in Sutter Creek. A red-brick pathway winds to the front entrance and weaves its way through a lovely back garden with fountains, vine-covered arbors, and a patchwork of flowers. Inside, the inn's ambiance reflects the owners' heritage—the Garlicks hail originally from the Cotswolds, and they have brought a touch of the English countryside to the Mother Lode. Seven of the eight guestrooms are named for an English poet. Browning, Byron, Wordsworth, and Shelley are located on the main floor, just off the entry, while Keats, Brontë, and Tennyson are found on the lower garden level. Garden-level rooms have fewer windows. Secluded away on the top floor is the Victorian Suite. All the rooms are decorated with floral spreads in hues of greens, rose, and mauve. All rooms have fireplaces, most have garden views, and some enjoy claw-foot tubs. Guests settle in the formal dining room and parlor to enjoy an informal afternoon tea with cake and scones, wine and hors d'oeuvres in the evening, and a bountiful breakfast served on fine English china. *Directions:* From Sacramento, take Hwy 16 east to Hwy 49 south for 6 miles to Sutter Creek. Grey Gables Inn is on the west side of Hwy 49, one block north of the downtown area.

GREY GABLES INN
Owners: Sue & Roger Garlick
161 Hanford Street
P.O. Box 1687, Sutter Creek, CA 95685, USA
Tel: (209) 267-1039, (800) 473-9422
Fax: (209) 267-0998
8 rooms
Double: $110–$190
Open: all year, Credit cards: all major
karenbrown.com/california/greygablesinn.html

The Cottage Inn, built as a resort in 1938, offers a number of storybook cottages nestled under the trees on the edge of Lake Tahoe. Parking is limited, so unfortunately the drive that weaves through the grounds is hampered by guests' cars. The lovely cottages, all with individual themes, capture the mountain-cabin atmosphere with their exposed knotty-pine walls, rich fabrics, Swedish pine furniture, and a variety of beds (brass, willow, or pine). The Fireplace Room has the added attraction of a wood-burning fireplace. The Pomin House, the original home on the property, contains a reception area, a breakfast room, and a large sitting room with games, books, local restaurant menus, and a small sitting area where wine and cheese are set out in the afternoons before the blazing log fire. In summer you can happily while away the hours sunning yourself on the dock and swimming in Lake Tahoe's cool, clear waters—the inn has access to a private beach. The more energetic can take advantage of the lovely bicycle trail that passes in front of the inn and travels the lakeshore drive. Vikingsholm, Emerald Bay, and D.L. Bliss Park are a short car ride south. Ski resorts are between a five-minute and twenty-minute drive away. *Directions:* the inn is 2 miles along on your left.

COTTAGE INN
Owner: Susanne Muhr
1690 West Lake Boulevard
P.O. Box 66, Tahoe City, CA 96145, USA
Tel: (530) 581-4073, (800) 581-4073
Fax: (530) 581-0226
20 rooms
Double: $150–$280
Open: all year, Credit cards: MC, VS
karenbrown.com/california/cottageinn.html

Lake Tahoe is an exquisite, crystal-clear blue lake ringed by pines and backed by high mountains. The only outlet for this enormous body of water is the Truckee River, and standing at one of its broad bends some 3 miles downstream is River Ranch. This historic lodge enjoys a marvelous setting, best enjoyed from the circular bar with its picture windows and outdoor patio opening onto the river. Four of the five bedrooms in the lodge itself have sliding glass doors opening to small balconies and the rushing river. These lodge rooms are decorated with traditional antiques. The remaining bedrooms are decorated in a mountain-lodge style with lodgepole-pine beds (usually king-size)—be sure to request one with a balcony and/or a river view. (There are several rooms without the view that are less expensive.) In the mornings a Continental breakfast is served in a part of the dining room that is cantilevered over the river. The restaurant offers California-style cuisine and specializes in steaks, fresh seafood, and wild game. In winter Squaw Valley (5 miles) and Alpine Meadows (3 miles) operate shuttle buses to and from the lodge. In warm weather, enjoy lunch or a cocktail on the spacious deck over the river. In spring and fall room rates are discounted. *Directions:* From the Bay Area take I-80 to Truckee then Hwy 89 south, exiting toward Tahoe City. River Ranch is 11 miles south of the freeway on Hwy 89 at Alpine Meadows Road.

RIVER RANCH LODGE
Innkeeper: Jane Glynn
Director: Bric Haley
2285 River Road
P.O. Box 197, Tahoe City, CA 96145, USA
Tel: (530) 583-4264, (800) 535-9900
Fax: (530) 583-7237
19 rooms
Double: $80–$160
Open: all year, Credit cards: all major
karenbrown.com/california/riverranch.html

From the deck of this comfortable mountain lodge you can look over the crystal-clear blue waters of Lake Tahoe to pines and high mountains—an exquisite view at any time and magnificent when the mountains are capped with snow and pink and purple hues paint a spectacular sunset. Lake Tahoe has long been one of our favorite spots in California and since we found Sunnyside we have a base from which to go skiing in winter, water skiing, sailing, and hiking in the High Sierra in summer, and revel in the beauty of the area year round. A meal at Sunnyside is a real pleasure, for not only do the dining room and deck have magnificent lake views but the food is most enjoyable. It would be a shame to stay in such a lovely spot and not have a view of the lake, which Sunnyside's rooms offer you. Several bedrooms have wonderful river-stone fireplaces— what could be more romantic on a winter evening? Sunnyside has its own marina offering boat rentals and water skiing during the summer. In winter, discount tickets for nearby major ski resorts are available. If you are unable to bring your own mountain bike, you'll find no shortage of places to rent one. Nevada casinos with their gambling and super-star entertainment are less than an hour's drive away. *Directions:* From Truckee take Hwy 89 to Tahoe City. Turn right at the traffic lights and follow the lake shore south for 2 miles to Sunnyside.

SUNNYSIDE RESTAURANT & LODGE
Manager: Janet Gregor
1850 West Lake Boulevard
P.O. Box 5969, Tahoe City, CA 96145, USA
Tel: (530) 583-7200, (800) 822-2754
Fax: (530) 583-2551
23 rooms
Double: $100–$295
Open: all year, Credit cards: all major
karenbrown.com/california/sunnyside.html

Tiburon is an enchanting waterfront community that enjoys million-dollar views across the bay to Angel Island and San Francisco. Surprisingly, it has never drawn the crowds that its famous neighbor, Sausalito, does—but that is definitely part of its charm. It is a relatively undiscovered jewel and its network of small streets that navigate to the water's edge are home to some enticing shops, boutiques, restaurants, and a small theater. Sandwiched between two great restaurants, Sam's and Guaymas, this hotel is located right on the dock at the water's edge. Appropriately named, Waters Edge Hotel is a narrow, two-story building, two guestrooms wide, spanning the distance between Main Street and the dock. The filtered water views from the bedrooms (many of which enjoy snug, private balconies) gets better the closer the rooms are to the back. The two Grand King rooms are the choice end rooms and enjoy the magnificent and only truly unobstructed views. Guestrooms, cozy in size, all have fireplaces and a similar, clean, corporate decor with beds topped with white feather duvets and comfortable seating by the windows. A Continental breakfast is served in the rooms. *Directions:* Located to the north of San Francisco and the Golden Gate Bridge. From Hwy 101 north or south, take the Tiburon exit east. Follow it into town and take a right onto Main Street. The hotel is located on Main Street just before you get to the Corinthian Yacht Club.

WATERS EDGE HOTEL
Manager: Mariell Svensson
25 Main Street
Tiburon, CA 94920, USA
Tel: (415) 789-5999, (877) 789-5999
Fax: (415) 789-5888
23 rooms
Double: $180–$399
Open: all year, Credit cards: all major
karenbrown.com/california/watersedgehotel.html

The Lost Whale, a gray-wash Cape-Cod house with blue trim set on 5 acres of windswept Northern Californian coast, was designed by Susanne Lakin and Lee Miller who manage it with a refreshing, bountiful enthusiasm. The mood is set by the living room with its fir floors warmed by throw rugs and comfortable sofas arranged to enjoy not only the fireplace but also the magnificent view across the garden, through the towering pine trees to the ocean. Five rooms capture this same glorious view while three overlook the northern gardens. Whichever room you select, you will find it decorated in a light, airy style. Several rooms have an extra bed to accommodate a child and two have a sleeping loft. Whereas most inns discourage children, here at The Lost Whale they are made genuinely welcome. Relax on the deck or well-placed chairs in a quiet corner of the garden and listen to the crashing waves and the distant barking of sea lions. Stroll down the cliff path to the 2-mile private beach or pop into your car for the short drive up the road to Patrick's Point State Park with its miles of beaches, walking paths along rocky headlands, and the opportunity to explore a re-created Indian village. The Lost Whale is a homey inn in a spectacular setting. *Directions:* North from Trinidad, take the Seawood Drive exit, turn right on Patrick's Point Drive, and drive 1-1/8 miles north. South from Oregon, exit at Patrick's Point Drive and continue south 1 mile.

LOST WHALE
Owners: Guia Sandler & Gary Hiegerk
3452 Patrick's Point Drive
Trinidad, CA 95570, USA
Tel: (707) 677-3425, Fax: (707) 677-0284
6 rooms
Double: $180–$240
Open: all year, Credit cards: all major
karenbrown.com/california/lostwhale.html

The Trinidad Bay Bed and Breakfast is a homey Cape Cod-style inn with a great location—just across the road from the Trinidad Memorial Lighthouse. This cozy, unpretentious inn has four guestrooms, each with private bath, comfortable bed, reading chair, and spectacular ocean view. A collection of antique clocks adds to the charm of this lovely inn. Upstairs are two queen-bedded rooms, each with an alcove in the dormer with a view of the coast. Guests in these rooms enjoy a hearty breakfast downstairs. The room with king bed and private entrance has the best view from its long strip of windows overlooking the harbor. The fourth room, a large room on the ground floor, has a wraparound window, king-sized bed, a fireplace, and private entry. These two king-bedded rooms enjoy breakfast delivered to the door. Be sure to hike around Trinidad Head, walk along the sandy beaches, and explore the shops, restaurants, art gallery, and museum in town. Just up the road are ample opportunities for walking on isolated beaches and marveling at the height of coastal redwoods. *Directions:* Take the Trinidad exit west off Hwy 101 to Trinidad Memorial Lighthouse. The inn is across the street.

TRINIDAD BAY BED AND BREAKFAST
Owners: Corlene & Don Blue
560 Edwards Street
P.O. Box 849, Trinidad, CA 95570, USA
Tel: (707) 677-0840, Fax: (707) 677-9245
4 rooms
Double: $150–$180
Open: Feb to Nov, Credit cards: MC, VS
karenbrown.com/california/trinidadbay.html

The charming Carrville Inn, located in the splendid Trinity Alps, dates back to the mid-1800s when it was a popular stop for stagecoaches on their way to Oregon. You cannot help falling in love with this inn, an appealing wooden home with a romantic, two-tiered porch stretching across the front where guests relax in comfy, old-fashioned wicker chairs to soak in the idyllic view. A dark-green, densely wooded hill rises behind the hotel, setting off to perfection the pristine white of the building. In front, a meadow sweeps toward distant hills and farm animals graze in the pasture. On hot days, a swimming pool enclosed by a picket fence is a welcome sight, or you might prefer just to laze in the hammock and dream. The decor throughout is appropriately Victorian with many antiques of the period. The dining room is especially cheerful, with large windows opening onto the rose garden. Upstairs there are five individually decorated bedrooms, three with private bathrooms and two sharing a large bathroom. Your charming hosts, Sheri and Dave Overly, had never even stayed in a bed and breakfast before buying the inn, but the art of innkeeping comes naturally to them. In the evening your bed linens are turned down, the lamps softly lit, and chocolates are set on the pillow. *Directions:* Take Hwy 3 north from Weaverville and continue 6 miles past Trinity Center to the Carrville Loop Road (the first paved road on your left after passing the lake).

CARRVILLE INN
Owners: Sheri & Dave Overly
Carrville Loop Road
Rt. 2, Box 3536, Trinity Center, CA 96091, USA
Tel: (530) 266-3511, Fax: (530) 266-3778
5 rooms
Double: $125–$160
Open: mid-April to late-October
karenbrown.com/california/carrvilleinn.html

The McCaffrey House B&B Inn is a lovely country home nestled in a grove of giant oak, pine, and cedar trees. In 1996, Michael and Stephanie built this three-story house on the lot where Stephanie's family cabin sat for 35 years. The living room and other common areas are tastefully decorated and inviting for visiting with other guests or reading a book. You will also find over 500 videos for watching in your room. The warmth of the owners is apparent throughout the inn by the family photos hung on the walls and by their love of their two dogs. Because the McCaffreys designed the house as a bed and breakfast, its seven rooms are spacious, comfortable, and well appointed, each with an iron fire stove with a self-timer so that you can doze off in front of the fire, and a bathroom with tub and shower. A handmade Amish quilt sets the color scheme for each room, and robes and extra towels are provided for jaunts to the hot tub. Most rooms have a balcony or patio, and some have views down to a creek. The McCaffreys serve a complete breakfast at 9, but are happy to accommodate schedules by serving earlier. Thoughtful appointments, charming owners, and a picturesque setting make this a winner. *Directions:* From San Francisco take Hwy 580 east to 205, go east to 120, then east to 108. When you reach Sonora, travel east for 11 miles, and ½ mile above the East Twain Harte exit, make a right turn just beyond the 4,000-feet elevation marker.

MCCAFFREY HOUSE B&B INN
Owners: Stephanie & Michael McCaffrey
P.O. Box 67
23251 Highway 108, Twain Harte, CA 95383, USA
(888) 586-0757, Fax: (209) 586-3689
7 rooms
Double: $135–$180
Open: all year, Credit cards: all major
karenbrown.com/california/mccaffreyhouse.html

Elegant in its simplicity, Le Montrose is not an inn, but offers great value and exceptional accommodation in a safe neighborhood on the edge of Beverly Hills. Converted from an apartment complex, Le Montrose has a nondescript concrete square façade, which belies the charm of the interior. There are three sizes of guest suites: junior, executive, and one-bedroom. All have a sunken living room and come with welcome baskets of fruit, twice-daily maid service, color televisions equipped with VCRs and web TV, state-of-the-art multi-line phones, private email, fax and copy machines, gas fireplaces, great mattresses, excellent lighting, and comfortable sitting areas. The decor in the rooms is handsomely elegant—tones of browns, beiges, golds, and blacks are used in the furnishings against the soft hues of the subtly elegant wallpapers and the classically framed art. The intimate, private library restaurant serves fine cuisine in a quiet setting or will provide 24-hour room service. A small but well-equipped fitness center is available to guests at no charge, and there's a lighted tennis court and rooftop swimming pool. Please request the Karen Brown bed and breakfast rates when making a reservation. *Directions:* Located one block east of Beverly Hills. Take a long journey east on Sunset Boulevard off the I-405, then turn right on Hammond Street, just past Doheny.

LE MONTROSE SUITE HOTEL
Manager: John Douponce
900 Hammond Street
West Hollywood, CA 90069, USA
Tel: (310) 855-1115, (800) 776-0666
Fax: (310) 657-9192
132 rooms
Double: $199–$575*
*Breakfast not included: $10
Open: all year, Credit cards: all major
karenbrown.com/california/lemontrosehotel.html

While the attractions of staying in Yosemite Valley cannot be denied, a more serene, country atmosphere pervades the Wawona Hotel, located within Yosemite Park about a 30-mile drive south of the valley. With its shaded verandahs overlooking broad, rolling lawns and a nine-hole golf course, the hotel presents a welcoming picture that invites one to while away the afternoon beside the pool, fondly referred to as the swimming tank. Bedrooms are in several scattered buildings and private bathrooms are at a premium. Hotel rooms without private baths have bathroom and shower facilities located at the end of each building's verandah. The Annex building is being completely refurbished in 2003 as was the main dining room in a gracious turn-of-the-century style. This is the kind of wonderful old hotel that attracts lots of families. In the summer rangers give interpretive presentations on such topics as bears, climbing, and photography, and there are carriage rides, wonderful Sunday brunches, Saturday-night barbecues, and barn dances. Ask about the Wawona's "discounted lodging packages", which are very good value for money. Accommodation and golf packages are available in the spring and fall. *Directions:* Wawona is in Yosemite National Park, 30 miles south of Yosemite Valley on Hwy 41.

WAWONA HOTEL
Manager: Al Gonzalez
Yosemite National Park
Yosemite–Wawona, CA 95389, USA
Tel: (559) 252-4848, Fax: (559) 456-0542
104 rooms
Double: $112–$161*
 *Breakfast not included: $10.35–$16.60
Open: all year, weekends only Jan 5 to mid-Mar
Credit cards: all major
karenbrown.com/california/wawonahotel.html

The Ahwahnee with its 127 bedrooms hardly qualifies for inclusion in a country inn guide. It is a large, bustling resort with a level of activity in its lobby that is comparable to that at many airports, yet it merits inclusion because it is the most individual of hotels, with all the sophistication of a grand European castle, surrounded by the awesome beauty of Yosemite Valley. The lofty vastness of the lounge dwarfs the sofas and chairs and its huge windows frame magnificent views of the outdoors. The dining room has to be the largest in the United States: it is gorgeous with its massive floor-to-ceiling windows framing towering granite walls, cascading waterfalls, and giant sugar pines. In contrast to the surrounding wilderness, the dining room wears an air of sophistication in the evening when guests dress for dinner and flickering candlelight casts its magical spell. Bedrooms are in the main building or in little cottages in a nearby woodland grove. There is a small swimming pool just off the back patio and it is not unusual to see deer grazing on the lawn. This is undeniably a grand old hotel but if the price tag is a little rich for your blood, less expensive accommodations in Yosemite Valley are briefly outlined on page 72. *Directions:* The Ahwahnee is located in Yosemite Valley just east of Yosemite Village.

THE AHWAHNEE
Manager: Larry Ross
Yosemite National Park
Yosemite–Yosemite Village, CA 95389, USA
Tel: (559) 252-4848, Fax: (559) 456-0542
127 rooms, 24 cottages
Double: $357–$864*
*Breakfast not included: $18
Open: all year, Credit cards: all major
karenbrown.com/california/theahwahnee.html

Lavender is a simply delightful little inn with a superb location, just a short stroll to the boutiques and restaurants in the quaint town of Yountville. The house was built in the 1850s by the Grigsby family, early pioneers who came across the continent by covered wagon. The two-story, gray building, which exudes the flavor of a country farmhouse, is charming in its simplicity. The house was totally renovated and completely modernized inside, but great care was taken to retain the shell of the building, which still maintains its authentic historic character. On the old-fashioned verandah you will find an inviting porch swing where guests can sit back and relax. In the grounds are three cottages providing eight very private guestrooms, all with fireplaces, deep soaking tubs, air conditioning, and custom-made "old-world" furniture. The vibrant colors used throughout are reminiscent of Provence, a theme enhanced by nearly 200 feet of fragrant lavender planted in the garden, forming a seasonal garland of purple around the inn. The room price includes a scrumptious full gourmet breakfast, afternoon tea, wine and hors d'oeuvres, and the use of the inn's bicycles to explore the surrounding countryside. *Directions:* Coming north on Hwy 29, take the Yountville exit. Turn right at the bottom of the exit, then quickly left on Washington Street. Go to Webber Avenue and turn right. Lavender is on the corner of Webber and Jefferson, marked by a giant oak.

LAVENDER
Innkeeper: Rachel Retterer
2020 Webber Avenue
Yountville, CA 94599, USA
Tel: (707) 944-1388, (800) 522-4140
Fax: (707) 944-1579
8 rooms
Double: $150–$250
Open: all year, Credit cards: all major
karenbrown.com/california/lavenderinn.html

The location of the Maison Fleurie is superb—a short walk from the heart of the quaint town of Yountville. The inn (with a look of the French countryside) is a cluster of thick stone and brick buildings, entrancingly draped with ivy. From the moment you enter, the mood is conducive to a carefree holiday. You come into a parlor-like foyer with a corner fireplace, sofa, and chairs. When you begin to wonder if this is a hotel, you notice a discreet reception desk in the room beyond. To the right, a few steps lead down to an inviting lounge where two comfortable sofas (covered with a pretty floral fabric) flank a brick fireplace. The price of the bedrooms depends upon size. The most spacious rooms are found in the Bakery Building and feature king-sized beds, fireplaces, spa tubs, and DVD players. The friendly, well-managed Maison Fleurie offers many extras: not only is a hearty breakfast served in the morning, but also wine and hors d'oeuvres in the late afternoon. Cold and hot drinks are available all day, along with cookies. The morning paper, bathrobes, turn-down service, and the complimentary use of bicycles are additional amenities. Tucked into the courtyards behind the inn are a swimming pool and a hot tub. *Directions:* Coming north from Napa on Hwy 29, turn right into Yountville onto Washington Street. When the road splits, keep to the right onto Yount Street. The inn is on your left.

MAISON FLEURIE
Innkeeper: Rachel Retterer
6529 Yount Street
Yountville, CA 94599, USA
Tel: (707) 944-2056, (800) 788-0369
Fax: (707) 944-9342
13 rooms
Double: $125–$275
Open: all year, Credit cards: all major
karenbrown.com/california/maisonfleurie.html

The Vintage Inn is a large hotel complex nestled between Hwy 29 and the main street of Yountville. The 80 rooms are housed in an attractive mix of two-story green and blue, wood-sided and red-brick buildings, which are connected by meandering paths. We recommend the Vintage Inn as an alternative to bed and breakfast accommodation if you seek a bit more anonymity, privacy, and the full services of a luxury hotel. A concierge is present for assistance, a limited menu is offered poolside and through room service, and the stretch limousine parked at the front entry is available for hire. Guestrooms are very attractive in decor, spacious, and comfortable, equipped with television, fireplace, coffee maker, a complimentary bottle of wine, tub-shower with Jacuzzi jets, and terrycloth robes. Turn-down service is offered each evening and appreciated touches such as a fresh supply of towels and bedside chocolates are thoughtfully provided. Request an "interior" room for the best views and quietest location. In the mornings, an appetizing champagne breakfast buffet with juice, hot beverages, fresh-baked pastries, cereals, yogurt, and fruit is set out in the front lobby and you can sit either inside or at tables on the patio. The Vintage Inn has a capable management team, which extends a courteous welcome and strives to please. *Directions:* Take the Yountville exit off Hwy 29, turn right at the bottom of the exit, then left on Washington Street.

VINTAGE INN
Manager: Mary Crowe
6541 Washington Street
Yountville, CA 94599, USA
Tel: (707) 944-1112, (800) 351-1133
Fax: (707) 944-1617
80 rooms
Double: $210–$510
Open: all year, Credit cards: all major
karenbrown.com/california/vintageinn.html

Index

A

A B Seas Kayaks, 38
Afternoon Refreshments, 6
Agate Cove Inn, Mendocino, 174
Ahwahnee (The), Yosemite–Yosemite Village, 257
Ahwahnee, The, Yosemite National Park, 83
Albion
    Albion River Inn, 98
Alcatraz, 29
Alisal Guest Ranch & Resort, Solvang, 240
Amador City, 90
    Imperial Hotel, 99
Anderson Valley, 55
Andrew Molera State Park, 40
Angels Camp, 88
Año Nuevo State Reserve, 36
Aptos
    Seascape Resort–Monterey Bay, 100
Artists' Inn, Pasadena (South), 205
Atascadero
    Oak Hill Manor, 101
Auberge du Soleil, Rutherford, 215
Avenue of the Giants, The, 58

B

Babbling Brook Inn, Santa Cruz, 232
Balboa, 16
    Balboa Island, 16
    Balboa Pavilion, 16
    Pavilion Queen, 16
Ballard, 47
    Ballard Inn, 102
Barretta Gardens Inn, Sonora, 244
Bathrooms, 4
Beach House, Half Moon Bay, 139
Beach House, Hermosa Beach, 147
Beaulieu Vineyards, 68

Bed & Breakfast Inn at La Jolla (The), La Jolla, 158
Bel-Air (Hotel), Los Angeles, 166
Belle de Jour Inn, Healdsburg, 142
Beltane Ranch, Glen Ellen, 135
Benbow Inn, Garberville, 134
Benziger Winery, 75
Beringer Vineyards, 70
Beyond Limits Adventures, Coloma, 91
Big Sur
    Big Sur Coastline, 40
    Deetjen's Big Sur Inn, 103
    Nepenthe, 41
    Phoenix Shop, The, 41
    Ventana Inn & Spa, 104
Bissell House, Pasadena (South), 206
Bixby Creek Bridge, 41
Blackbird Inn, Napa, 188
Blackthorne Inn, Inverness, 151
Blue Heron Inn, Mendocino, 175
Blue Lantern Inn, Dana Point, 125
Blue Whale Inn, Cambria, 109
Bolinas Lagoon, 52
Breakfast, 4, 6
Brewery Gulch Inn, Mendocino, 176
Brigadoon Castle, Igo, 150
Buelleton, 46
    Andersen's Restaurant, 46
Buena Vista Winery, 78

C

Cable Cars, San Francisco, 30
Calaveras Big Trees State Park, 87
California Missions, 27
    Carmel Mission, 39
    Mission Dolores, 33
    Mission La Purisma Concepcion, 46
    Mission San Antonio de Pala, 23

California Missions (continued)
  Mission San Diego de Alcala, 20
  Mission San Francisco de Assisi, 33
  Mission San Francisco Solano de Sonoma, 77
  Mission San Juan Bautista, 37
  Mission San Juan Capistrano, 17
  Mission San Luis Obispo, 45
  Mission Santa Barbara, 48
  Mission Santa Ysabel, 22
California Petrified Forest, 74
Calistoga, 72
  Chateau de Vie, 105
  Christopher's Inn, 106
  Cottage Grove Inn, 107
  Dr. Wilkinson's Hot Springs, 72
  Indian Springs, 72
  Lavender Hill Spa, 72
  Meadowlark Country Inn, 108
  Mount View Spa, 72
  Old Faithful Geyser, 72
Cambria, 43
  Blue Whale Inn, 109
  J. Patrick House, 110
  Squibb House, 111
Cancellation Policies, 5
Cannery Row, 38
Capitola
  Inn at Depot Hill, 112
Car Rental, 2
Carlsbad (San Diego)
  Legoland, 19
Carmel, 39
  Carmel Mission, 39
  Cobblestone Inn, 113
  Mission Ranch, 114
  Normandy Inn, 115
  Point Lobos State Reserve, 40
  Sea View Inn, 116
  Seventeen-Mile Drive, The, 39
  Vagabond's House Inn, 117

Carmel Highlands
  Tickle Pink Inn, 118
Carmel Valley
  Stonepine Estate, 119
Carmody McKnight Winery, 44
Carrville Inn, Trinity Center, 253
Carson City, 96
  Nevada State Museum, 96
Carter House Inns, Eureka, 130
Casa Cody, Palm Springs, 199
Casa Malibu, Malibu, 168
Castoro Winery, 44
Catalina Island–Avalon
  Inn on Mt. Ada, 120
Cedar Street Inn, Idyllwild, 148
Centerville Beach, 60
Channel Road Inn, Santa Monica, 233
Charm of Inns, 5
Chateau de Vie, Calistoga, 105
Chateau du Sureau, Oakhurst, 194
Château Montelena Winery, 73
Château St. Jean Winery, 74
Chaw'se Indian Grinding Rock State Park, 89
Check-in, 5
Cheshire Cat, Santa Barbara, 228
Children, 5
Chinese Camp, 85
Christopher's Inn, Calistoga, 106
City Hotel, Columbia, 87
Clos Pegase Winery, 71
Cobblestone Inn, Carmel, 113
Coloma, 90
  Coloma Country Inn, 121
  Marshall Gold Discovery State Historic Park, 90
  Rafting
    Beyond Limits Adventures, 91
  Sutter's Sawmill, 90
Columbia, 87
  City Hotel, 87
  Columbia City Hotel, 122

Columbia (continued)
  Fallon Hotel, 123, 87
Comfort, 6
Cornelius Daly Inn, Eureka, 131
Corona del Mar, 17
Coronado (Hotel del), San Diego–Coronado, 219
Cottage Grove Inn, Calistoga, 107
Cottage Inn, Tahoe City, 247
Credit Cards, 6
Cromberg
  Twenty Mile House, 124
Crystal Pier Hotel & Cottages, San Diego–Pacific Beach, 220
Cuyamaca Rancho State Park, 21
Cypress Inn on Miramar Beach, Half Moon Bay, 140

D

Daffodil Hill, 89
Dana Point
  Blue Lantern Inn, 125
Dark Star Winery, 44
Davenport, 36
  New Davenport Cash Store, 36
Deer Creek Inn, Nevada City, 192
Deetjen's Big Sur Inn, Big Sur, 103
Del Coronado, Hotel, San Diego-Coronado, 18
Desert Hills Hotel, Palm Springs, 200
Dietary Requirements, Special, 6
Disneyland, 12
Domaine Chandon, 65
Donner Lake, 93
Donner Pass, 93
Dover Canyon Winery, 44
Drakesbad
  Drakesbad Guest Ranch, 126
Driving Times, 2
Drytown, 90
Dunbar House, 1880, Murphys, 187

E

Eagle Mine, 22
Eagle's Landing, Lake Arrowhead, 161
East Brother Light Station, Point Richmond, 211
Eberle Winery, 45
Elephant Seals, Año Nuevo Reserve, 36
Elk, 56
  Elk Cove Inn, 127
  Griffin House, 128
  Harbor House Inn, 129
Eureka, 60
  Carson Mansion, 60
  Carter House Inns, 130
  Cornelius Daly Inn, 131
  Old Town, 60

F

Fallon Hotel, Columbia, 123, 87
Farmhouse Inn, Forestville, 133
Felton, 36
Fern Valley Inn, Idyllwild, 149
Ferndale, 59
  Gingerbread Mansion, 132, 60
  Museum, 60
  Repertory Theater, 60
  Shaw House Inn, 60
Fess Parker's Wine Country Inn, Los Olivos, 167
Forestville
  Farmhouse Inn, 133
Fort Bragg, 56
  Mendocino Coast Botanical Gardens, 56
  Skunk Railroad, 57
Fort Ross, 54
Foxes, Sutter Creek, 245
Frank Family Vineyards, 70
Fratelli Perata Winery, 44

G

Gables Wine Country Inn, Santa Rosa, 235
Gaige House Inn, Glen Ellen, 136
Garberville
    Benbow Inn, 134
Georgetown, 90
Gerstle Park Inn, San Rafael, 227
Gingerbread Mansion, Ferndale, 132, 60
Glen Ellen, 75
    Beltane Ranch, 135
    Gaige House Inn, 136
    Jack London State Park, 76
Glendeven, Little River, 163
Gloria Ferrer Winery, 78
Golden Gate Bridge, 32, 50
Goosecross Cellars, 65
Gosby House Inn, Pacific Grove, 196
Grandmere's Inn, Nevada City, 193
Grass Valley, 91
    Empire Mine State Park, 91
Green Gables Inn, Pacific Grove, 197
Grey Gables Inn, Sutter Creek, 246
Grey Wolf Winery, 44
Griffin House, Elk, 128
Groveland, 85
    Groveland Hotel, 137
Gualala
    North Coast Country Inn, 138
Guerneville, 54

H

Half Moon Bay, 35
    Beach House, 139
    Cypress Inn on Miramar Beach, 140
    Half Moon Bay Feed and Fuel, 35
    Old Thyme Inn, 141
Harbor House Inn, Elk, 129
Haydon Street Inn, Healdsburg, 143
Healdsburg, 55
    Belle de Jour Inn, 142

Healdsburg (continued)
    Haydon Street Inn, 143
    Healdsburg Inn on the Plaza, 144
    Honor Mansion, 145
    Madrona Manor, 146
Hearst Castle, 41
Hermosa Beach
    Beach House, 147
Hess Collection Winery, 63
Historic National Hotel, 1859, Jamestown, 86
Honor Mansion, Healdsburg, 145
Hop Kiln Winery, 55
Huck Finn Sport Fishing, Princeton Harbor, 35
Humboldt Redwoods State Park, 58
    Rockefeller Forest, 58

I

Icons, 7
Idyllwild, 23
    Cedar Street Inn, 148
    Fern Valley Inn, 149
Igo
    Brigadoon Castle, 150
Imperial Hotel, Amador City, 99
Ingleside Inn, Palm Springs, 201
Inn Above Tide, Sausalito, 237
Inn at 213 Seventeen Mile Drive, Pacific Grove, 198
Inn at Depot Hill, Capitola, 112
Inn at Occidental, Occidental, 195
Inn at Playa del Rey, Playa del Rey, 210
Inn at Rancho Santa Fe, Rancho Santa Fe, 212
Inn at Schoolhouse Creek, Little River, 164
Inn at Sonoma, Sonoma, 242
Inn at Union Square, San Francisco, 221
Inn on Mt. Ada, Catalina Island–Avalon, 120
Innkeepers
    Professionalism, 8
Introduction, 1
    About Inn Travel, 4
    About Itineraries, 2

Inverness
    Blackthorne Inn, 151
    Manka's Inverness Lodge, 152
    Ten Inverness Way, 153
Ironstone Vineyards, 88
Itineraries
    Leisurely Loop of Southern California, 11
    North from San Francisco, 49
    San Francisco to Los Angeles via the Coast, 27
    Wandering through the Wine Country, 61
    Yosemite, the Gold Country & Lake Tahoe, 81

J

J. Patrick House, Cambria, 110
Jack London State Park, 76
Jackson, 89
    Amador County Museum, 89
Jamestown, 86
    1859 Historic National Hotel, 86
    Jamestown Hotel, 86
    National Hotel, 154
    Railtown 1897 State Historic Park, 86
Jarvis Winery, 64
John Dougherty House, Mendocino, 177
Joshua Grindle Inn, Mendocino, 178
Julia Pfeiffer Burns State Park, 41
Julian, 22
    Eagle Mine, 22
    Julian White House (The), 155
    Orchard Hill Country Inn, 156
Just Inn, Paso Robles, 207
Justin Winery, 44

K

Kayaking
    A B Seas Kayaks, 38
Kenwood
    Landmark, 157
Korakia Pensione, Palm Springs, 202

Korbel Winery, 54
Kunde Winery, 74

L

La Jolla
    Bed & Breakfast Inn at La Jolla (The), 158
    George's Ocean Terrace, 19
    Museum of Contemporary Art, 19
    Scripps Inn, 159
    Scripps Institution of Oceanography, 19
    Valencia Hotel (La), 160
Laguna Beach, 17
Lake Arrowhead, 26
    Eagle's Landing, 161
    Saddleback Inn, 162
Lake La Quinta Inn, Palm Springs-La Quinta, 204
Lake Tahoe, 93
    Eagle Falls and Lake, 95
    Emerald Bay, 94
    Sugar Pine State Park, 94
    Vikingsholm, 94
Landmark Vineyards, 74
Landmark, Kenwood, 157
Lavender, Yountville, 258
Leggett, 57
Legoland, San Diego (Carlsbad), 19
Little River
    Glendeven, 163
    Inn at Schoolhouse Creek, 164
Livermore
    Purple Orchid Inn, 165
Lompoc
    Mission La Purisma Concepcion, 46
Los Angeles, 12, 48
    Bel-Air (Hotel), 166
    Disneyland, 12
    Getty Museum, The, 13
    Huntington Library, Gallery, Gardens, 13
    NBC Television Studios, 14

Los Angeles (continued)
  Norton Simon Museum Of Art, The, 14
  Pueblo de Los Angeles, 14
  Queen Mary, The, 15
  Universal Studios, 15
Los Olivos, 47
  Fess Parker's Wine Country Inn & Spa, 167
Lost Whale, Trinidad, 251

M

MacArthur Place, Sonoma, 243
Madrona Manor, Healdsburg, 146
Maison Fleurie, Yountville, 259
Majestic (Hotel), San Francisco, 222
Malakoff Diggins, 92
Malibu
  Casa Malibu, 168
  Malibu Beach Inn, 169
Manchester
  Victorian Gardens, 170
Manka's Inverness Lodge, Inverness, 152
Maps, 2
Marin Headlands, 51
Marina
  Marina Dunes Resort, 171
Marine Mammal Center, 51
Martin-Weyrich Winery, 45
McCaffrey House B&B Inn, Twain Harte, 254
McCloud
  McCloud Guest House, 172
  McCloud Hotel, 173
Meadowlark Country Inn, Calistoga, 108
Meadowood Napa Valley, Saint Helena, 216
Mendocino, 55
  Agate Cove Inn, 174
  Blue Heron Inn, 175
  Brewery Gulch Inn, 176
  John Dougherty House, 177
  Joshua Grindle Inn, 178
  Mendocino Farmhouse, 179

Mendocino (continued)
  Packard House, 180
  Stanford Inn by the Sea, 181
  Whitegate Inn, 182
Mercer Caverns, 88
Meridian Vineyards, 45
Mexico Sightseeing, 19
  Tijuana, 19
Midnight Cellars Winery, 44
Milliken Creek, Napa, 189
Mission Ranch, Carmel, 114
Moaning Cavern, 87
Monarch Butterfly, 39
Monterey, 37
  Aquarium, 38
  Cannery Row, 38
  Fisherman's Wharf, 38
  Kayaking
    A B Seas Kayaks, 38
  Old Monterey Inn, 183
  Old Town, 38
  Spindrift Inn, 184
Montrose Suite Hotel (Le), West Hollywood, 255
Moss Beach
  Seal Cove Inn, 185
Muir Beach, 51
  Pelican Inn, 186, 51
Muir Woods, 51
Mukulumne Hill, 88
Murphys, 88
  Dunbar House, 1880, 187
  Old Timers' Museum, 88

N

Napa, 63
  Blackbird Inn, 188
  Copia, 63
  Milliken Creek, 189
  Oak Knoll Inn, 190
  Residence (La), 191

Napa Valley Wine Region
  Beaulieu Vineyards, 68
  Beringer Vineyards, 70
  Château Montelena, 73
  Clos Pegase, 71
  Domaine Chandon, 65
  Frank Family Vineyards, 70
  Goosecross Cellars, 65
  Hess Collection, 63
  Jarvis Winery, 64
  Nichelini, 68
  Niebaum-Coppola Estate, 67
  Opus One, 66
  Plumpjack, 66
  Robert Mondavi Winery, 66
  Rutherford Hill, 69
  Schramsberg Vineyards, 71
  Sterling Vineyards, 71
  Trefethen Vineyards, 64
  V. Sattui Winery, 69
  Vincent Arroyo, 73
National Hotel, Jamestown, 154
Navarro Winery, 55
NBC Television Studios, 14
Nepenthe, Big Sur, 41
Nevada City, 91
  Deer Creek Inn, 192
  Grandmere's Inn, 193
Newport Beach, 15
  Dory Fleet, 15
  Oyster Bar & Grill, 16
Nichelini Winery, 68
Niebaum-Coppola Winery, 67
Normandy Inn, Carmel, 115
North Bloomfield, 93
North Coast Country Inn, Gualala, 138
Noyo Harbor, 56
  Telstar Charters, 56

O
Oak Hill Manor, Atascadero, 101
Oak Knoll Inn, Napa, 190
Oakhurst
  Chateau du Sureau, 194
Oakville, 66
  Oakville Grocery, 66
Occidental
  Inn at Occidental, 195
Old Coast Road, 40
Old Faithful Geyser, 72
Old Monterey Inn, Monterey, 183
Old Stonewall Mine, 21
Old Thyme Inn, Half Moon Bay, 141
Opus One Winery, 66
Orchard Hill Country Inn, Julian, 156
Orchard Hill Farm, Paso Robles, 208

P
Pacific Grove, 38
  Gosby House Inn, 196
  Green Gables Inn, 197
  Inn at 213 Seventeen Mile Drive, 198
  Monarch Butterfly, 39
Pacific Lumber Company, 58
Pacing, 3
Packard House, Mendocino, 180
Pala, 23
  Mission San Antonio de Pala, 23
Palm Springs, 23
  Aerial Tramway, 24
  Casa Cody, 199
  Desert Hills Hotel, 200
  Ingleside Inn, 201
  Korakia Pensione, 202
  Living Desert Wildlife and Botanical Park, 24
  Willows (The), 203
Palm Springs-La Quinta
  Lake La Quinta Inn, 204
Palomar Observatory, 22

Pasadena (South)
    Artists' Inn, 205
    Bissell House, 206
Paso Robles, 45
    Carnegie Library, 45
    Estrella Warbird Museum, 45
    Just Inn, 207
    Orchard Hill Farm, 208
    Paso Robles Hot Springs, 45
    Pioneer Museum, 45
    Summerwood Inn, 209
    Sycamore Farms, 44
Paso Robles Wine Region, 44
    Carmody McKnight Winery, 44
    Castoro Winery, 44
    Dark Star Winery, 44
    Dover Canyon Winery, 44
    Eberle Winery, 45
    Fratelli Perata Winery, 44
    Grey Wolf Winery, 44
    Justin Winery, 44
    Martin-Weyrick Winery, 45
    Meridian Winery, 45
    Midnight Cellars Winery, 44
    Tobin James Winery, 45
    Treana Winery, 44
    Wild Horse Vineyards, 45
Pebble Beach Golf Course, 39
Pelican Inn, Muir Beach, 186, 51
Petite Auberge, San Francisco, 223
Pfeiffer Big Sur State Park, 41
Phoenix Shop, The, Big Sur, 41
Pismo Beach, 45
    State Park, 46
Placerville, 90
Playa del Rey
    Inn at Playa del Rey, 210
Plumpjack Winery, 66
Point Lobos State Reserve, 40

Point Reyes National Seashore, 52
    Drakes Bay, 53
    Johnson Oyster Company, 53
    Lighthouse, 52
    Morgan Ranch, 52
Point Reyes Station, 53
    Station House Café, 53
Point Richmond (San Francisco Bay)
    East Brother Light Station, 211
Princeton Harbor, 35
    Huck Finn Sport Fishing, 35
Purple Orchid Inn, Livermore, 165

Q

Queen Mary, The, 15

R

Rafting
    Beyond Limits Adventures, 91
Rancho Santa Fe
    Inn at Rancho Santa Fe, 212
    Rancho Valencia Resort, 213
Rancho Valencia Resort, Rancho Santa Fe, 213
Red and White Fleet, 34
Redding
    Tiffany House, 214
Reservations, 8
Residence (La), Napa, 191
Responsibility, 8
Rim of the World Highway, 25
River Ranch Lodge, Tahoe City, 248, 93
Roaring Camp Railroad, 36
Robert Mondavi Winery, 66
Rochioli Winery, 55
Room Rates, 9
Russian River, 54
Rutherford
    Auberge du Soleil, 215
Rutherford Hill Winery, 69

S

Saddleback Inn, Lake Arrowhead, 162
Saint Helena, 70
    Dean and Deluca, 70
    Library and Museum, 70
    Meadowood Napa Valley, 216
    Vineyard Country Inn, 217
    Wine Country Inn, 218
San Diego, 17
    Balboa Park, 18
    Coronado, 18
    Heritage Park, 18
    Hotel del Coronado, Coronado, 18
    La Jolla, 19
    Legoland, 19
    Mexico Sightseeing, 19
    Mission San Diego de Alcala, 20
    Museums, 18
    Old Town, 18, 19
    Sea World, 21
    Seaport Village, 20
    The Embarcadero, 18
    Visitors Bureau, 17
    Wild Animal Park, 21
    Zoo, 18
San Diego–Coronado
    Coronado (Hotel del), 219
San Diego–Pacific Beach
    Crystal Pier Hotel & Cottages, 220
San Francisco, 28
    Alcatraz, 29
    Beach Chalet, 32
    Cable Cars, 30
    California Academy of Sciences, 32
    California Historical Society, 34
    Cannery, The, 31
    Chinatown, 30
    Coit Tower, 31
    Fisherman's Wharf, 31
    Fort Point, 32

San Francisco (continued)
    Ghiradelli Square, 32
    Golden Gate Bridge, 32
    Golden Gate Park, 32
    Hyde Street Cable Car Turnaround, 32
    Hyde Street Pier, 31
    Inn at Union Square, 221
    Japanese Tea Garden, 32
    Lombard Street, 33
    Majestic (Hotel), 222
    Maritime Museum, 32
    Mission San Francisco de Assisi, 33
    Morrison Planetarium, 32
    Museum of Modern Art, 34
    Museum of Natural History, 32
    Palace of the Legion of Honor, 30
    Petite Auberge, 223
    Pier 39, 31
    Sausalito, 34
    Steinhart Aquarium, 32
    Stores, 35
    Theater, 34
    Tiburon, 34
    Union Square, 35
    Union Street, 35
    Union Street Inn, 224
    Visitors Bureau, 29, 34
    Washington Square Inn, 225
    White Swan Inn, 226
    Yerba Buena Gardens and Galleries, 34
San Juan Bautista
    Mission San Juan Bautista, 37
San Juan Capistrano, 17
    Mission, 17
San Luis Obispo
    Mission San Luis Obispo, 45
San Rafael
    Gerstle Park Inn, 227
San Simeon
    Hearst Castle, 41

Santa Barbara, 47
   Cheshire Cat, 228
   County Courthouse, 48
   Mission Santa Barbara, 48
   Santa Barbara (Hotel), 229
   Secret Garden Inn, 230
   Simpson House Inn, 231
Santa Cruz, 36
   Babbling Brook Inn, 232
   Boardwalk, 36
   Roaring Camp Railroad, 36
Santa Inez, 47
Santa Monica
   Channel Road Inn, 233
   Shutters on the Beach, 234
Santa Rosa
   Gables Wine Country Inn, 235
   Vintners Inn, 236
Santa Ysabel, 22
   Dudley's Bakery, 22
   Mission Santa Ysabel, 22
Sausalito, 34
   Inn Above Tide, 237
   Sausalito (Hotel), 238
Schramsberg Vineyards, 71
Scotia, 58
Scripps Inn, La Jolla, 159
Sea View Inn, Carmel, 116
Seal Beach
   Seal Beach Inn, 239
Seal Cove Inn, Moss Beach, 185
Seascape Resort–Monterey Bay, Aptos, 100
Secret Garden Inn, Santa Barbara, 230
Seventeen-Mile Drive, The, Carmel, 39
Shaw House Inn, Ferndale, 60
Shutters on the Beach, Santa Monica, 234
Simpson House Inn, Santa Barbara, 231
Skunk Railroad, 57

Smoking, 9
Socializing, 9
Solvang, 46
   Alisal Guest Ranch & Resort, 240
   Storybook Inn, 241
Sonoma, 76
   Barracks, 76
   Cheese Factory, 78
   Inn at Sonoma, 242
   Lachryma Montis, 78
   MacArthur Place, 243
   Mission San Francisco Solano de Sonoma, 77
   Toscano Hotel, 76
Sonoma Valley Wine Region
   Benziger Winery, 75
   Buena Vista Winery, 78
   Château St. Jean, 74
   Gloria Ferrer Winery, 78
   Kunde Winery, 74
   Landmark Vineyards, 74
   Viansa Winery, 79
Sonora
   Barretta Gardens Inn, 244
Spindrift Inn, Monterey, 184
Squibb House, Cambria, 111
Stanford Inn by the Sea, Mendocino, 181
Sterling Vineyards, 71
Stinson Beach, 51
Stonepine Estate, Carmel Valley, 119
Storybook Inn, Solvang, 241
Summerwood Inn, Paso Robles, 209
Summerwood Winery, 44
Sunnyside Restaurant & Lodge, Tahoe City, 249
Sutter Creek, 89
   Foxes, 245
   Grey Gables Inn, 246
Sycamore Farms, 44

Index

T

Tahoe City, 94
   Cottage Inn, 247
   Fanny Bridge, 94
   Gatekeeper's Cabin, 94
   River Ranch Lodge, 248, 93
   Sunnyside Restaurant & Lodge, 249
Telstar Charters, 56
Templeton
   Wild Horse Vineyards, 45
Ten Inverness Way, Inverness, 153
Tiburon, 34
   Waters Edge Hotel, 250
Tickle Pink Inn, Carmel Highlands, 118
Tiffany House, Redding, 214
Tijuana, 19
Tobin James Winery, 45
Tomales, 53
   Bakery, 53
Tomales Bay, 53
Trefethen Vineyards, 64
Trinidad, 60
   Lost Whale, 251
   Seascape Restaurant, 60
   Trinidad Bay Bed and Breakfast, 252
Trinity Center
   Carrville Inn, 253
Truckee River, 93
Twain Harte
   McCaffrey House B&B Inn, 254
Twenty Mile House, Cromberg, 124

U

Union Street Inn, San Francisco, 224
Universal Studios, 15

V

V. Sattui Winery, 69
Vagabond's House Inn, Carmel, 117
Valencia Hotel (La), La Jolla, 160

Ventana Inn & Spa, Big Sur, 104
Viansa Winery, 79
Victorian Gardens, Manchester, 170
Vincent Arroyo Winery, 73
Vineyard Country Inn, Saint Helena, 217
Vintage Inn, Yountville, 260
Vintners Inn, Santa Rosa, 236
Virginia City, 96
Visitors Bureau
   San Diego, 17
   San Francisco, 29, 34
Volcano, 89
   Saint George Hotel, 89

W

Washington Square Inn, San Francisco, 225
Waters Edge Hotel, Tiburon, 250
Wawona Hotel, Yosemite–Wawona, 256, 84
Weather, 3
Website, Karen Brown, 10
West Hollywood
   Montrose Suite Hotel (Le), 255
Wheelchair Accessibility, 10
White Swan Inn, San Francisco, 226
Whitegate Inn, Mendocino, 182
Wild Horse Vineyards, 45
Willits, 57
   Skunk Railroad, 57
Willows (The), Palm Springs, 203
Wine Country Inn, Saint Helena, 218

Y

Yosemite National Park, 83
   Ahwahnee, The, 83
   Cathedral Rock, 84
   Clouds Rest, 84
   El Capitan, 84
   Glacier Point, 85
   Half Dome, 84
   Mariposa Grove, 85

Yosemite National Park (continued)
    Wawona Hotel, 84
    Yosemite Concessions Services, 83
    Yosemite Lodge, 84
    Yosemite Valley, 83
Yosemite–Wawona
    Wawona Hotel, 256
Yosemite–Yosemite Village
    Ahwahnee (The), 257
Yountville, 65
    Lavender, 258
    Maison Fleurie, 259
    Vintage 1870, 65
    Vintage Inn, 260

Enhance your Guides—Visit us Online

www.karenbrown.com

- Hotel specials
- Color photos of hotels and B&Bs
- 20% online discount for book purchases
- Discount airfare, both business and coach class
- Direct links to individual property websites and e-mails
- Up-to-the-minute phone, fax, and e-mail information
- Rental cars, travel planning, trip insurance, itineraries, maps, and more

Become a Member of the Karen Brown Club

- Additional specials and offers from our travel partners
- Exclusive access to "new discoveries" from our current research
- An additional 20% savings on purchases from our online store

A complete listing of member benefits can be found on our website

Don't delay, join online today!

www.karenbrown.com

KB Travel Service

❖ **KB Travel Service** offers travel-planning assistance using itineraries designed by *Karen Brown* and published in her guidebooks. We will customize any itinerary to fit your personal interests.

❖ We will plan your itinerary with you, help you decide how long to stay and what to do once you arrive, and work out the details.

❖ We will book your airline tickets and your rental car, arrange rail travel, reserve accommodations recommended in *Karen Brown's Guides,* and supply you with point-to-point information and consultation.

Contact us to start planning your travel!

800-782-2128 or e-mail: info@kbtravelservice.com

Service fees do apply

KB Travel Service
16 East Third Avenue
San Mateo, CA 94401 USA
www.kbtravelservice.com

Independently owned and operated by Town & Country Travel
CST 2001543-10

Travel Your Dreams · Order Your Karen Brown Guides Today

Please ask in your local bookstore for Karen Brown's Guides. If the books you want are unavailable, you may order directly from the publisher. Books will be shipped immediately.

_____ *Austria: Charming Inns & Itineraries* $19.95

_____ *California: Charming Inns & Itineraries* $19.95

_____ *England: Charming Bed & Breakfasts* $18.95

_____ *England, Wales & Scotland: Charming Hotels & Itineraries* $19.95

_____ *France: Charming Bed & Breakfasts* $18.95

_____ *France: Charming Inns & Itineraries* $19.95

_____ *Germany: Charming Inns & Itineraries* $19.95

_____ *Ireland: Charming Inns & Itineraries* $19.95

_____ *Italy: Charming Bed & Breakfasts* $18.95

_____ *Italy: Charming Inns & Itineraries* $19.95

_____ *Mexico: Charming Inns & Itineraries* $19.95

_____ *Mid-Atlantic: Charming Inns & Itineraries* $19.95

_____ *New England: Charming Inns & Itineraries* $19.95

_____ *Pacific Northwest: Charming Inns & Itineraries* $19.95

_____ *Portugal: Charming Inns & Itineraries* $19.95

_____ *Spain: Charming Inns & Itineraries* $19.95

_____ *Switzerland: Charming Inns & Itineraries* $19.95

Name _____ Street _____

Town _____ State_____ Zip _____ Tel _____

Credit Card (MasterCard or Visa) _____ Expires: _____

For orders in the USA, add $5 for the first book and $2 for each additional book for shipment. Overseas shipping (airmail) is $10 for 1 to 2 books, $20 for 3 to 4 books etc. CA residents add 8.25% sales tax. Fax or mail form with check or credit card information to:

KAREN BROWN'S GUIDES
Post Office Box 70 · San Mateo · California · 94401 · USA
tel: (650) 342-9117, fax: (650) 342-9153, e-mail: karen@karenbrown.com, www.karenbrown.com

KAREN BROWN wrote her first travel guide in 1976. Her personalized travel series has grown to 17 titles, which Karen and her small staff work diligently to keep updated. Karen, her husband, Rick, and their children, Alexandra and Richard, live in Moss Beach, a small town on the coast south of San Francisco. They settled here in 1991 when they opened Seal Cove Inn. Karen is frequently traveling but when she is home, in her role as innkeeper, enjoys welcoming Karen Brown readers.

CLARE BROWN was a travel consultant for many years, specializing in planning itineraries to Europe using charming small hotels in the countryside. The focus of her job remains unchanged, but now her expertise is available to a larger audience—the readers of her daughter Karen's country inn guides. When Clare and her husband, Bill, are not traveling, they live either in Hillsborough, California, or at their home in Vail, Colorado, where family and friends frequently join them for skiing.

JUNE EVELEIGH BROWN'S love of travel was inspired by the *National Geographic* magazines that she read as a girl in her dentist's office—so far she has visited over 40 countries. June hails from Sheffield, England and lived in Zambia and Canada before moving to northern California where she lives in San Mateo with her husband, Tony, their daughter Clare, their two German Shepherds, and a Siamese cat.

JANN POLLARD, the artist responsible for the beautiful painting on the cover of this guide, has studied art since childhood, and is well known for her outstanding impressionistic-style watercolors, which she has exhibited in numerous juried shows, winning many awards. Jann travels frequently to Europe (using Karen Brown's Guides) where she loves to paint historical buildings. Jann's original paintings are represented through The Gallery, Burlingame, CA, 650-347-9392 or www.thegalleryart.net. Fine-art giclée prints of the cover paintings are also available at www.karenbrown.com.

BARBARA TAPP, the talented artist who produces all of the hotel sketches and delightful illustrations in this guide, was raised in Australia where she studied in Sydney at the School of Interior Design. Although Barbara continues with freelance projects, she devotes much of her time to illustrating the Karen Brown guides. Barbara lives in Kensington, California, with her husband, Richard, and daughter, Georgia.

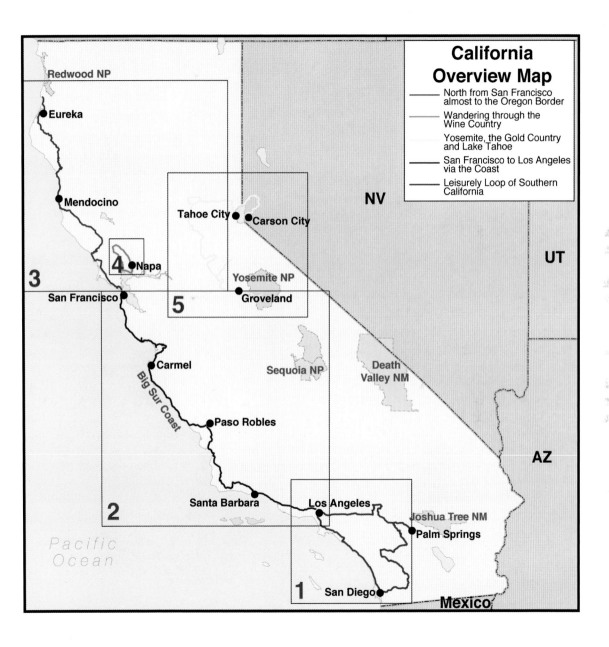

California Map 1

- ● Places to Stay
- — Leisurely Loop of Southern California
- –·– Ferry Route

0 ——— 10 Miles
0 ——— 10 KM

California Map 2

- Places to Stay
- San Francisco to Los Angeles via the Coast

0   20 Miles

0   20 KM

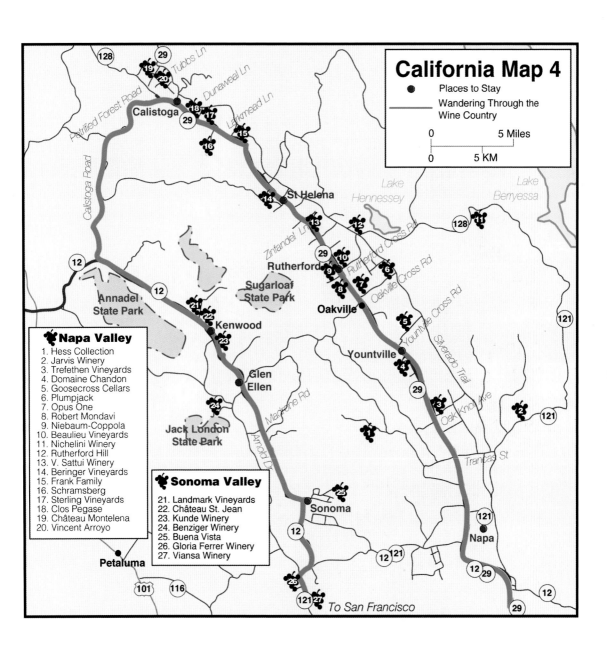

California Map 4

● Places to Stay
━━ Wandering Through the Wine Country

0 _____ 5 Miles
0 _____ 5 KM

Napa Valley
1. Hess Collection
2. Jarvis Winery
3. Trefethen Vineyards
4. Domaine Chandon
5. Goosecross Cellars
6. Plumpjack
7. Opus One
8. Robert Mondavi
9. Niebaum-Coppola
10. Beaulieu Vineyards
11. Nichelini Winery
12. Rutherford Hill
13. V. Sattui Winery
14. Beringer Vineyards
15. Frank Family
16. Schramsberg
17. Sterling Vineyards
18. Clos Pegase
19. Château Montelena
20. Vincent Arroyo

Sonoma Valley
21. Landmark Vineyards
22. Château St. Jean
23. Kunde Winery
24. Benziger Winery
25. Buena Vista
26. Gloria Ferrer Winery
27. Viansa Winery

Karen Brown Presents Her Own Special Hideaways

Karen Brown's Seal Cove Inn

Spectacularly set amongst wildflowers and bordered by cypress trees, Seal Cove Inn (Karen's second home) looks out to the distant ocean. Each room has a fireplace, cozy sitting area, and a view of the sea. Located on the coast, 35 minutes south of San Francisco.

Seal Cove Inn, Moss Beach, California
toll free telephone: (800) 995-9987
www.sealcoveinn.com

Karen Brown's Dolphin Cove Inn

Hugging a steep hillside overlooking the sparkling deep-blue bay of Manzanillo, Dolphin Cove Inn offers guests outstanding value. Each room has either a terrace or a balcony, and a breathtaking view of the sea. Located on the Pacific Coast of Mexico.

Dolphin Cove Inn, Manzanillo, Mexico
toll free telephone: (888) 497-4138
www.dolphincoveinn.com

Icons Key

We have introduced the icons listed below in the guidebooks and on our website (*www.karenbrown.com*). These allow us to provide additional information about our recommended properties. When using our website to supplement the guides, placing the cursor over an icon will in many cases give you further details.

❄	Air conditioning in rooms	🍴	Restaurant
⛱	Beach	❀	Spa
☕	Breakfast included in room rate	🏊	Swimming pool
🏃	Children welcome	🎾	Tennis
☕	Cooking classes offered	📺	Television w/ English channels
CREDIT	Credit cards accepted	🔔	Wedding facilities
☎	Direct-dial telephone in room	♿	Wheelchair friendly
🐕	Dogs by special request	⛳	Golf course nearby
🛗	Elevator	🚶🚶	Hiking trails nearby
🤸	Exercise room	🐎	Horseback riding nearby
🔥	Fireplaces in some rooms	⛷	Skiing nearby
🍷	Mini-refrigerator in room	⛵	Water sports nearby
🚭	Some non-smoking rooms	🍇	Wineries nearby
P	Parking available		